The Impact of Modern Paints

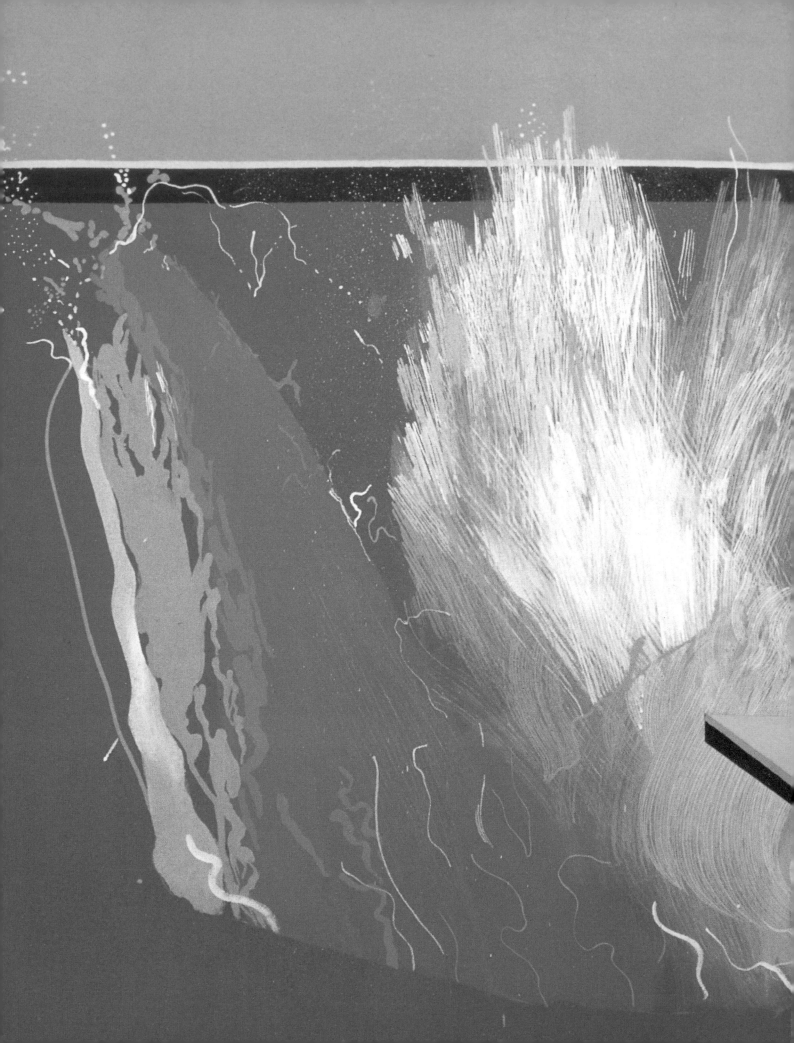

Jo Crook and Tom Learner

The Impact of Modern Paints

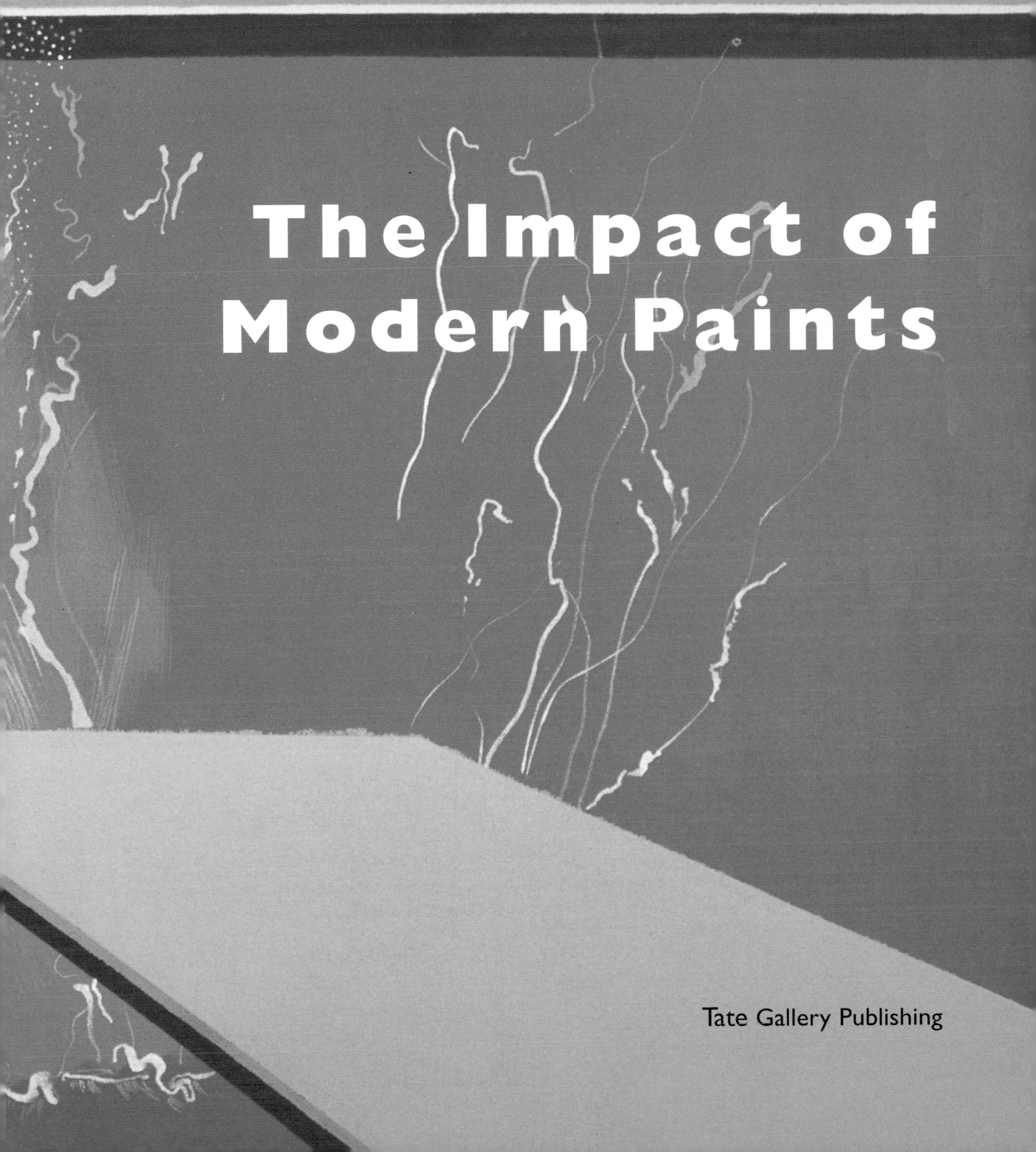

Tate Gallery Publishing

Published by order of the Trustees of the Tate Gallery by

Tate Gallery Publishing Ltd

Millbank

London SW1P 4RG

© 2000 Tate Gallery. All rights reserved

ISBN 1 85437 287 4

A catalogue record for this book is available from the

British Library

Designed and typeset by Harry Green

Printed in Hong Kong by South Seas International Press

Front cover: Detail from *Saracen* (1977)

by John Hoyland, taken in raking light from above

Back cover: Detail from *Pottery* (1969)

by Patrick Caulfield, taken in raking light from above

Frontispiece: Detail from *A Bigger Splash* (1967)

by David Hockney

Contents

Acknowledgements

Much of the content of this book has been developed from our direct contact with several of the artists featured, and we have been overwhelmed by the generosity of those involved. Many gave lengthy interviews specifically for the book (often on more than one occasion), read through draft versions of the relevant chapters and were generous in allowing us to reproduce images of their paintings. We could not have written this book without their assistance and support.

In addition, we are extremely grateful to the following artists, artists' assistants and family, conservators, curators, paint-makers, paint suppliers, photographers and researchers for providing recollections, thoughts, photographs or other additional information: Gillian Ayres, Ronnie Cutrone, Anne Baldassari, Patrick Baty, Marcella Louis Brenner, Ed Brickler, Brian Butson, Earl Childress, Marion Faller (acting on behalf of the Hollis Frampton estate), Alan Fitzpatrick, Alun Foster, Alan French, Helen Frankenthaler, Ann Garfinkle (acting on behalf of the Morris Louis estate), Nathan Gluck, Mark Golden, Timothy Hunt, William Hunt (acting on behalf of the Edward Wallowitch estate), Karen Khulman, Ray Leggetter, Jorge Lewinski, Jon Lloyd, Cassandra Lozano, Emma Pearce, Herman Reich, Steve Steinberg, Gerard Malanga, National Archives of American Art, Piccia Neri, Kenneth Noland, Neil Printz, Brian Rogerson, Will Shank, Andrew Smith, George Stegmeir, Jeanne-Yvette Sudour, Carol Mancusi-Ungaro, Diane Upright, Thomas Vonderbrink and Matt Wrbican.

Our research included scientific analysis of paintings in the Tate Gallery Collection. We are therefore indebted to the generosity of the Cloth-workers' Foundation, whose financial assistance enabled the purchase of the FTIR spectrometer, and Professor Dr Jaap Boon, from the FOM Institute in Amsterdam, who arranged the loan of the PyGCMS instrument.

We would also like to thank several of our Tate Gallery colleagues. High quality photographs of paintings and details have ensured the book's visual impact; everyone from the Tate's Photographic Department con-tributed and we thank particularly Marcella Leith for her assistance and David Lambert who photographed approximately three-quarters of the book's colour illustrations. We thank the art handlers of the Tate Store for enabling access to the paintings themselves, and the Tate Library staff for their support in answering our requests. We also thank the follow-ing Tate conservators, conservation scientists and curators for their invaluable comments and suggestions to our text: Monique Beudert, Stephen Hackney, Sam Hodge, Catherine Kinley, Paul Moorhouse, Roy Perry, Graham Peters and Joyce Townsend. And finally Sarah Derry and Susan Lawrie, from Tate Gallery Publishing Ltd, who assisted in turning our work into such a stunning book.

Jo Crook and Tom Learner

Introduction

When asked to describe his method of painting in an interview in 1950, Jackson Pollock replied:

My opinion is that new needs need new techniques. And the modern artists have found new ways and new means of making their statements. It seems to me that the modern painter cannot express this age, the airplane, the atom bomb, the radio, in the old forms of the Renaissance or of any other past culture. Each age finds its own technique … Most of the paint I use is a liquid, flowing kind of paint. The brushes I use are used more as sticks rather than brushes – the brush doesn't touch the surface of the canvas, it's just above.[1]

Pollock's working methods are remarkably well documented. Many people will have seen excerpts from Hans Namuth's series of films of 1950 showing the execution of his 'drip' paintings and will therefore be familiar with Pollock's technique of pouring, dripping and splashing paint onto the canvas. These fascinating images clearly illustrate the importance of his technique to his work.

It is now generally accepted that an overall awareness of the ways in which artists apply their materials is crucial to an appreciation of twentieth-century art. However, the role played by the choice of those materials has frequently been overlooked. Indeed, most of the effects that characterise Pollock's drip paintings relied heavily on the use of household and industrial 'enamel' (i.e. gloss) paints, and not (as some might assume) on the traditional medium of oil paint. Apart from being much cheaper than oils, these enamel paints are formulated to a much thinner consistency and therefore have a greater ability to flow, both crucial to Pollock's work.

The enamel paints also differed chemically from oil paint: they all contained a synthetic resin instead of a drying oil to hold the pigments in place. In fact, the majority of paints that have appeared throughout the twentieth century, especially those formulated for the household and industrial markets, have been based on synthetic resins. The names of some of these resins, such as acrylic, may already be familiar to many, while others, such as alkyd, are less so. Synthetic paints started to replace traditional housepaints (which were also based on oil) in America during the 1930s, although it was not until the end of the 1950s that they became available in Britain.

The first artists to use synthetic paints were therefore those who worked with housepaints or materials that had been designed for other uses. Often this choice was determined by economic necessity, particularly during and immediately after the Second World War, when the availability of conventional artists' materials was severely restricted. The American painter Kenneth Noland reflected on the strain imposed on the Abstract Expressionists working in America during the 1940s: '[with] no money coming in from painting … they couldn't get good art materials and there was a necessity almost to go out and start using housepaint, enamel paint'.[2] The relative cheapness of the paints was especially important for artists working on a larger scale. The use of such paints certainly enabled artists like Pollock and Willem de Kooning to carry out more experimental application techniques than they might have attempted with expensive artists' quality materials.

It is clear, however, that cost was not the only factor to determine the choice of materials. Noland also notes that the Abstract Expressionists' use of commercial paint was motivated by the desire to employ 'something besides the conventional means of art … other kinds of paint, or kinds of canvas, or ways of making pictures that weren't the usual ways'.[3] For some artists the choice was influenced by considerations such as durability or visual impact. The Mexican muralist David Alfaro Siqueiros experimented with industrial paints in the 1930s, such as those used for cars, to make his early exterior mural paintings more weather-resistant. Pablo Picasso frequently used a particular brand of French commercial paint, Ripolin, in his works. Gertrude Stein, writing in 1933, remembers Picasso 'talking a long time about the Ripolin paints. There are, said he gravely, *la santé des coleurs*, that is why they are the basis of good health for paints. In those days [1912 onwards] he painted pictures and everything with Ripolin paints, as he still does, and as so many of his followers young and old do.'[4]

These artists often also explored novel application techniques, ranging from staining, silk-screening and spraying – where thin and fluid paints are required – to high impasto and hard-edge painting, incorporating thicker and more viscous paints. In 1936, Siqueiros set up a painting workshop in New York to encourage participating artists such as Pollock and Morris Louis to engage in experimental techniques using commercial paints. Alex Horn, an artist and contemporary of Pollock's, attended the workshop that existed 'for the express purpose of experimentation with new technological developments in materials and tools. Paints including the then new nitro-cellulose lacquers and silicones … and paint applicators including airbrushes and sprayguns, were some of the materials and techniques to be explored and applied … We used [lacquer] in thin glazes or built it up into thick globs. We poured it, dripped it, spattered it, hurled it at the picture surface … What emerged was an endless variety of accidental effects. Siqueiros soon constructed a theory and system of "controlled accidents".'[5]

This use of materials and methods more often employed in industry became associated with an initiative in British painting that aimed to replace the established hierarchies of taste in art with a pluralistic approach that is still much in evidence today. From the mid-1950s the Independent Group, of whom Richard Hamilton was a leading member, advocated an art that embraced the resources of popular culture along with modern scientific and technological developments. Hamilton's relief paintings of automobiles, for example, were sprayed with car paint to make the image more real.

The small companies – known as artists' colourmen – that specialised in making artists' paints could not afford to invest in the development of their own synthetic resins. However, they followed progress in the house-paint industry with great interest, and by carefully considering the needs and expectations of artists, started to use synthetic resins to make their own paints soon after the Second World War. Perhaps the closest relationship between an artist and a paint manufacturer was that between Morris Louis and Leonard Bocour in America during the early 1950s. Louis's acrylic paints were custom-made by Bocour for much of his career. However, it was not until the 1960s that acrylic emulsion, a synthetic paint intended specifically for artists' use, became readily available in both Britain and America.

The 1960s is therefore a particularly interesting decade to consider, since by this time all the major classes of modern paint had become available, and their impact can be more accurately assessed. The purpose of this book is to introduce the various types of modern paint used in art by focusing on ten influential artists who all rejected oil paint in favour of at least one of the available synthetic alternatives in the 1960s. The painters are Peter Blake, Patrick Caulfield, Richard Hamilton, David Hockney, John Hoyland, Roy Lichtenstein, Morris Louis, Bridget Riley, Frank Stella and Andy Warhol. The ways in which each artist used these paints are considered through examples of their paintings in the Tate Gallery collection.

What becomes clear is that these modern paints provided artists with a whole range of new possibilities to explore, and their impact on the unfolding history of late twentieth-century art has been greatly underestimated. Each type of paint has its own unique set of properties. Household gloss paint, for example, tends to produce a flat, glossy surface that is largely devoid of brushmarks. This quality suited the sign-painterly style of Patrick Caulfield's early work and the decorative fairground references of some of Peter Blake's Pop art compositions, whereas the varied properties of industrial paints were exploited by Frank Stella and Richard Hamilton at several points in their careers. Bridget Riley discovered that the accelerated drying rate of emulsion housepaint assisted her painting. For Roy Lichtenstein and Andy Warhol, the flat surface that was easily produced with acrylic paint was important, while David Hockney and John Hoyland both expanded the perceived limitations of this new material by manipulating and modifying it in experimental ways. For Louis, acrylic paint was essential. The intensely coloured stains that characterised his painting simply could not have been produced with traditional oils.

Wherever possible, paints and techniques are described in the artists' own words, from recent interviews conducted by the authors. The result is an illuminating account of exactly how these paintings were made.

Modern Paints

Paint is made of two principal components: the pigments, which are finely ground powders that provide colour (and sometimes opacity), and the binder (or binding medium), which is a transparent, film-forming component into which the pigments are dispersed. The crucial function of the binder occurs during the drying process, when it converts from a liquid, fluid state into a flexible and transparent solid film. This surrounds and binds the pigments and bonds them to the painting's support.

New types of binding material became available throughout the twentieth century. At the start of the century, the binder used for most artists' paints, as well as for paint formulated for other markets, such as interior and exterior housepaints, was oil. However, as the century proceeded, the housepaint industry rapidly expanded, especially with the emergence of the do-it-yourself market; enormous investment in the development of new paints followed. Most of these advances depended on using synthetic resins as binders, which offered several advantages over traditional oil colours, such as rapid drying and reduced yellowing with age. The advancement of artists' paints followed from this, albeit at a much slower rate, but by the early 1960s, when acrylic emulsion paint became established in the artists' paint market, synthetic paints started to challenge the dominance of oil.

A huge assortment of such man-made materials has been developed. However, only four important classes of synthetic resin have been widely used in twentieth-century paints. These are (in order of their introduction) nitro-cellulose (or pyroxylin), alkyd, polyvinyl acetate (PVA) and acrylic. Of these, acrylic has been the most important synthetic resin used in paint of artists' quality, whereas the other three have been used principally in housepaints (and in other commercial paint products). Although other classes of synthetic resin have also been used in the manufacture of paint, including polyurethane, ethyl silicate, chlorinated rubber and epoxy, their use has normally been restricted to specialised industrial formulations, and they are rarely encountered in works of art.

The history and handling properties of paints made with these four

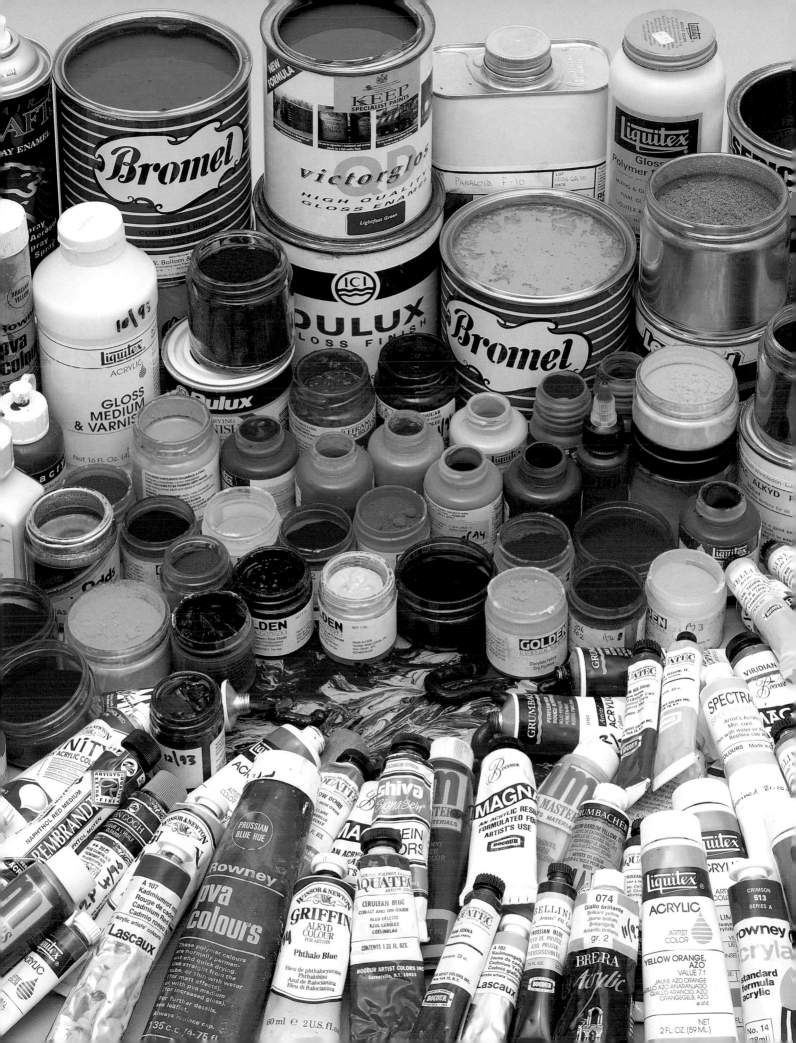

types of synthetic polymers are discussed below. For comparison, the properties of oil paint are also briefly outlined. Although oil is a natural product and is considered a traditional binding medium, it remains the binder most widely used in artists' paints.

Oil paint

There can be little doubt that oil paint has been the most important artists' medium over the last five hundred years. The use of drying oils in painting materials – that is, oils that dry to a solid film if left exposed to the air – is now thought to have been already well established by the start of the fifteenth century. For many artists oil paint still remains the preferred choice. Even in the housepaint market, the use of linseed oil as the principal binder was not surpassed in the United Kingdom until the 1950s.

Perhaps the main reason for the continued dominance of oil as a binding medium lies in its great versatility. The oil medium readily accepts a vast range of pigments, guaranteeing both opaque and transparent colours, and capable of producing deep, saturated colour. When used straight from the tube, its texture is characteristically 'buttery' and is readily manipulated during application to achieve a variety of effects. It can be spread across a canvas to produce smooth or textured layers, using a brush or other tools such as a painting knife. When used thickly, its inherent viscosity ensures that it holds the form in which it was applied. Many artists have taken advantage of this property to produce three-dimensional surfaces through large build-ups of paint and 'impasto', such as those commonly seen in the work of Frank Auerbach (fig.1) and Leon Kossoff. Oil paint can also be modified to produce a range of colour saturation and surface gloss, which can be increased by the addition of further medium and reduced by thinning with an appropriate diluent. It is possible to thin an oil paint to such an extent that it becomes little more than a stain. The diluent has traditionally been turpentine, but nowadays solvents such as white spirit are more commonly used. Other artists have achieved textural effects with oil paint by adding materials like sand, as seen, for example, in paintings by Jean Dubuffet or Cedric Morris.

Oil paint dries via a series of complex chemical reactions that involve the incorporation of atmospheric oxygen into the film. The process is relatively slow: it can take weeks for some oil paints to feel even touch dry. If oil paint is not in contact with oxygen, it will not dry. It therefore tends to dry from the surface, and it is not unusual for a thicker application of oil paint to form a skin on its surface while the inner part remains fluid. When this happens, wrinkling can occur as the paint contracts with further drying, a property that Auerbach is aware of and accepts as an inevitable result of his technique: 'I imagine that the paint has shrunk as it has oxidised – the wrinkling does not seem to alter the image'.[1]

There are a number of drying oils that exhibit appropriate properties

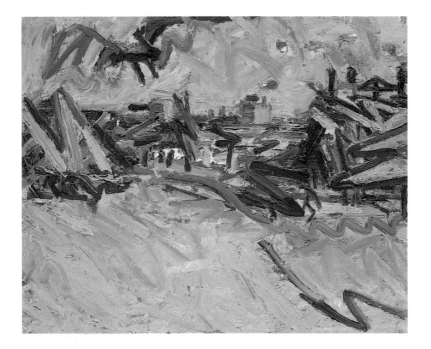

fig.1 Frank Auerbach, *The Origin of the Great Bear* 1967–8, oil on hardboard 114.6 x 140.2 cm.

for use as a binding medium. Linseed oil (extracted from the flax plant) has been used most widely due to its relatively rapid drying time. However, this is unfortunately accompanied by a tendency to yellow with age. Other, less yellowing oils have therefore sometimes been used, especially for white paints and other light colours. At the start of the century, these oils were typically walnut or poppy, but during the twentieth century others such as safflower, sunflower and soyabean have also been used. In their use of these binders, the oil paints available today are similar to those used by the Old Masters. The differences are usually in the other components, such as the pigments and extenders. In addition, many ranges will contain small amounts of 'driers' – typically lead, cobalt or manganese salts – which increase the rate of drying. A recent development is a water-mixable oil paint formulated with an oil binder that has been modified to mix with water instead of repelling it.

Nitro-cellulose (pyroxylin)

Nitro-cellulose and pyroxylin are terms used to describe a range of materials that consist of blends of different types of cellulose nitrate. Cellulose nitrate is often considered a synthetic material, as it is formed by treating natural cellulosic materials, such as paper, wood pulp or cotton, with nitric and sulphuric acids, and is therefore actually a modified natural material. It was the first 'plastic' material to be developed (around 1875) and was used extensively for early cinematic films, when it was often referred to as 'celluloid'. However, by adding a resin (initially a natural resin such as copal or mastic, but later an alkyd resin) and a plasticiser (initially camphor), and then dissolving it in an organic solvent, it can be modified into a form that is appropriate for use as a binding medium.

Nitro-cellulose first made an impact into the paint market in the 1920s, after a method had been discovered for lowering its viscosity and a wider range of solvents had become available. It became widely used as car paint and as a lacquer on furniture, although its popularity in these industries was due more to its rapid drying abilities than to its durability. The housepaint market soon adopted the medium, selling it as a gloss 'enamel' paint for interior decoration. As with all types of gloss paint, nitro-cellulose is referred to as lacquer when clear and as enamel when pigmented.

Nitro-cellulose paint was used by a number of important artists, notably those who attended David Alfaro Siqueiros's workshop in New York, established in the mid-1930s. Siqueiros had started to use car paints for his murals in the late 1920s and his workshop persuaded artists to explore these and other commercial paints. Much experimentation was carried out particularly with pyroxylin paints, often through unconventional methods of application, such as staining, dripping and pouring the fluid paint onto a support. For Siqueiros, the new synthetic resin-based paints were the appropriate means for expressing modern ideas in painting: 'to a new society must correspond new material solutions'.[2] The paint most frequently used at the workshop was Duco, the trade name of the pyroxylin-bound enamel paint made by the industrial paint manufacturers, DuPont. Its fluid viscosity and flexible handling made it ideal for trials with a variety of application methods. Through personal experience, Siqueiros gained much knowledge about the handling properties of pyroxylin paint and the potential it could offer other twentieth-century artists. Soon after the workshop had been set up, he contacted the general manager of DuPont:

I told him categorically: I am the first artist to lay claim to the use of painting materials with a synthetic resin base. And already at this moment there are at least some fifty American or American-based painters who are following my example. What will happen when all the painters of the world ... grasp the convenience of using these modern materials?[3]

Jackson Pollock's idiosyncratic technique of dripping paint onto a horizontally placed canvas suited the flow properties of gloss pyroxylin paint and by 1947 he was using Duco enamel extensively in his paintings. His wife, the artist Lee Krasner, recalled that he liked the characteristic flow of commercial paint:

He could do what he wanted to do with it. He also at one point got DuPont to make up very special paints for him and [a] special thinner that [was] not turpentine. I don't know what it was ... The paint Jackson used for the black-and-whites was commercial too – mostly black industrial enamel, Duco or Davoe & Reynolds. There was some brown enamel in a couple of the paintings.

So his 'palette' was typically a can or two of this enamel, thinned to the point he wanted it, standing on the floor beside the rolled-out canvas. Then, using sticks and hardened or worn-out brushes (which were in effect like sticks) and basting syringes, he'd begin. His control was amazing. Using a stick was difficult enough, but the basting syringe was like a giant fountain pen. With it he had to control the flow of paint as well as his gesture.[4]

Pollock's choice of gloss household and industrial enamels, applied with innovative methods, evolved as 'a natural growth out of a need, and from the need the modern artist has found new ways of expressing the world about him. I happen to find ways that are different from the usual techniques of paintings, which seems a little strange at the moment, but I don't think there's anything very different about it'.[5] Pollock continued to use gloss enamel paint for the rest of his career. From the end of the 1940s alkyd resins began to replace nitro-cellulose in many of the household and industrial enamel paint formulations. However, nitro-cellulose continued to be the principal resin for car spray paints and it was in this form that artists such as Richard Hamilton used it in the late 1950s and throughout the1960s to achieve very smooth finishes.

Alkyd
Alkyd resins are forms of polyester. The term 'alkyd' is derived from the two principal components that make an ester linkage, namely an *alc*ohol and an ac*id*. When used as paint binders they are modified with significant amounts of oil to make them sufficiently flexible, typically over 60% by weight; they are therefore often termed oil-modified alkyds. The drying process of alkyd paint is similar to that of a pure drying oil, in that it requires the incorporation of oxygen into the film. However, far fewer reactions are needed before the resin starts to solidify, so the drying time of an alkyd is significantly lower than that of a pure drying oil. A short drying time is an important factor in housepaints, and this was the reason for their widespread use.

The first of these 'oil-modified' alkyd resins was produced in 1927, but the conservative housepaint industry did not use them to replace drying oils immediately. Alkyd paints did not become commercially available in America until shortly before the Second World War, and it was not until the mid-1950s that the UK and other European paint industries became convinced that the alkyd resins were sufficiently stable. Since the early 1960s, however, alkyds have become the standard binder in all oil-based housepaints – i.e. those requiring white spirit for their dilution – and have remained so to this day. Although they have revolutionised the technology behind housepaints, they have been of limited success in the artists' paint market.

The replacement of nitro-cellulose housepaints by alkyds in enamel paint was far more immediate. Although alkyds did not dry any quicker (in fact their drying time was increased due to the drying oil content), they had vastly superior handling properties over pyroxylin. For example, the viscosity of the alkyd formulations was typically higher than nitrocellulose enamels, which meant the paint was easier to apply with a brush. The longer drying time of the alkyd paints significantly reduced the likelihood of wrinkling and helped to produce a flatter finish. In addition, a

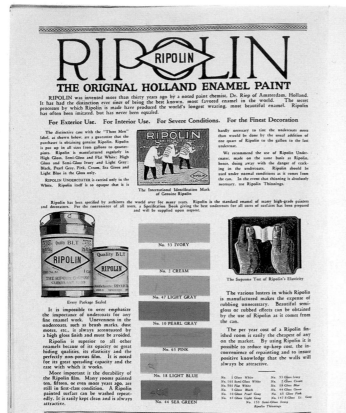
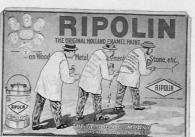

fig.2 An advertisement for Ripolin paints from c.1930.

far wider range of pigments could be successfully dispersed into alkyd resins, and the pigment content in general could be significantly increased, which resulted in more intense and/or more opaque colours.

Perhaps the most famous artist to work with housepaint was Pablo Picasso, who used it before alkyd resins had replaced drying oil. Picasso preferred Ripolin gloss paint made by a French company of the same name, although it originated in Holland (fig.2). In several letters to his dealer Daniel Henry Kahnweiler, written in 1912, Picasso mentions the paint by brand name and admires its visual quality. In one letter he refers to his 'Ripolin paintings, or *Ripolin genre*, which are the best ones'.[6] The presence of housepaint has been inferred by its distinct optical properties, evident in many paintings executed throughout his *oeuvre*. He also occasionally used boat paint, applied with house painter's brushes onto plywood panels. His wife, Françoise Gilot, recalled in 1946: 'he went down to the harbour ... and laid in a supply of boat paint because, he said, that would stand up better in the environment in which it was going to live'.[7]

Many other important artists chose to use housepaints in preference to artists' paints, which were expensive and often inaccessible. The American Abstract Expressionist Willem de Kooning discovered that housepaint was an appropriate medium with which to express expansive fields of colour and experiment with technique. The presence of alkyd resins has been detected in several of his paintings.[8] Many more artists adopted the use of alkyd housepaints during and after the 1950s, when exhibitions began to tour around the world and different types of paints and techniques were communicated to a wider audience. The 1956 exhibition *Modern Art in the United States*, which toured eight European cities including London, revealed bold imagery as well as new paint-surface effects. The impact of synthetic paints on the work of the American artists now had an irresistible allure for a young generation of artists working in the drab, austere Britain of the mid-1950s. British artists responded by introducing 'Brutalist' methods into their painting – burning, dripping and spraying household and industrial paint materials – influenced by the work of European artists such as Jean Dubuffet as well as American painters like Pollock and de Kooning.

The Australian artist Sidney Nolan incorporated commercial gloss paints in his work throughout his career, especially the range made by Ripolin, although he exploited the availability of different paint types by changing brands every three or four years. His style and technique favoured a fast-drying paint, which could be worked with speed so that the composition could be resolved quickly. Ripolin seems to have achieved an almost legendary status among many artists. Indeed, Gillian Ayres, who used Ripolin gloss paints for a number of works, including *Distillation* (fig.3), recalls doing so 'because Picasso had used it and there's a sort of trust in Picasso'. Executed in 1957, shortly after Ayres completed a commission to paint an eighty-foot mural at South Hampstead High School also using Ripolin housepaints, *Distillation* is the earliest painting in the Tate Gallery collection by a British artist in which alkyd resin has been detected. Ayres combined housepaint with areas of artists' oil colour that was often squirted directly from the tube. She employed a range of techniques, such as pouring, dripping and splashing the housepaint onto the hardboard support that she placed on the studio floor. The overall gloss of the housepaint was varied, the matt areas achieved by diluting the paint with significant quantities of turpentine: 'I liked gloss and matt'.[9] Those areas that were applied as puddles of paint often dried to wrinkled films. Although she was unable to control the surface precisely, Ayres recalls varying her techniques 'because I like [to see] what paint could do'.[10]

For those artists who wished to remove the painted image from the refined, elegant fine-art tradition commonly associated with artists' oil

paints, the household alkyd paints were a preferred option. Peter Blake, in his evocation of the fairground sign, chose to paint with enamel paints, 'rather than lacquers. Later you could buy small pots of lacquer paint, which was very quick drying, but this was an ordinary kind of enamel housepaint, gloss housepaint'. In his attempt to paint in an anonymous style similar to that of a commercial sign-writer, Patrick Caulfield also selected gloss paints, often in bold, bright colours. 'I used commercial oil when I was a student … I [bought] thick tubes of oil paint that were commercial oil paints … they were marvellous colours.' The gloss paint produced an uninterrupted paint surface: 'I'm not asking for brushstrokes. I haven't got any brushstrokes, you know; I'm not Rembrandt.'

Frank Stella's paintings frequently incorporated industrial materials such as aluminium panels as supports, and he fully exploited the range of effects produced by the various alkyd-based paints, which often presented a challenge to work with: 'We got started using lacquers … it was a beautiful color and it came through the aluminum in a really nice way, it was very transparent. But it was very, very fickle, you know; sometimes it would stay down, sometimes it would be gone in a flash.'

Few artists' colourmen have produced ranges of alkyd colours, which is perhaps surprising given their huge success in the housepaint market and their popular use by artists. An exception is Winsor and Newton's Griffin range, though this was not brought onto the market until the 1980s. Alkyds have, however, been more widely used in the manufacture of artists' primers and oil painting media. Products such as Wingel, Liquin and Oleopasto (Winsor & Newton) and Spectraflow (Spectrum) are media that can be added to oil paints to modify their properties: some will simply speed up the drying process, others ensure a more uniform gloss, and some impart a thicker consistency or thixotropic (non-drip) character.

Polyvinyl acetate

Polyvinyl acetate (PVA) resins were first introduced in the 1930s. When dissolved in an appropriate organic solvent they make useful varnishes and paint binders. However, this form of *solution* paint was never successful and PVA only became widely used by the paint industry when it came onto the market as a water-borne *emulsion* at the start of the 1950s. It is important to distinguish between the solution and emulsion forms of PVA (and indeed of any polymer), as they have quite different handling properties.

A solution paint dries simply by the evaporation of the solvent. The drying time is therefore much quicker than oil (and alkyd) paint, typically creating a touch-dry paint film after an hour. The dried film can be re-dissolved in the same solvent in which it was initially dissolved. However, in the emulsion form the PVA polymer is not dissolved but *dispersed* in water; emulsions are often, and more correctly, called dispersions. The concept of dispersion is an important one, since PVA is insoluble in

fig.3 Gillian Ayres, *Distillation* 1959, oil and alkyd housepaint on hardboard 213.4 x 152.4 cm.

water. In an emulsion, the PVA polymer exists as distinct spherical particles that are mixed in the water phase with significant quantities of surfactant, which is basically a detergent. It is the same principle that enables water to clean greasy plates when detergent is added. When an emulsion dries, the water first evaporates, but this is accompanied by the polymer spheres fusing together to form a continuous film. This means that although it can be thinned with water, once the film has dried it cannot be re-dissolved in water.

The main advantage of emulsions is simply that water is the principal liquid component, so the amount of organic solvent, which is typically toxic and has a stronger odour, is drastically reduced. Emulsions also dry rapidly, typically within an hour, although subsequent layers can often be applied sooner than this. Thus it is difficult to paint wet-in-wet with emulsion paint due to this short working time. An important visual difference between solutions and emulsions in the wet state is seen when the two forms are unpigmented. The solution form appears as a clear solution, while the emulsion is white and opaque (although it dries to a transparent coating). This characteristic opacity is the result of the inability of light to pass through the emulsion without being reflected and refracted by the polymer particles. One of the more familiar types of PVA emulsion is that used for white wood glues such as Resin W (in the UK) or Elmer's Glue-All and Rivit Glue (in the USA).

As with the alkyds, PVA has had fairly limited use in the artists' paint market. Alfred Duca, an American artist, worked with the paint manufacturers Borden Co. to develop an artists' PVA emulsion paint, Polymer Tempera, which was first produced in 1945. Problems with the effective distribution of the pigments in the medium, however, meant that the paint never achieved success among artists. In 1966, Rowney introduced a range of pre-mixed PVA colours in the UK, but these never caught on either, presumably because they offered no advantages over acrylic emulsion paint (see Acrylic section below), other than relative cost. In the early 1960s, Rowney had also marketed an unpigmented artists' PVA emulsion binding medium (the first in the UK), into which artists could mix their choice of pigments. This system offered artists an extremely quick-drying paint combined with a great deal of control over the colours and gloss. However, the necessary grinding process was laborious. Spectrum Oil Colours, a small paint company in the UK, soon followed, promoting a similar system of pigments and binder in component parts. However, their pigments were supplied as aqueous dispersions, which meant that they were readily mixed into the media, and they provided a choice of binders, namely a PVA emulsion, an acrylic emulsion and a blend of the two called a acrylic-vinyl copolymer. This permitted far greater control over the consistency, gloss and colour intensity of the paint.

Despite its limited use in the artists' paint market, PVA has remained

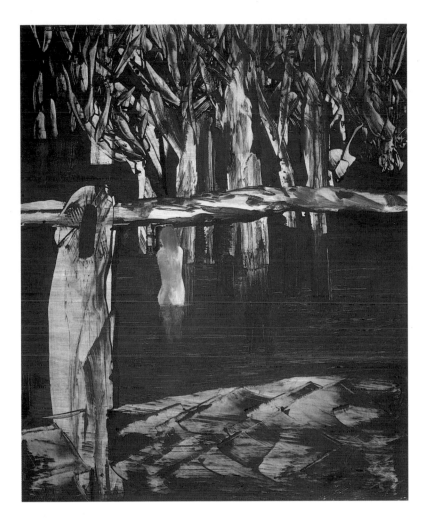

the principal type of binder in most emulsion interior housepaints in the UK since the early 1960s (hence the term '*vinyl* emulsion'). They are generally agreed to possess slightly inferior properties to the acrylic emulsion paints in terms of toughness, binding power and resistance to weathering, but are far less expensive, and perfectly adequate for standard interior use. In other countries there have been some slight variations, such as in Germany, where a 'copolymer' of acrylic and styrene is more commonly used, and in the United States immediately following the Second World War when emulsions based on synthetic rubber (butadiene-styrene) were developed in an attempt to use up the massive excess of this material that had been produced for the war effort.

The use by artists of PVA emulsion housepaints does not appear to have been as widespread as the solvent-borne alkyd type. This is probably due to the availability of a very limited colour range and because they were soon followed by the introduction of the artists' quality acrylic emulsion paints, which essentially offered all the same advantages. One of the more notable users was Bridget Riley, who used PVA emulsion housepaint for her black-and-white paintings in the early 1960s.

A number of important artists combined commercial unpigmented

PVA emulsions and dry pigments to make up their own paints, employing a similar principle to the Rowney/Spectrum PVA component paints. One of the earliest was Alberto Burri, who from 1950 used a brand of PVA called Vinavyl. Sidney Nolan, who had painted for a number of years with Ripolin enamel paint, changed to PVA in 1957, describing it as a 'very fluent kind of emulsion medium'.[11] *Women and Billabong* (fig.4), painted in May of that year, was one of his first works to be painted in the new medium. As Nolan recalled:

I used polyvinyl acetate because it was such a fast-drying medium that I had to work very quickly against it. It was like cooking a soufflé. There was a point at which it bubbled and hardened and you couldn't use it anymore; it was like lava. So one had a specified time for producing images, and this was quite exciting ... I like to work against the medium, so I keep changing. I think it's partly a result of working with different mediums as a boy in factories; all kinds of commercial synthetic substances so that now I have a taste for them.[12]

In America, Kenneth Noland recalls using a similar approach, particularly when large areas of colour were needed:

They started selling a kind of glue called Elmer's Glue. It was one of those water-soluble glues. It was kind of like the beginning of latex [emulsion] paints. They were using it in water-soluble paints to paint houses. Well ... you could buy it by the gallon. I used to put dry pigment in it ... David Smith gave me some dry pigment.

Although this system was inexpensive, thereby facilitating experimentation, Noland recalls that 'the water-soluble paints dried milky; it made the colours stay opaque ... It was something that was very hard to get around because you couldn't get into looking right into a colour as if it were glass.'[13] PVA has been detected in the background yellow colour of *Gift* (fig.5), painted in 1961.

Acrylic

The term acrylic covers a diverse range of materials that first became widely available in the 1930s. One of the more familiar types is Perspex (known as Plexiglass in the USA), a rigid and brittle material, too hard for use as a paint binder. Conversely, many of the current pressure-sensitive adhesives are also acrylic, but these remain tacky and would therefore be too soft for paint. Between these two extremes lie a number of acrylic resins whose flexibility and other physical properties are appropriate for use as a paint binder. Acrylic paint is the most important type of synthetic paint developed for artists' use. However, due to their relatively high cost compared to other synthetic resins, the use of acrylic resins in housepaint formulations has normally been restricted to coatings that require superior durability, such as paints designed for bathrooms and kitchens, or exterior coatings.

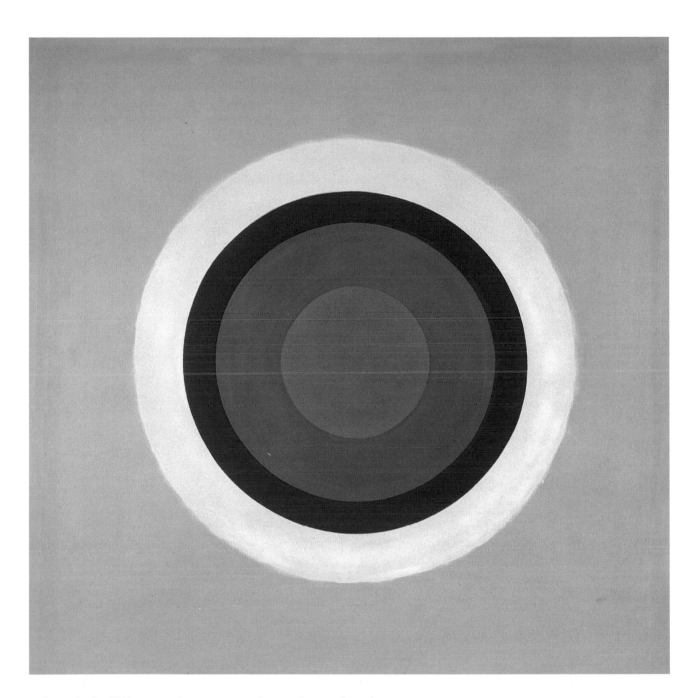

As with the PVA paints, there are two distinct forms of acrylic paint: the solution and the emulsion. However, unlike PVA, the solution type had a huge impact on twentieth-century painting. The first artists' acrylic paint, known as Magna, was an acrylic solution type. Magna was developed by the American paint makers Leonard Bocour and Sam Golden in the late 1940s and marketed as 'the first new painting medium in 500 years' (fig.6). The acrylic resin they used was a polybutyl methacrylate called Acryloid F-10 (or Paraloid F-10 in the UK), and this was dissolved in turpentine to make a clear solution. Bocour and Golden recall being given a jar of the acrylic resin in 1941 by an artist who asked if they could add pigment to it. So Bocour approached the American company Rohm

fig.5 Kenneth Noland, *Gift* 1961–2, acrylic solution and PVA emulsion on canvas 182.9 x 182.9 cm.

and Haas, the principal manufacturers of acrylic resins. He remembers telling them that he 'wanted something with viscosity, something that could simulate oil, and they thought in terms of housepaint, something that was very loose and liquidy and very, very flat. However, with a few trips they did help me and I did have a paint that was very, very good.'[14] Presumably Bocour wanted a resin that simulated oil paint so that artists could switch easily from oil to his acrylic paint without significantly affect-

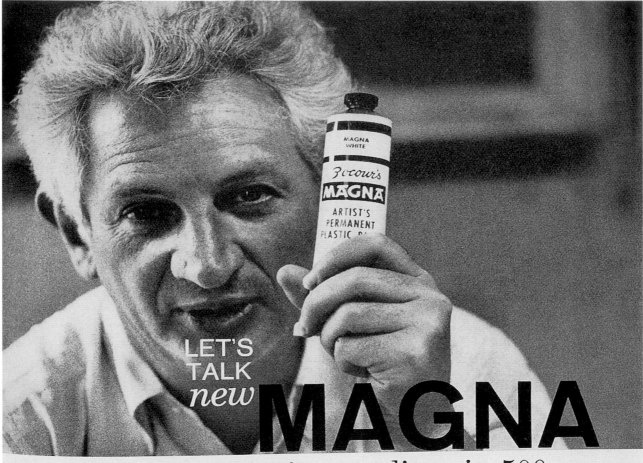

fig.6 A 1956 advertisement for Magna acrylic solution paint.

ing their technique, and he advertised that Magna paint could be mixed into oil paint. He also marketed it as an alternative to oil, with its rapid drying qualities and superior flexibility.

Bocour and Golden kept the pigment concentration in Magna paints deliberately high, so that the paint could be thinned with considerable amounts of solvent and still produce a saturated, intense colour. Whenever possible, they also chose pigments that were transparent, so the colours of the dried films were typically deep and pure, providing that the pigment was properly dispersed in the medium. The Magna paint film does, however, remain soluble in turpentine or mineral spirits after drying, which could present problems in overpainting, since the subsequent layer of paint has a tendency to re-dissolve the underlayer. An effective method of reducing this problem is to isolate each layer with a retouching varnish (made with an acrylic solution not soluble in mineral spirits). Lichtenstein employed this technique in his almost exclusive use of Magna paint: 'I always used the sealing varnish in between the layers of Magna. I think you would almost have to; it gets very sticky if you don't.'

Bocour enjoyed a close association with several artists who worked in New York:

I had what I now refer to as the Bocour Bread Line. You see we used to grind the paint … and you could not make just the right amount of colour to fit the tube. There would always be a little bit of paint left over and if it was enough to fill half a tube, I would put it in a tube. But if it was not enough, then I would put it in a piece of wax paper and throw it in this basket.[15]

Artists such as Mark Rothko, Willem De Kooning, Barnett Newman, Kenneth Noland and Morris Louis would visit the shop on 15th Street in New York to obtain the paint and discuss their use of it with Bocour. Noland, who used the paint extensively, remembers that one of the principal reasons for this preference was that 'when you thinned Magna it held its intensity. If you thinned oil, it dispersed the pigments'.[16] The circles in *Gift* (fig.5), painted in 1962, were all executed in Magna. The close collaboration that developed between Bocour and Morris Louis resulted in the paint being modified to suit Louis's technique, which demanded a thinner, more finely ground paint, crucial for creating the transparent stain effects on canvas made by thinning the Magna with turpentine.

Magna is the best-known of the acrylic solution range of paints. Bocour later sold Bocour Artist Colours, Inc. to Zipatone of Chicago, but they ceased making Magna paint in the early 1990s. Lichtenstein immediately bought up all available supplies and contacted Mark Golden of Golden Artist Colours to discuss the possibility of making the paint for him following the original formula. Golden Artist Colours now produces a mineral spirit-borne acrylic paint called MSA Colours, which is very similar to the original Magna. This satisfied Lichtenstein, who was concerned about his dwindling supplies of Magna: 'I could paint in something else but I'd have to learn to paint all over again.'

Acrylic emulsions were initially developed for use in exterior housepaint and first introduced by Rohm and Haas in 1953. One of the earliest emulsions they developed was called Rhoplex (or Primal in the UK) AC-34 and this was used by Permanent Pigments, another American paint company, to formulate the first artists' acrylic emulsion paint, known as Liquitex. Their founder and chemist, Henry Levinson, recalls the moment he realised the distinct stability of the acrylic emulsions: 'I had a cracked

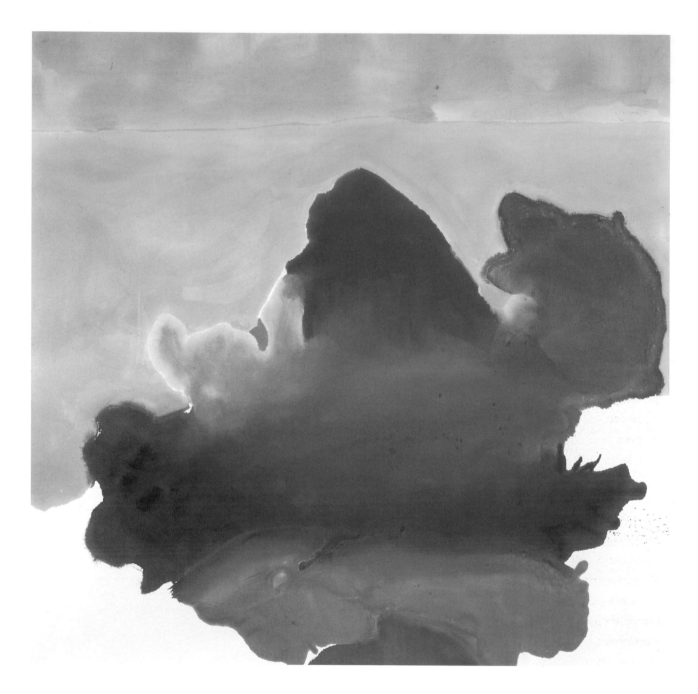

fig.7 Helen Frankenthaler, *The Bay* 1963,
acrylic on canvas 205.1 x 207.7 cm.
The Detroit Institute of Arts.
Founders Society Purchase,
Dr and Mrs Hilbert H. DeLawter Fund

jar of acrylic emulsion that didn't solidify even though the lid was cracked. It was there for close to a year so I decided that this was stable enough to make artists' colours'.[17]

When first introduced, Liquitex was rather thin and runny, and was not immediately successful. However, several artists did experiment with it, such as Andy Warhol and Helen Frankenthaler. In the 1950s Frankenthaler had created her stained canvases using thinned oil paint on sized canvas, which left halos of oil around the colour. As her technique developed, it demanded a paint that was 'thinner and more fluid, and cried out to be soaked, not resting'.[18] Unlike oil paint, acrylic emulsion tends not to produce this halo effect. It could also be applied directly to a fabric support (the inherent acidic nature of oil can cause a fabric to deteriorate when in direct contact), which was a very important feature for artists wishing to apply thin stains. Indeed, acrylic emulsions can be applied directly to a whole range of supports, including paper, hardboards and aluminium panels in addition to the usual fabric supports, so long as they are not oily or greasy.

Frankenthaler's second trial with acrylic emulsion paint in the early 1960s was successful and from then on she continued to paint with it. The paint could be 'scratchy, tough, modern, once-removed – you're not as involved in métier, wrist, or medium as is often the case with oil. At its best, it fights painterliness for me.'[19] The effect of the acrylic medium could be 'often very cold and often without feeling', but she soon adapted to it, discovering that she 'would rather cope with the lack of sentiment' in her painting than have too much of it.[20] One of her earlier works from this second period of painting with Liquitex was *The Bay*, painted in 1963, in which most areas of the acrylic emulsion have created precise regions of staining in the cotton canvas (fig.7). Although there are a few areas where a slight feathering of the edges has occurred, the halo that had characterised many of her earlier oil paintings is clearly not present.

Liquitex introduced a new formulation in 1963. This had a much thicker consistency, which was closer to that of oil paint, and Liquitex rapidly became an established artists' paint (fig.8). Several other artists' colourmen had realised the potential of acrylic emulsion paints when the first version of Liquitex had appeared and, having carried out their own development, introduced their own brands in 1963–4. These were mainly the other big American paint companies, such as Grumbacher (their range was called 'Hyplar'), Shiva ('Shiva') and Bocour ('Aqua-tec'). Bocour had by then formed his own company. New Masters, another American company, also brought out a range of emulsion paint at this time, although it was slightly different to the pure acrylic paints. Their brand was bound in an acrylic-vinyl emulsion, a material that combines the components of acrylic with those of PVA, and was formulated as a much

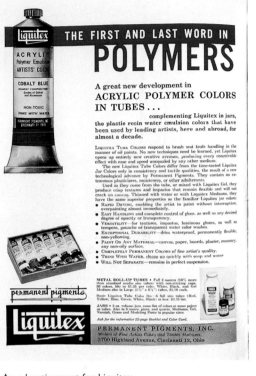

fig.8 An advertisement for Liquitex acrylic emulsion tube paints from 1964.

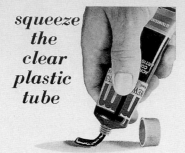

fig.9 A 1963 advertisement for New Masters acrylic-vinyl paints.

thicker consistency, a feature that was clearly stressed in their early advertisements (fig.9).

The advantages of an emulsion system were perhaps never in doubt. Many of the properties of acrylic emulsion paints are similar to those of the PVA emulsions. For example, they can be thinned with water when wet, but cannot be re-dissolved in water once dried. With water as the diluent, emulsion paints are simple and convenient to use, and can be applied without the stringent safety precautions required for paints dissolved in organic solvents. They dry extremely rapidly – even thick applications are usually dry within a few hours. They often become touch dry far more quickly than this, which means that subsequent layers can be applied in rapid succession, although this makes wet-in-wet working of the paint technically difficult.

David Hockney made the departure from oil to acrylic emulsion paint when he moved to America in 1963. His oil paintings were characterised by variations in the paints' thickness, and other materials were often incorporated to introduce different textures. In his subsequent paintings he required a more consistent, smooth surface to avoid distraction from the image. He found he could apply acrylic paint more thinly and efficiently: 'When I worked with oil paints I always had to work on at least three or four pictures at the same time because then you could keep working every day ... you had to wait for things to dry. Whereas now it's possible to work on one all the time.'[21]

The availability of acrylic emulsion paints was not restricted to America. In 1963, George Rowney and Sons introduced the first range in Britain: Cryla (fig.10). Spectrum introduced their binder/pigment component paints soon after, of which the acrylic emulsion binder proved to be by far the most successful: the PVA and acrylic-vinyl copolymer were both discontinued in the 1970s. John Hoyland, who was painting in Britain at this time, recalls being aware of Magna and Liquitex, the early acrylic products in America, and made a rapid switch from oil to acrylic emulsion when it first became available in the UK. His thinly painted layers of oil paint on canvas already suggested an acrylic paint surface imitating the stained acrylic surface of the American abstract painters, such as Morris Louis. When Cryla was introduced in the UK in 1963 he immediately adopted it, having abandoned the 'voluptuary of paint and surface that was generally considered to be fairly old hat at that time'. His switch from oil to acrylic emulsion was also connected to 'this idea that historically, art always changed when techniques changed, from gesso to oil and so on and so forth, and this had the faint hum of new technology about it that was behind the new philosophy.' When he later started to use thicker applications of paint, the acrylic's reduced drying time was clearly an important advantage, as was its resistance to wrinkling on drying. Acrylic emulsion is far more likely to dry with air pockets in its films, due to the significant quantities of surfactant that is present in it which can easily start to lather if stirred up vigorously.

Nowadays, there are a number of relatively large international artists' paint companies whose trade relies upon the sale of acrylic emulsion paint to the amateur art market. Most of them offer an assortment of

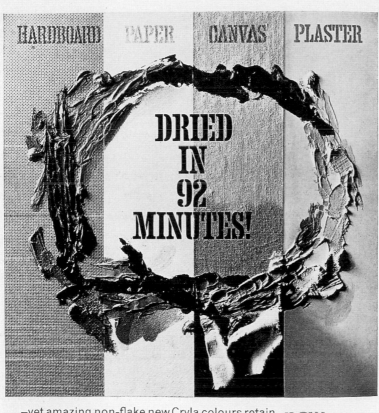

fig.10 Rowney Cryla advertisement from 1964.

acrylic media, such as gels and pastes, that can be added to the tube colours, so that a range of consistencies can be created. However, there remains a place for the more specialised paint company, such as Golden in the USA, which has attempted to meet the specific requirements of the artist in terms of technical flexibility and has provided custom-made acrylic products for individual painters.

Methods of Examination

For more than ten years, the Tate Gallery's Conservation Department has recorded (from written questionnaires and extensive conversations) artists' recollections of the exact materials and techniques they used when creating works belonging to the collection. For this book their memories were augmented with a review of published literature, and the authors have conducted further focused interviews with most of the artists and/or their assistants, giving them an opportunity to discuss the comparative merits of various paints and the artists' techniques in greater detail.

Unless otherwise indicated, the quotations used in this book have been taken from these recent interviews. Information obtained in this way,

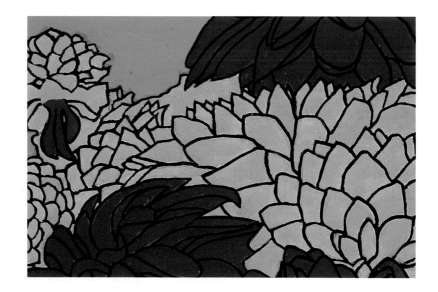

fig.11 Detail from *Vases of Flowers* by Patrick Caulfield (see fig.33 for full image).

however, may not be complete, and is occasionally misleading: memories are often accurate but sometimes not. To support the recollections of the artists, all the descriptions of paint-type have been corroborated by scientific analysis of the paints themselves.

The scientific analysis of paint used in late twentieth-century works is a recent development. Although many museums around the world regularly analyse traditional painting materials, the examination of synthetic paints is not widely practised. The Scientific Section of the Tate Gallery Conservation Department has developed two techniques for differentiating between the various types of synthetic binding media: Fourier transform infrared spectroscopy (FTIR) and pyrolysis-gas chromatography-mass spectrometry (Py-GC-MS). Whilst studying the works of the ten artists assembled here, these methods generally confirmed information obtained from other sources. There were, however, occasions when this information was found to be either incomplete or inaccurate. Inevitably, the reliance on analytical results was greater for the artists whom it was not possible to interview.

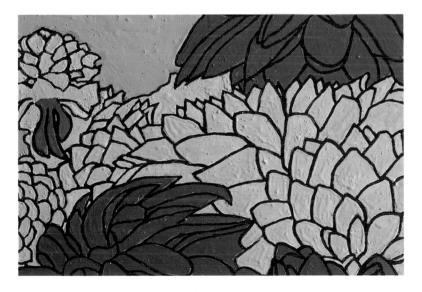

fig.12 The same detail from *Vases of Flowers* taken in raking light from the right.

There are a number of different photographic techniques that can be used to illustrate a painting. For this book 'normal' light and 'raking' light photography were used extensively, although occasionally the more sophisticated techniques of ultraviolet (UV) and infrared (IR) photography were employed.

For normal light photography, a light source is placed on either side of the painting to ensure that the colours are accurately recorded. Fig.11 shows a detail of Patrick Caulfield's 1962 painting, *Vases of Flowers* (see p.54), taken under normal lighting conditions, replicating the turquoise of the background and the red and yellow of the flowers.

It might be inferred from this photograph that the paint surface is completely flat. With raking light photography, a single light source is

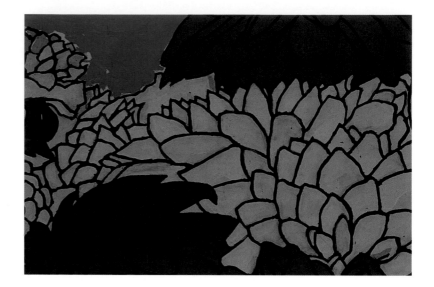

fig.13 The same detail from *Vases of Flowers* under ultraviolet (UV) radiation.

placed to one side or above the painting at an acute angle. The light picks out the texture of the surface, so that it becomes possible to distinguish between high build-ups of paint and very thin layers where the texture of the painting's support might become visible (this is particularly true for paintings on canvas). When the same area of the Caulfield painting is viewed under raking light (fig.12), the texture of the paint surface is exaggerated. Marks left by Caulfield's brush become visible, particularly in the petals. The paint surface is fundamentally flat and is characteristic of a housepaint applied to a solid support (such as hardboard, which is used here). It can be seen that an appreciable quantity of dust and dirt has been absorbed into many areas of the paint, giving it a more granular texture. In the top left corner, the turquoise paint film has wrinkled. Raking light photography also helps determine the order in which different colours were applied. For example, the yellow paint extends slightly over the black outlines of the petals in a number of places, indicating that it was applied after the black.

Raking light photography is invaluable as a means of illustrating texture. However, an unfortunate consequence of this lighting process is that colours can appear altered (compare the colours in figs.11 and 12). To compensate for this, a 'partial' raking light is sometimes used, when two light sources are set up (as in normal lighting conditions), but one is placed in the raking position, so that an indication of texture is still given without affecting the colours to the same extent.

In fig.13 the same area of *Vases of Flowers* is viewed under UV illumination. This is an established examination technique. UV can cause materials to fluoresce to varying degrees, depending on the nature of

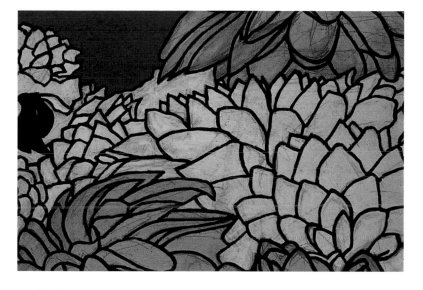

fig.14 The same detail from *Vases of Flowers* taken with infrared (IR) film.

the binding medium and pigments. Two paints that look identical under visible light can often appear slightly different under UV lighting. It is a particularly useful device for detecting repainting over a layer of varnish: most varnishes fluoresce quite strongly, and any subsequent retouching will appear dark in comparison. In fig.13, the turquoise used in the background appears dark because of its complete lack of fluorescence under UV. There are a number of areas around the yellow flower in the top left corner which appear lighter in colour because of a higher UV fluorescence. These areas correspond to a green paint that was used over the entire background before the turquoise was applied. If the normal light photograph is now re-examined (fig.11), the green colour is visible.

Fig.14 is a photograph taken in normal lighting conditions using infrared film. This gives an image whose colours are dependent on the amount of infrared radiation reflected or absorbed by the various materials. Because graphite is a particularly strong absorber of IR radiation, IR imaging techniques are frequently used to detect the presence of preparatory drawings underneath paint layers. In this detail, a large number of pencil lines can be seen. Some of these are visible under normal lighting, but IR photography makes them far more prominent.

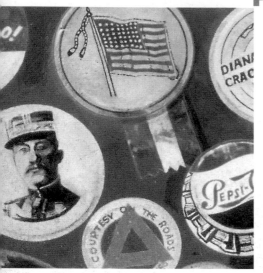

Peter Blake born 1932

Peter Blake is probably best known for his Pop art works, produced in the mid-to-late 1950s, a time when the visual art world was becoming heavily influenced by advertising and mass communication. Blake endeavoured to translate this popular imagery into a fine art style, and the incorporation of non-traditional materials and techniques into his working methods played an integral part in this. Although most of these works involved areas of collage, his use of paint was just as important and he usually chose a type of paint with a particular surface effect in mind. Blake has always placed great significance on the surface qualities of his paintings, even though he has 'never been interested in the preparation side of things … I've never made a rabbit [skin] glue in my life. I've never stretched a canvas'.

While a student at the Royal College of Art in London, Blake was instructed in the traditional techniques of oil painting on canvas. However, the early Pop art works that followed were a clear departure from his figurative oil studies, particularly in terms of the materials he used to make them. 'I was using wood and photographs and enamel paints and in fact I even used bitumen at one point.' He was aware that some of his contemporaries, such as William Green and Robyn Denny, had also started to look for alternatives to oil, but claimed, 'I was using different new materials … I think the thing was no one was using enamel. I think that was the breakthrough'.

One of Blake's earliest Pop art pieces, *The Fine Art Bit* (fig.16), was typical of works from this period, combining collage with horizontal bands of gloss housepaint. By this time, he had been introduced to colour-field painting, particularly through the work of Richard Smith, with whom he shared a flat for three years. He recalls that 'at that point all my contemporaries were interested in the first Rothkos they were seeing'. He had also recently seen the work of other American artists shown for the first time in London.

I wouldn't have thought at the time that it influenced me but it clearly did in

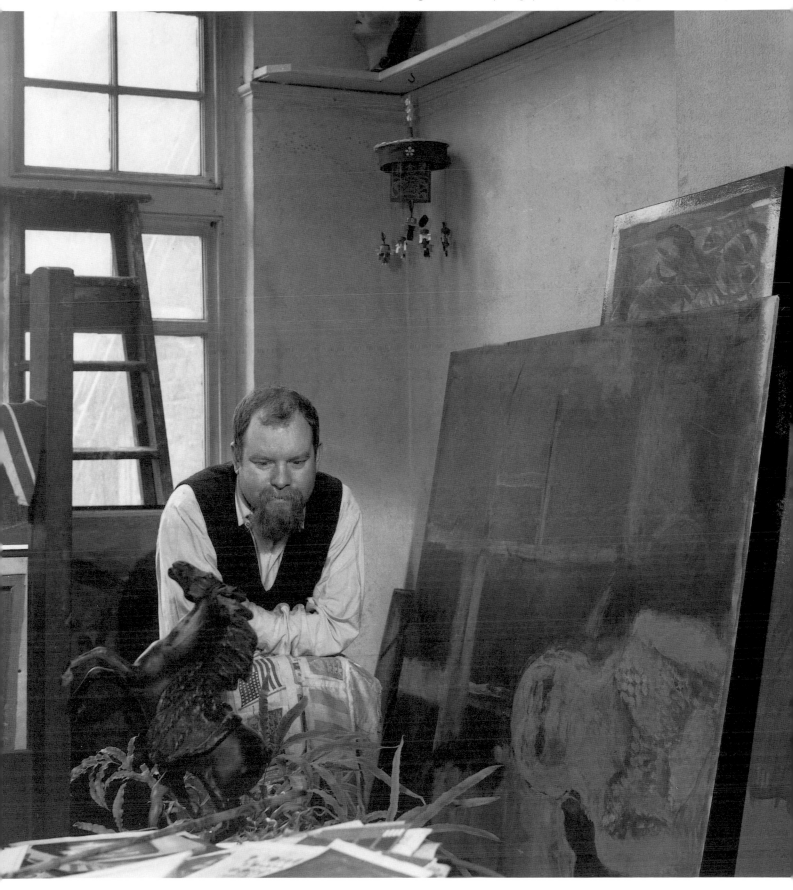

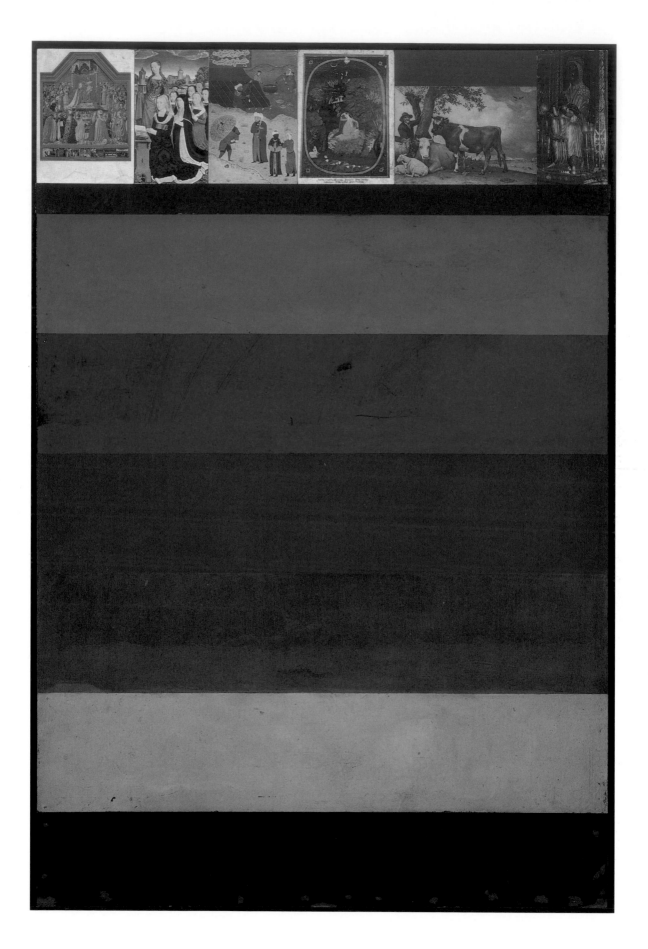

some ways. [*The Fine Art Bit*] is about some kind of hard-edged painting that was just starting to happen then. Even someone like Ellsworth Kelly was an influence in some way … Along with my contemporaries and friends I was seeing these pictures and it was coming into my work in a very subtle way.

The painted area in *The Fine Art Bit* consists of six horizontal bands of colour on a single piece of hardboard, used as a support for economic reasons: 'The financial situation changes things. I can buy canvas now; I couldn't then'. The panel was primed with a dark grey undercoat. He remembers that 'you could only get grey undercoat then. Grey or probably white'. It is separated from the series of collaged images at the top by a strip of gloss-painted wood. Blake recalls that the paint he used was 'an ordinary kind of enamel housepaint', probably taken from Humbrol's range of alkyd housepaints, which he used frequently throughout his career. He chose this type of paint largely for aesthetic reasons: 'I was interested in fairground painting. They used gloss paint'.

Before the application of gloss paint, Blake marked the boundaries of the bands of colour with incised lines, scored into the hardboard surface. These are still visible, particularly when viewed under raking light, for example between the pink and yellow bands seen in fig.17. He then applied paint directly from the tin, without any mixing of colours, lying the panel flat on a table to prevent excessive running of the very liquid paint. At each intersection of colour, the first painted band extended well into the area of the next band, and the straight edge of each top colour was 'painted by hand, just taking it up to the side of the [incised] line. Sometimes [the paint] would run into [the line]'. By viewing two adjacent bands in raking light, it is possible to see which colour extends underneath the other, and therefore which was applied first. For example, in fig.17 the lower part of the pink band appears thicker compared to the upper part because the yellow band runs underneath it. From the examination of each border it can be deduced that the order of application was from the black band at the bottom of the panel, through each colour in turn to the green band at the top. For every band he applied a number of individual paint layers: 'I would have kept going until I got what I wanted'. The only modification to this order was that after all the bands had been painted, additional applications of colour were made to the black and red bands. Subsequently these two colours appear more opaque than the others.

An important feature of *The Fine Art Bit* is that various surface effects have been deliberately incorporated into the otherwise smooth bands of colour. 'I partly wanted it to be like a hard-edged painting but I wanted different surfaces … I was interested in the surfaces on old paintings, whether they were Renaissance paintings, or walls that had paintings on them that had been scratched away'. He 'consciously sandpapered away'

fig.17 Detail from *The Fine Art Bit* taken in raking light from below, showing the texture of the paint surface and incised lines.

fig.16 *The Fine Art Bit* 1959, alkyd housepaint and collage on hardboard 91.4 x 61 cm.

fig.18 A second raking light detail from *The Fine Art Bit* (this time from the left), showing evidence of Blake's use of sandpaper.

fig.19 Detail from *Tuesday* taken in raking light from below, showing edges left by masking tape, wrinkling in yellow paint and debris absorbed into the paint.

the blue layer to leave a scratched surface, contrasting with the adjacent green band, which is reasonably flat and glossy (fig.18). The scratches extend well into the lower green band, although the green paint was applied in sufficient thickness to cover most of them.

Each colour displays a slightly different surface texture. The yellow paint, for example, has a surface indicative of a very fluid paint, characterised by 'tide marks' as well as drips, some of which were subsequently covered by the adjacent pink band (fig.17). The drips were formed as a result of placing the painting upright before the paint had dried. The small circular marks in the yellow band, visible in the top-left corner of this detail, were probably caused by bubbles that were present in the wet paint on application. The yellow band has also absorbed a certain amount of dirt into its surface. The pink paint, on the other hand, is transparent and brushmarks are visible in its surface. Blake discovered that fairground painters used 'a paint called Flamboyant, which is like a coloured varnish, and that was the effect I was probably trying to get on the pink [band] … It's literally like a varnish stain. They use it over gold leaf a lot on the fun fairs'.

Blake had intended to retouch a few areas in the black band where he had hammered pins through the hardboard to a supporting batten frame behind. He used the grey undercoat paint as the first layer of retouching, but the process was abandoned before the black gloss topcoat was applied because he decided that he actually 'liked the effect of the [grey] retouching'. This illustrates Blake's desire to distress the work so that it looked 'like an old piece from a fun fair'. In contrast to the distressed bands of colour, the strip of painted wood and frame were painted 'as immaculately as possible'. The frame was just a 'simple way of edging the picture' and consists of thin strips of wood. These were painted in black gloss paint and their surface, unlike those of the painted bands, 'should be pristine'.

When Blake painted *Tuesday* (fig.20) two years later, he 'was making [a] point of using primary colours, which people simply didn't use [at that time] and using enamels to get them as simple [as possible] … It was making a statement about colour … to suddenly start using red, yellow and blue in that context was very strange'. Compared to *The Fine Art Bit*, the paint is more opaque and the execution of the bands of colour 'was meant to be much more precise', resulting in a surface that 'would have been very pristine'. The paints are again alkyd housepaints and several thin applications were used to achieve the very smooth surface. However, there are still some drying effects that are visible in the paint surfaces, such as the wrinkles in the lower part of the yellow band and the minor tide marks in the blue band (fig.19).

For this piece, Blake abandoned his previous technique of scoring lines into the panels to mark out the positions of bands. Instead, he used mask-

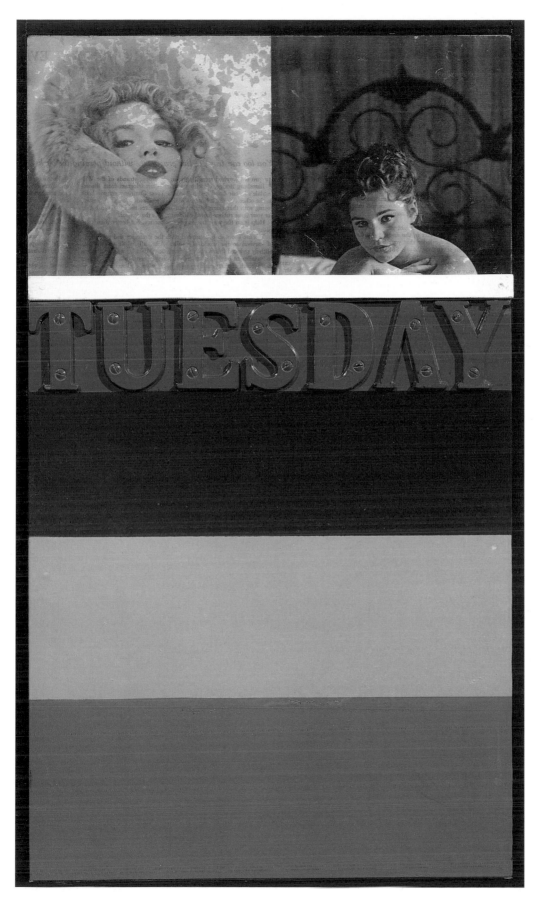

fig.20 *Tuesday* 1961,
alkyd housepaint and
collage on hardboard
47.6 x 26.7 cm.

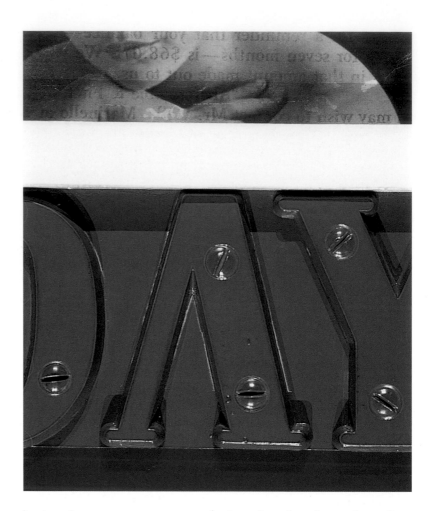

fig.21 Detail from *Tuesday* showing the inverted 'V' letter used for the 'A' in Tuesday, taken in raking light from above and below. The extent of the red paint beneath the green is also visible.

fig.22 *Self-Portrait with Badges* 1961, oil on hardboard 174.3 x 121.9 cm.

ing tape in an attempt to prevent the intrusion of marks on the surface. These bands consequently display a slightly raised edge, characteristic of the use of masking tape. The upper line, seen in fig.19, was formed by masking tape used when the blue paint was applied over the yellow band, whereas the lower line indicates the lower border of the yellow band beneath the blue. Once again he used a strip of gloss-painted wood to separate the painted surface from the collaged photographs, which he took from *Playboy* magazine. He bought the plastic letters used to spell 'Tuesday' from Woolworths, whose stock of the alphabet was incomplete: 'I couldn't get an 'A' so I just used a 'V' [inverted]'. A detail of the letter 'A' is seen in fig.21, which also shows the upper border of the red band of colour that lies beneath the green that was used to paint the letters.

The liquid adhesive used to attach the image of the actress Tuesday Weld to the panel face has caused the paper to become translucent over time, exposing the printed type on the reverse of the image, an effect neither anticipated nor intended. But Blake considers this 'the natural ageing of a picture. I've always treated that as a part of the process … that pictures get their own patina during their life, and that I usually accept. Certainly in a collage, if a paper changes colour, I accept that'.

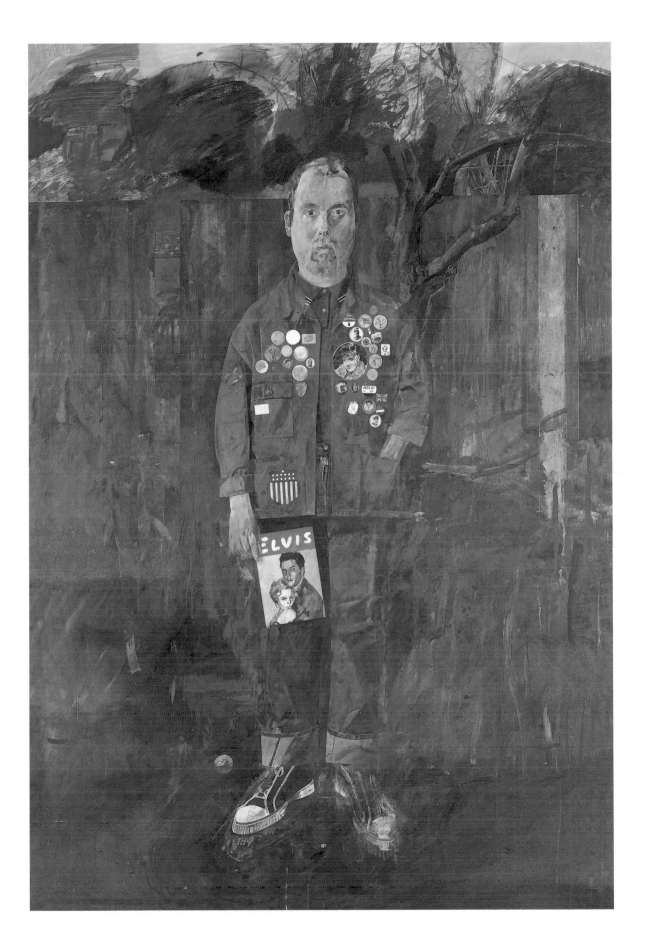

fig.23 Detail from *Self-Portrait with Badges*, showing exposed areas of hardboard and drips in the paint.

Throughout the period in which he used collage and housepaints, Blake continued to paint in oil colours and to work with more traditional techniques to make paintings such as *Self-Portrait with Badges* (fig.22). As he explains, 'I've always had this core of being a straight figurative painter, but I've made excursions from that. They might be wood engraving, they might be Pop art'. In this painting, he 'started with a very rough drawing in pencil, just to establish more or less where the figure would go'. He then 'painted straight onto the hardboard' without any sort of priming or further preparation. He painted his head, shoes, trousers and shirt from his reflection in a mirror, but dressed a dummy in the jacket decorated with badges, in order to paint it. The thin, sketchily applied paint was initially intended to be underpainting; 'eventually the fence would have been very solid and the tree and the plants would have been much more like plants'. But Blake had a three-month deadline for the John Moores Exhibition that year and had to submit the painting unfinished. On its return, however, he decided to leave it as it was: 'Whereas some of the others stay works in progress until I finish them, I accepted that is how it should stay'.

Blake painted many areas of the picture in thin glazes of oil paint, heavily diluted with turpentine; this method of applying the paint as a repeated build-up of thin layers was similar to watercolour technique. The hardboard surface is still visible through some of the more transparent areas. He recounts that he 'actually used the brown [of the hardboard] as a colour. It comes through quite a bit and that was deliberate'. The brown seen in fig.23, a detail from the lower-right part of the painting, is the bare hardboard. Also shown in this detail are several paint drips. 'The fact that I was sharing a flat with Dick Smith at that point probably accounts for the dribbled paints.' The transparency of oil paint tends to increase slightly with time and he feels that this effect has already resulted in a more pronounced contrast between dark and light areas than was originally intended.

A number of other techniques have also been used in this work. For example, the 'circles [of the badges] were done with a compass filled with paint [whereas] the lettering would have just been copied [freehand] rather than traced or anything like that'. Fig.24 shows a detail of some of the badges viewed in a raking light, which reveals holes caused by the compass point at the centre of each badge and the remarkable detail in which the badges were copied. 'I didn't need glasses then, my eyes were incredibly good'. It also shows the clean, crisp and very straight lines of the fence. The paint used for these is slightly raised compared to surrounding areas and is characteristic of paint applied with a ruling pen. In addition, the raking light picks up some brushmarks at the top of the denim jacket and just beneath the red shirt collar, both of which indicate that Blake made a number of compositional changes during its execution.

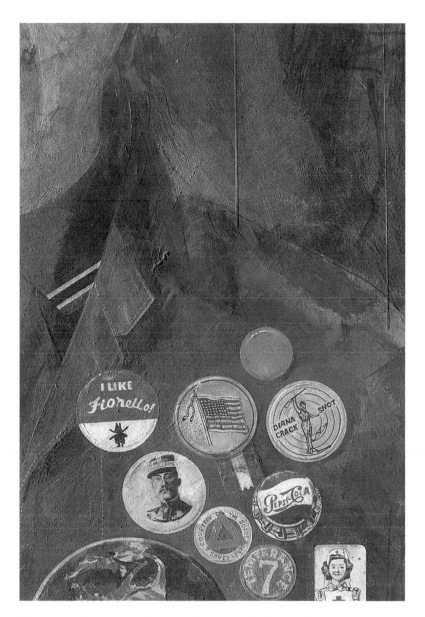

fig.24 Detail from *Self-Portrait with Badges* taken in partial raking light from the left, revealing changes made to the positioning of the collar and Blake's use of a compass and ruling pen.

The artist also recalls using a technique he had adopted at college to produce a slightly higher sheen in some areas of paint, such as his face. 'What I used to do at that time was to give it a gloss … just as it was at the point of drying I'd polish it slightly with my hand, which gave it a gloss like a varnish'.

Blake also produced works that incorporated ready-painted objects. *The First Real Target* (fig.25) consists of a Slazenger archery target bought from a sports shop, 'probably the big one on Piccadilly [Lilleywhites]', and then stuck to a piece of hardboard. 'Jasper Johns had done his target at that point and Ken Noland had done targets but nobody kind of accepted that they were targets. They always talked about circular motifs. Even Jasper Johns didn't accept the image was a target. The simple joke was that this was the first real target'. (Blake confesses that in fact, 'technically it's the second real target because I bought one and went drinking and

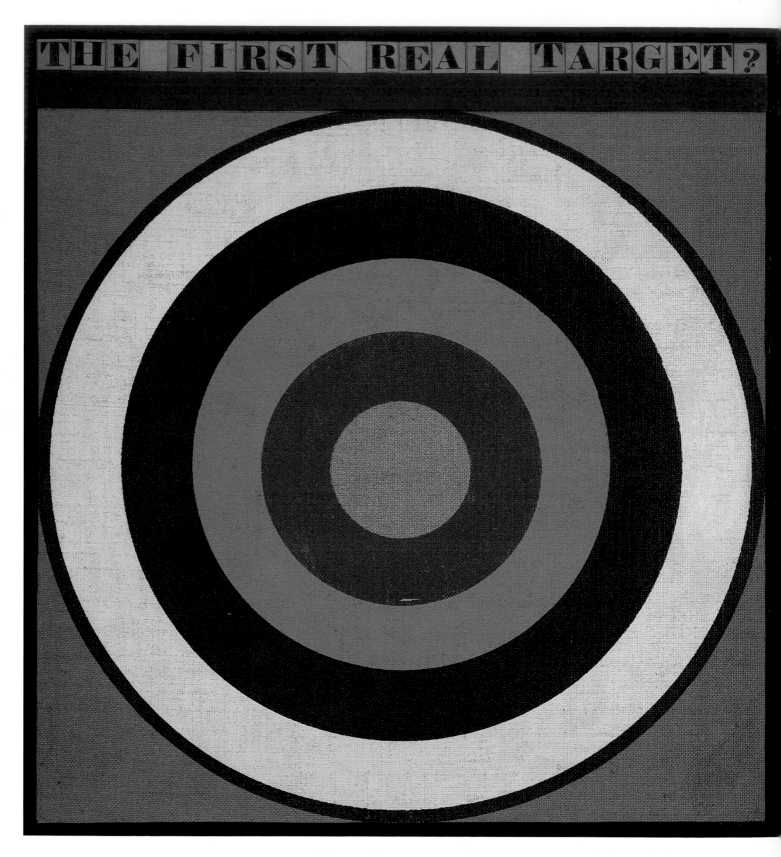

fig.25 *The First Real Target* 1961, commercial oil-based paint on canvas and collage 53.7 x 49.3 cm.

lost it, so I bought another one'.) The paint used by Slazenger was an oil-based paint that has been modified with rosin, a natural resin obtained from pine trees. Paint makers frequently incorporated rosin into their formulations at this time, often as an alternative to synthetic resins such as alkyds.

The paint was chosen by the manufacturers primarily for its flexibility and excellent adhesion to the canvas support. However, its visual properties would also have been important. The paint displays a uniform gloss and opacity that exhibits the texture of the canvas on which it is painted, but displays no signs of brushstrokes whatsoever (fig.26). In some places, for example in the red and light-blue paint, the canvas itself is visible. The paint on the target was not applied by Blake himself, but he considers it to be 'such a beautiful object … it's beautifully painted. It must have been painted by hand'. The exposed areas of canvas are somewhat dark – they may well have discoloured slightly, although Blake claims 'it looks as new as the day I bought it'. The letters along the top 'would have been quite brown anyway, because they were Victorian letters … thick wooden letters … The ones in between I might have painted. So you get different colouration'.

When UK paint manufacturers first introduced artists' acrylic emulsion onto the market in 1963, Blake was approached to test different brands: 'I think I tested every one'. But of the two early UK brands, he soon developed a preference for Rowney's Cryla. He found it a more 'solid' paint, and continued to use it between 1963 and 1968, even after he had tried out some of the American brands. He recalls the 'enormous hype about Liquitex at the time; it was more like an oil paint … and there was a great kind of craze to use it but I didn't get caught up in that'. He frequently came into contact with other artists who were using acrylic emulsions – 'I think Bernard Cohen at one point was the agent for Liquitex and he gave me a sample set and I tried them' – but he doesn't recall ever having used them on a painting. He also met Larry Bell and Claes Oldenburg in 1963 who 'were probably using them … but I don't think we talked technically'. He continued to work in much the same technique with the acrylic as he had done with oil, diluting the paint with water ('obviously water [for acrylic] equals white spirit [for oil]') and building up the image with repeated applications of thin glazes. Using the palm of his hand and the ball of his thumb over the glaze while it was still tacky, he continued to polish the paint surface in his manipulation of the paint to make it 'do what I wanted it to do'.

Blake started painting *The 1962 Beatles* (fig.27) in 1963. He copied the portraits from photographs taken of the Beatles for the magazine *Pop Pics* and the coloured edges, the gingery tone of the faces, and apparently mis-registered lines of the shoulders, imitate the printing process in the origi-

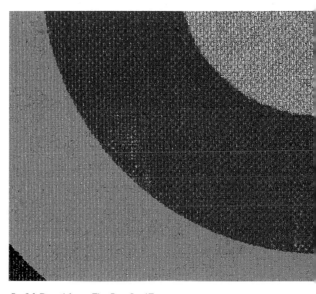

fig.26 Detail from *The First Real Target* taken in partial raking light from the left, showing exposed areas of canvas.

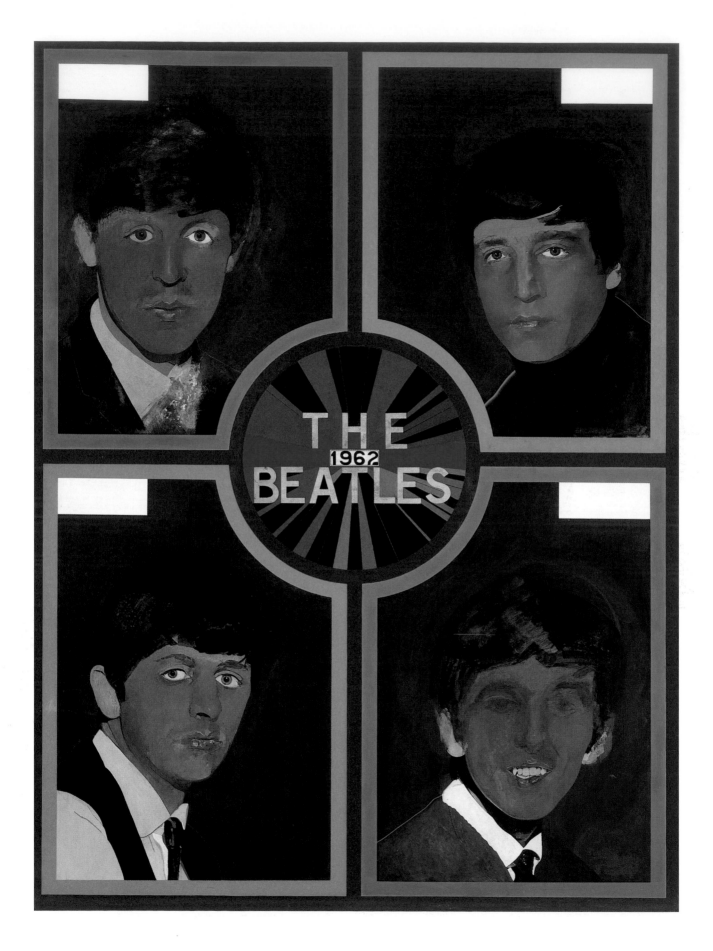

nal photographs. For this he required a paint that would produce a matt flat surface and turned to acrylic emulsion paint.

He painted the images onto the hardboard in a fairly loose manner, then gradually developed and refined them. He achieved the hard, straight lines using masking tape and the circle in the centre was made with a compass and ruling pen. The acrylic paint was diluted with water and dropped into the drawing pen, which was used with the compass and ruler. The areas of colour were then brushed up to the line for a crisp, sharp edge. Fig.28 shows a detail of the lower right part of McCartney's portrait, photographed in a slightly raking light. The very straight edges of the blue, red and orange areas are apparent, as is the more textured paint that fills these areas, especially for the curved part. The area of the actual portrait was painted in a much looser style. Also visible in this detail are pencil lines at the top of the chin and lower lip, as well as areas such as the tie and shirt, where Blake scraped the paint back to the underlayers.

Blake has always maintained an interest in printing and lettering, initiated by his training as a graphic designer: 'it's a standard [lettering technique]; you dip the brush in and you write it'. The central panel and lettering were designed to resemble a record sleeve. They were first established in pencil, using a compass to draw the outer circle. Masking tape was then added to the primed surface, cut with a scalpel to the shape of each letter. The acrylic paint was then applied by brush. The surface texture in some areas, such as the blue and yellow (see fig.29), suggests that the paint was of a rather thick and stiff consistency. In addition, a pencil line and an incised line (from the scalpel) can be seen in the top of the letter 'A', shown in the lower-left corner of this detail. Other areas where masking tape was used are indicated by the slightly raised edges of the painted areas, such as the two diagonal borders of the blue area on the left.

When the painting was first exhibited, Blake attached a sign to it saying 'This painting is not finished'. Several elements in the painting have an unfinished look, such as the abraded area of McCartney's tie (fig.28). But Blake acknowledges that 'there was a certain point that, rather than finish it, if I distress it that's giving the clue that it's meant to be like that'. The white rectangles are blank for the Beatles autographs. 'The original idea was that the Beatles signed in those panels. Paul saw it first and I think wasn't very flattered and without actually saying "I won't sign it" managed to go without signing it. After that the others never did. I didn't bother after that' and the sign was removed.

In 1965 Blake painted *The Masked Zebra Kid* (fig.30) whose appearance and construction is typical of early Pop art works. The photographs used in the collage and for the painted portrait in the top half of the composition, came from *Boxing and Wrestling Illustrated*, an American glossy magazine. Blake recalls working from the photograph for the portrait of the

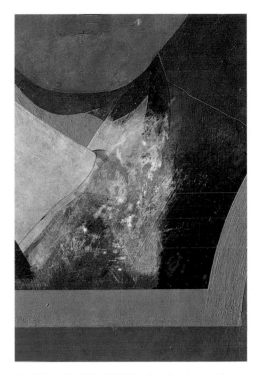

fig.28 Detail of *The 1962 Beatles* taken in partial raking light from the left. There is intentional abrasion of the area around the tie.

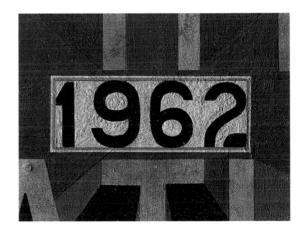

fig.29 A second raking light detail (from the left) of *The 1962 Beatles*, showing aspects of Blake's lettering technique.

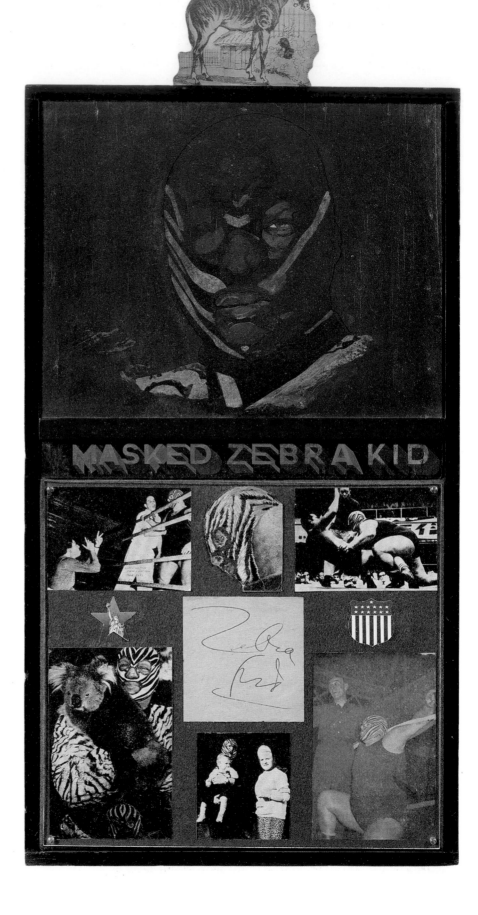

fig.30 *The Masked Zebra Kid*
1965, acrylic emulsion,
alkyd housepaint and collage
on plywood and hardboard
55.2 x 26.7 cm.

Masked Zebra Kid, which 'was no clearer than that one, so I think it was very deliberately done as a fragment … I think I probably focused on the mouth, the nose and one eye, and then applied a very dirty glaze, a sort of umber glaze. So that was deliberate, that was always dark'. The image is painted in thin layers of acrylic emulsion paint, applied directly to a sheet of plywood, and then glazed with a dilute mix of black and white paint, to 'put a kind of controlled bloom over it'. This technique, which Blake had first used to describe atmospheric landscapes, was only possible with the water-based acrylic emulsion paints. He recalls he would 'force a bloom to happen by using water in a certain way … probably more water than paint, and then as it dries the pigmentation makes that kind of strange bloom'. In fact, the portrait has lost some of its original 'soft and lost' character due to a later application of varnish; Blake's response to this new surface was 'I saw it, didn't like it and then accepted it'.

The support is a softwood frame with the plywood attached to the top half and a piece of hardboard to the bottom half. The heads of the panel pins used to attach the plywood have been deliberately left visible beneath the paint. A thin batten of wood was painted with red gloss housepaint, which was then pinned to the plywood section. Beneath it the lettering was painted in acrylic, with a glaze applied over the colour in imitation of the fairground signwriting, 'antique' look. The differences in surface between the two types of paint become apparent when viewed under a raking light (fig.31). The red housepaint is characteristically smooth and glossy, whereas the acrylic was applied to produce a significantly textured surface. As with *The 1962 Beatles,* masking tape was used to cover the letters while Blake applied paint around them.

The lower half of the panel is covered in a piece of green baize, which is folded round the edges of the hardboard. Photographs, an autograph (acquired by Blake after a wrestling match) and an embroidered version of the mask in one of the photographs (made by the artist Jann Haworth, his wife at the time) were then stuck onto the fabric using double-sided adhesive tape. The collage material and Victorian toy zebra placed on the top of the frame were old and already slightly yellowed when Blake applied them to the piece, and their aged patina was further enhanced by a yellow-tinted Perspex cover placed over the collaged elements, which had the effect both of 'putting a glaze over it' and unifying the composition.

At the end of the 1960s, Blake moved out of London to the country, where he formed the Brotherhood of Ruralists. He stopped painting with acrylic emulsion and returned to using oil colour. He perceives the two changes to have been directly related. 'Maybe it was just the 'sixties were coming to an end, maybe the Cryla ties in pretty much with the 'sixties and the Pop art period. I moved back to oil because the seventies pictures became the Ruralist pictures and were quite different'.

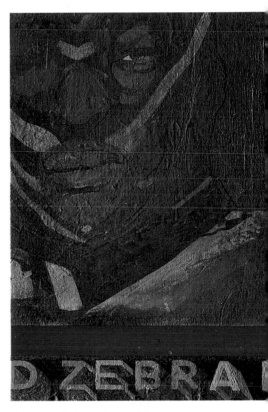

fig.31 Detail of *The Masked Zebra Kid* taken in raking light from the left, showing variations in the paint.

Patrick Caulfield born 1936

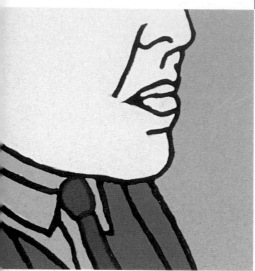

The paintings of Patrick Caulfield are characterised by their highly stylised representations of traditional subject matter, such as still lifes, interiors, landscapes and portraits, in an effort to produce images that are 'still and timeless'.[1] As was the case with many of his Pop art contemporaries, such as Peter Blake and David Hockney, his style developed partly in reaction to the expressive gestures of the abstract painters before him. 'I was aiming at reducing the means by which one described things … although the Pop art idiom became a fact and it was identified with commercial art, I thought … a very reduced and banal, straightforward way of describing things … would not be interesting enough for the realms of commercial art, it wouldn't be seductive.'[2] He was also influenced by the painter Juan Gris, whose work depicted 'a formalised image which was full of warmth and invention, again and again. He did more or less the same image always but there was always a plus'.[3]

Caulfield describes his early paintings, such as *Vases of Flowers* (fig.33), as 'usually rather banal in their conception'.[4] The images are often laid onto a background of solid colour and bound up in a series of parallel lines, an effect that makes the subject matter more emphatic. It also 'knitted the surface of the painting together so that whether an object was depicted in the foreground or the background, the evenness of the line was the same, so it rather denied the illusion of space, although it represented it'.[5] Caulfield borrowed his pictorial style from the ancient Minoan frescoes in Crete, which he had seen in postcards. 'The postcards from Crete were highly decorative … I felt that even if the murals did not exist in their original form it was likely that the paint was applied in flat areas, so that the interpretation on the postcards was probably accurate and what you had was flat areas of colour and linear imagery.'[6]

For these images, Caulfield 'wanted to choose something that was alien to my actual daily circumstances, something that had a more decorative quality than art was supposed to have'.[7] His choice of painting materials was consistent with this: a piece of hardboard as a support and alkyd gloss housepaint, both of which are materials manufactured principally for

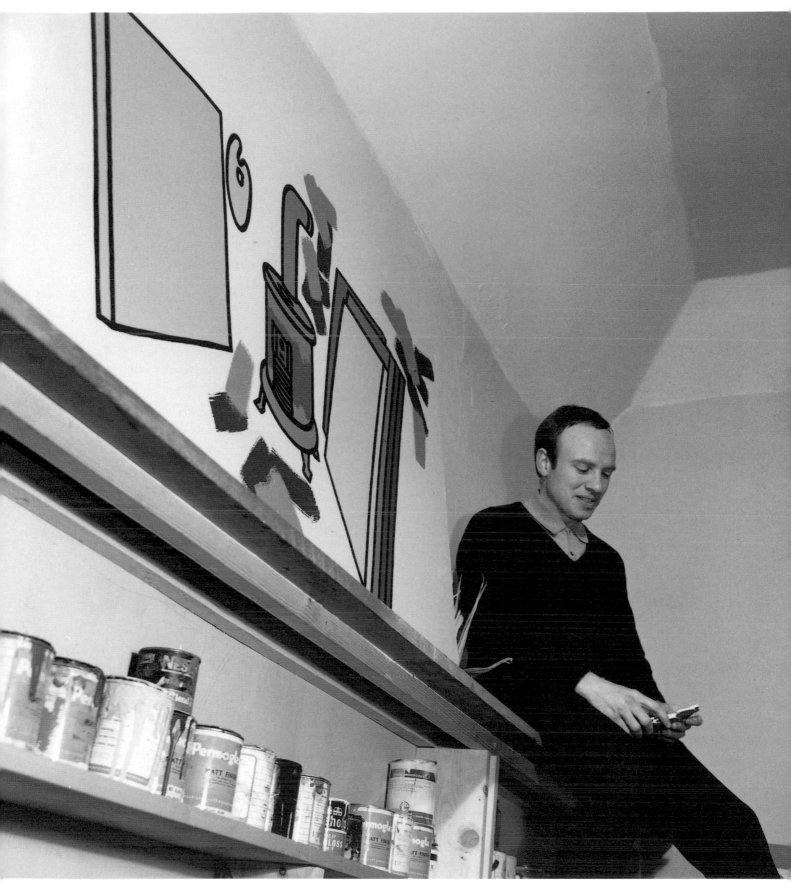

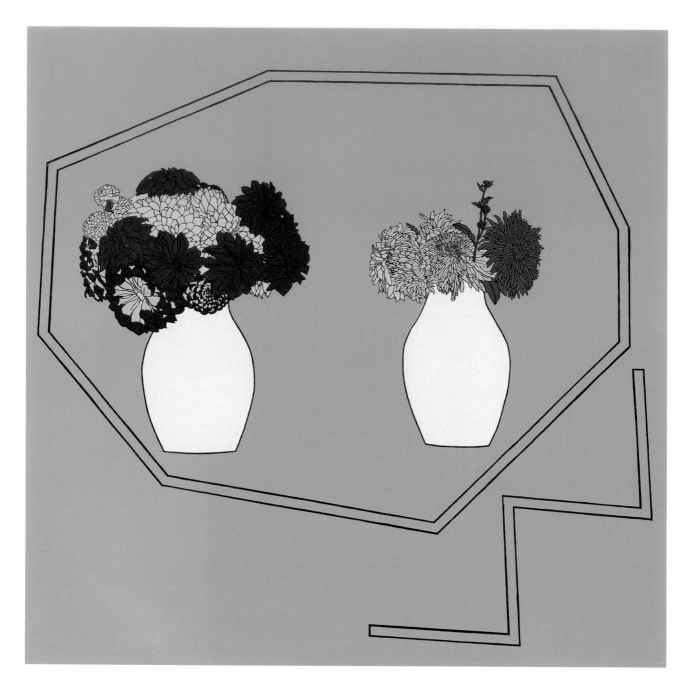

fig.33 *Vases of Flowers* 1962, alkyd
housepaint on hardboard 121.9 x 121.9 cm.

commercial use. As he recalls, 'I used to paint on hardboard because it was cheap and, I thought, an anonymous surface, the nearest equivalent to a wall'.[8] His choice of alkyd housepaint 'was an aesthetic decision, not anything to do with the technique. I wanted a very impersonal surface, I didn't want any obvious brushstroke work … It was more like a sign-painter's technique'. Alkyd housepaints were appropriate here because they are designed to level off after their application to produce a topo-graphically flat, high-gloss finish.

During the early 1960s Caulfield had no particular preference for any specific brand of paint; his selection was made according to those paints that were freely available to him: 'the gloss paints were just standard ones

… any commercial brand like Crown or Dulux etc. … they were often chosen for convenience'. He used many paints straight from the can, but 'I did mix colours as well, I didn't just use colours from a colour chart … I would have mixed brands if I had needed to'. He was aware that many artists considered Ripolin paints to be amongst the best available, but he preferred other brands that gave a higher opacity. 'I know [Ripolin] was used by Sidney Nolan. It suited him. He used to use it rather like a varnish. He leaned heavily on the transparency of the paint'.

The preparation of the support was somewhat unrefined. 'I used to nail these bits of hardboard to wooden battens … that's one of the crudest elements of the work I did at that time.' In these early works, Caulfield chose a square format to further enhance the anonymity of the work: 'once you do a picture that is horizontal, it's a landscape format. If you do it vertically, it's a figure, so this avoided these associations'.[9] The hardboard was sanded down and then 'I prepared the surface of the board as you might a door, with commercial undercoat'.[10] Before he started to paint he often made preliminary drawings 'in order to establish the image'. A number of techniques were then used to transfer the image onto the primed hardboard. 'I might have squared [the image] up or I might have done a tracing. I never projected anything. I drew onto the hardboard and just transferred it visually … [and] fairly freely, making corrections until I got it'. When infrared photography is used to examine the painting, the true extent of this drawing becomes apparent (fig.34). In this detail, freely applied pencil lines are seen everywhere. In the upper left quarter, the centre of a flower has been drawn in a completely different position to the flowers in the final painted image, indicating that Caulfield continued to make corrections well past the drawing stage. Some of these pencil lines remain visible around areas of paint, or occasionally, through it, if the paint is translucent (see the yellow paint in fig.35), but Caulfield always attempted to cover them completely: 'I wouldn't have wanted them to have been very evident, or evident at all'.

The primed hardboard was laid flat as he painted the image, due to the high fluidity of the gloss housepaint, which would inevitably have caused significant paint drips had the painting been vertical. The paint was brushed on in smooth, even applications, with very little alteration, in an attempt to get a flat surface. 'Basically I would have been after a uniform effect. I wasn't into underpainting. For me that was a Post-Impressionist hangover.' For each colour, he normally applied more than one coat, until it reached the desired opacity. 'If I saw it was evidently transparent I would go over it again'. These gloss housepaints were designed to be used in very thin layers; when they were applied slightly too thickly, the film dried to a wrinkled surface (see top left corner, fig.35).

Caulfield's order of painting was the same for all his early works: 'I would have drawn the whole thing in with black lines and then filled them

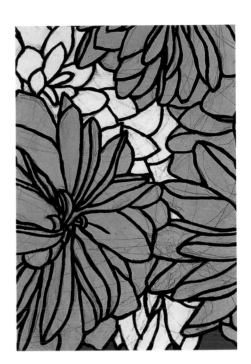

fig.34 Detail from *Vases of Flowers* showing the extensive pencil underdrawing.

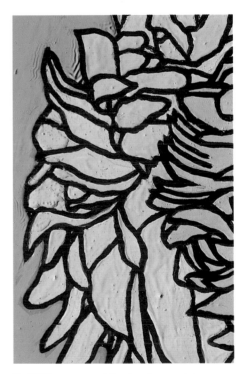

fig.35 The texture of the gloss housepaint is revealed in this detail from *Vases of Flowers* taken in raking light from above.

Patrick Caulfield   **55**

fig.36 *Portrait of Juan Gris* 1963,

alkyd housepaint on hardboard 122 x 122 cm.

Private Collection, on loan to the Tate Gallery

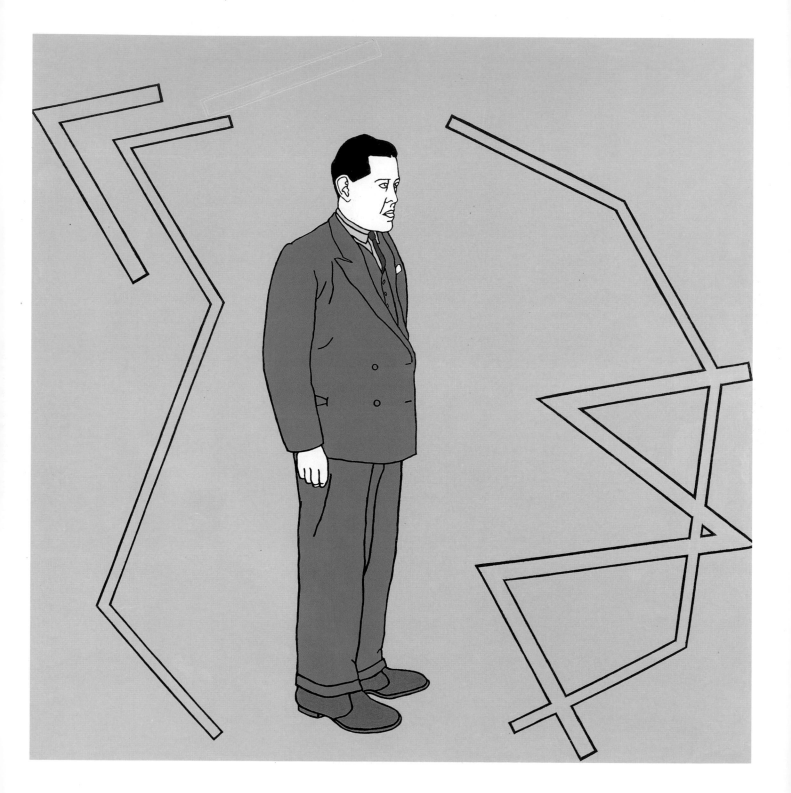

in with colour, but then I would have to go over it again and touch it up. I was continually touching them up; I never got them accurate at the first go.' In *Vases of Flowers*, an earlier background colour of green around the vases is visible in places beneath the turquoise colour that now covers it (fig.35). This occurred frequently, 'there were paintings where the background was a different colour [to begin with]'. Sometimes this initial colour may simply have been the recommended undercoat for the gloss paint that formed the final layer. He painted the flowers from a detailed drawing he made by studying real chrysanthemums, using approximately the same colours, but also referring to seed packets. 'I wouldn't have made up a chrysanthemum. The colours would have been influenced by the seed packets.' Finally, he used masking tape, an aid he refers to as 'my little delight', to paint the straight lines, the final details of the composition.

In *Portrait of Juan Gris* (fig.36) the fluidity of the gloss paint is particularly apparent in the brushmarks when viewed in raking light. The detail in fig.37 shows a subtle undulation of the background yellow paint, revealing the drag of the brush around the outline of the figure: 'the paint would be slightly wavy being gloss paint, you would have to spray it on to get it completely flat'. Also evident in the detail is the granular texture of the paint surface, probably caused by the residue debris from the preparation of the hardboard support. To paint the black parallel lines, Caulfield used only a single piece of masking tape positioned between the lines (the same technique had been used for *Vases of Flowers*). The inner edge of each line is therefore sharp and slightly raised, whereas the outer edges, which were painted freehand, are somewhat irregular. 'People are always surprised that they are so precise. Actually, I was quite shaky then, but when people are not watching me I can take my time'. An impression from the masking-tape adhesive ('sometimes it can be *very* adhesive!') is still visible in the yellow layer, which must have still been slightly wet when the tape was applied, as is evident in the raking-light detail (fig.38). The black paint has also bled slightly under the tape during its application, an effect exacerbated by the yellow 'being a light colour, so the surface may have picked it up a bit'. The colours are a combination of pure and mixed paints, for example 'the blue I would have mixed. I would have darkened it down from a colour you might find in a tin. The yellow was probably straight from the can'.

In *Greece Expiring on the Ruins of Missolonghi, after Delacroix* (fig.39), Caulfield abandoned the square format. The image is based on a black and white reproduction of the painting by Delacroix, which he transferred by drawing directly onto the hardboard support. The pencil lines guided him in placing the initial lines of black paint. Infrared photography reveals only a few areas, such as the folds in some of the drapery, where Caulfield altered the composition. He recalls: 'usually I worked things out very precisely and hardly deviated, but on certain works I would have changed

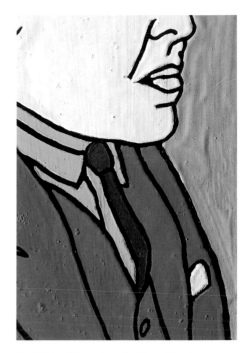

fig.37 Detail from *Portrait of Juan Gris* taken in raking light from the left, revealing the order of layers and the fluidity of the housepaint.

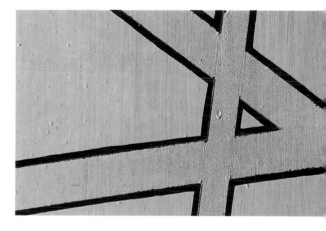

fig.38 Detail from *Portrait of Juan Gris* taken in raking light from the left, showing evidence of Caulfield's use of masking tape.

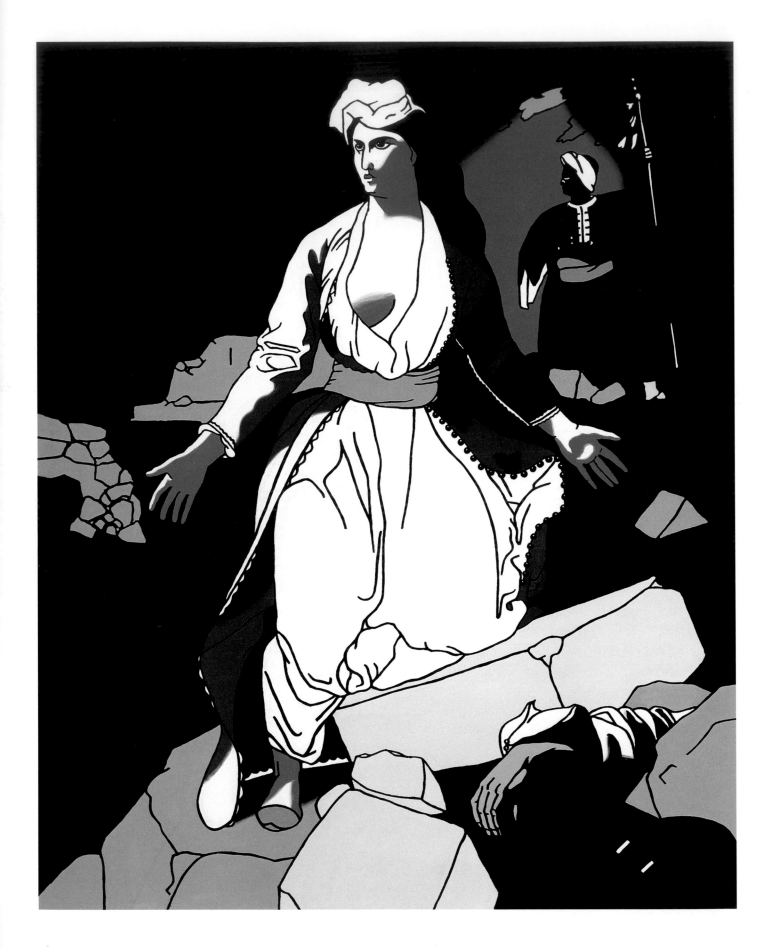

things around ... [with Greece's robe] I would have fiddled around to get it right. Probably Delacroix had the same problems!'

Although Caulfield had seen Delacroix's painting, the colours are not true to the original. 'I imagined the colours I associated with Delacroix, using a lot of black and white' from a limited range of household gloss colours. The flat surface quality of the paint accentuates the solid tones of the black and white reproduction. 'My idea was to do a transcription which was very close to the original, only emphasising the propaganda poster quality of it.' He hoped to achieve this 'by substituting for the dark, amorphous background a flat black gloss colour',[11] which differed from Delacroix's emotive brushstrokes. Unlike Caulfield's other works from this period, there is some suggestion of shading in the figure made by 'two wet colours going into each other to create a little bit of gradation. But being a copy, I made it as little as possible'. The raking-light detail (fig.40) shows that the white paint of the sleeve and forearm was blended with the colours while the paint was still wet. The angle of light accentuates the texture in the surface and reveals the layering and sequence of colour.

Towards the end of the 1960s, Caulfield made a change in his choice of both paint medium and support, although the two did not occur simultaneously. The first development was a switch to canvas as a support, the main reason for which appears to have been a practical one: 'At that time you couldn't get hardboard more than four foot wide. I wanted more freedom to do bigger things.' For a period, he continued to paint with alkyd housepaint, although by this time he sought a matt surface and began to use 'a matt alkyd decorator's paint'. Bromel had a store located behind Olympia, 'the people who set up the exhibitions there would use it. It was a good clean colour and it dried pretty quickly'. *Pottery* (fig.41) was painted with the Bromel household paint onto cotton canvas (also called 'cotton duck'); 'initially I wasn't using a very fine canvas'. Caulfield prepared his own canvases, usually with acrylic primer, which he stretched onto commercially made stretchers. 'I've never ever bought prepared canvas ... I haven't got round to finding someone who does it ... I nearly always stretch my own canvases, not from any puritanical viewpoint, just because I got used to doing it.' He used cotton canvas because of its availability in widths of up to twelve feet, later changing to linen canvas when cotton was supplied only in shorter widths. He was no longer painting on the flat but propping his paintings against the wall as 'the paint was less flowy and the canvas would soak up the paint'. The texture of the canvas is apparent in the raking-light detail (fig.42), beneath the smooth application of paint. '*Pottery* was an excuse for me to use a lot of colour.' Caulfield liked the 'delicacy' of the Bromel paint surface, but it was vulnerable to scratches and other minor surface abrasions.

fig.39 *Greece Expiring on the Ruins of Missolonghi (after Delacroix)* 1963, alkyd housepaint on hardboard 152.4 x 121.9 cm.

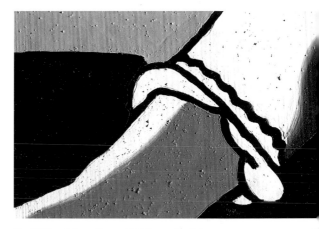

fig.40 Detail from *Greece Expiring on the Ruins of Missolonghi* taken in raking light from the right. Caulfield's wet-in-wet working of the housepaint and the absorption of dirt into the paint film are evident.

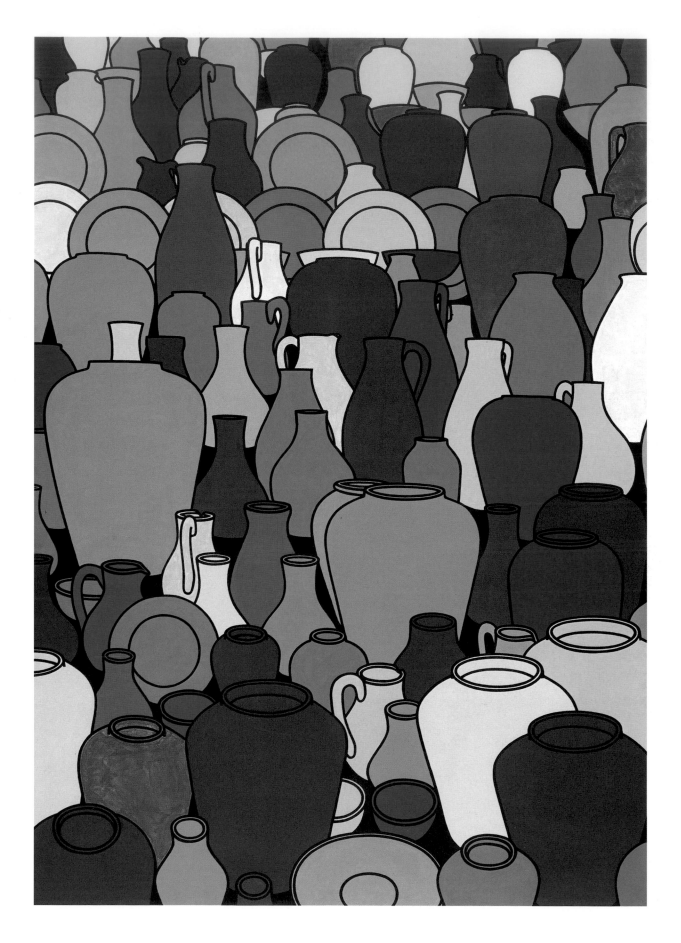

The artist recalls that he was 'probably aware of acrylic, but there were a lot of doubts expressed about them, such as, if they were exposed to cold temperatures they would just fall off. So I was put off them for a while. I was very cautious. I wouldn't leap from one technique to another'. Despite his close friendship with John Hoyland, who started using acrylic paint as soon as it became available in the UK, Caulfield recalls: 'I wouldn't have connected with his technique. Maybe it was something that abstract painters use. I would never want to stain a canvas'. He first began to use acrylic paint around 1969, initially incorporating it into paintings executed with housepaint, 'always the white because I thought it would yellow less'. However, from the early 1970s, he began to use acrylic exclusively in his paintings, 'when I realised it was a useable medium … It had a really good colour range – decorator's colours have an odd range. It was very dense and covered well and would dry quickly – all good things! I remember people would complain about the shiny plastic surface. I thought I could live with that.' The acrylic emulsion paints were less glossy but thicker in consistency than the alkyd housepaints. He found them more flexible to work with and he no longer had to purchase his paint in trade quantities for his fairly modest requirements: 'there was often a lot of wastage with housepaints. However firmly you put the lid back on, you would always get a skin forming'. The use of acrylic was also far more suited to canvas. Alkyds are primarily made for solid surfaces, and are therefore more likely to crack if used on a flexible support. Caulfield recognised the resilient qualities and durability of these acrylic paints over the alkyd paints he had been using. 'Acrylic is so tough. If you have splodges of acrylic you can beat it around and it just survives forever. I would have thought that [household] paint was much less plastic.'

In accounting for his use of housepaints at the start of his career Caulfield admits that, 'when I did these works with gloss paint I had an attitude. I was much younger and I would make paintings which were like oil paint, all textured and stuck on to make it something like a commercial object. I don't have that attitude anymore, but I still use a medium [acrylic] which is very adaptable.' Perhaps the delayed switch in his choice of paint can be explained in part by a certain reluctance to abandon this 'attitude'. His approach to materials is now very different: 'I use paints I think are good on supports I think are good. My attitude is in my mind, it's not to do with the materials.'

In the early 1970s, Caulfield began to paint interiors, outlining his imagery with a black line against a flat coloured background. *After Lunch* (fig.43), was worked out in a series of drawings. The final drawing, in which the composition was resolved, was squared up in the traditional manner. After applying a ground colour in heavily thinned acrylic ('I only used rollers to prime canvases'), he would 'cover the canvas with polythene and then square that up with felt-tip pen, then transfer the draw-

fig.41 *Pottery* 1969, alkyd housepaint on canvas 213.4 x 152.4 cm.

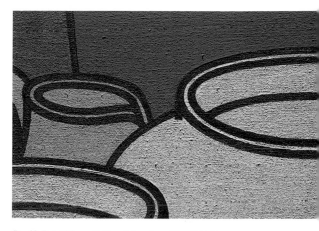

fig.42 Detail from *Pottery* taken in raking light from above, showing the texture of the paint surface.

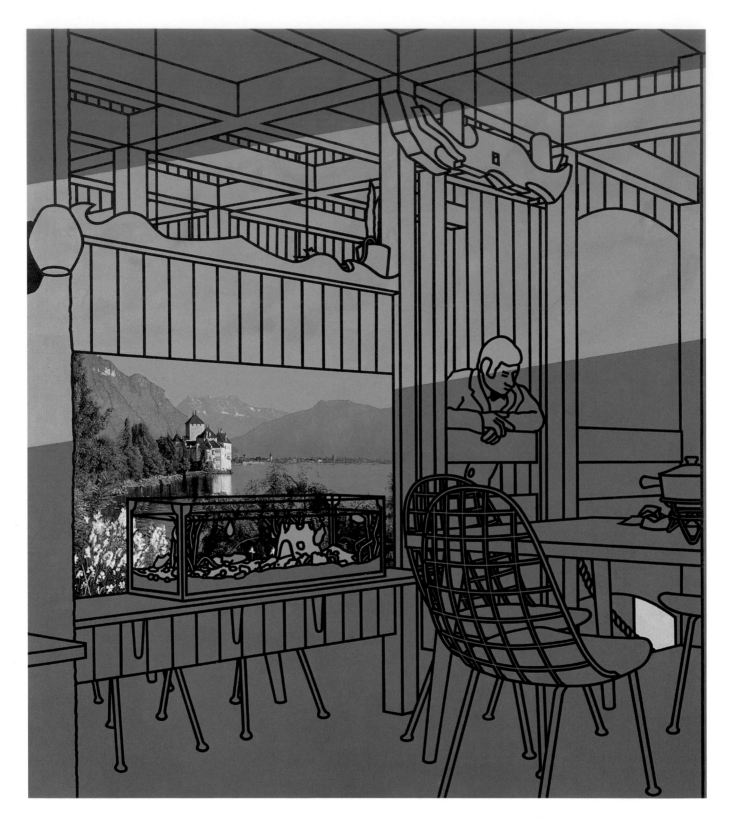

fig.43 *After Lunch* 1975, acrylic emulsion
on canvas 248.9 x 213.4 cm.

ing to the polythene with felt-tip pen and trace it onto the canvas so that the image, with only a few minor alterations, was established'.[12] Caulfield employed this preparatory technique in a number of his interior paintings at this time. Sometimes, only one section of the grid would be applied to the canvas, followed by a general area of colour, after which he would transfer the rest of the drawing. Pencil lines are visible on the blue background around the black lines in the detail of the carving of the room divider (fig.44).

The restaurant interior is a frequent subject in Caulfield's work. 'One reason I chose restaurant interiors is that they give one more scope to introduce space and objects than in a normal domestic setting.'[13] The objects in *After Lunch* initially included a photograph of a mural, bought from a photo-mural supplier in Chiswick, London, depicting the chateau of Chillon on Lake Geneva. 'First I was going to cheat; I tried to stick it onto the canvas but the next morning the canvas had buckled badly at the back. Somehow I managed to get it off then I painted it instead – it took me ages.' The mural is a painstaking copy of the original photograph done in acrylic paint, 'as a gesture to photo-realism which was going on at that time'. The copy of the photograph was the first thing to be painted. 'Because had it gone disastrously wrong I would have had to think again.' This was then carefully covered up with masking tape before the rest of the composition was executed. The raking-light detail (fig.45) reveals the raised edges of paint around the rectangle where the masking tape was used. The naturalistic depiction of the Swiss landscape view contrasts with the blue static interior, in which the 'rather smoky light you get after lunch' is represented in the thinly applied bands of matt acrylic colour. 'I am conscious of formalising lighting effects which of course are imagined.'[14]

By the early 1980s, Caulfield's use of the delineated black outline, which enhanced the anonymity of his style, occurred less frequently in his compositions. 'I use it more as an area of paint. I use the line thicker: it doesn't merely divide two spaces, it is in itself a space, something I use where I want to be emphatic.'[15] His style became more varied and the surface changed noticeably. Caulfield continues, however, to work with acrylic: 'I work in acrylic because it's incredibly flexible. If one wants to deal in different styles it's probably the best medium – different manners of working in the same painting. And it dries very quickly of course, which is a marvellous thing. [My paintings] tend not to have the richness of oil paint.' He found the acrylic surface to be less 'seductive ... I wouldn't want it to run away with the actual paint quality taking over.'[16]

Different kinds of brushwork began to feature in Caulfield's painting in the mid-1980s, in which he exploited the ability of acrylic paint to display a varied range of consistencies. 'You can do anything with acrylic. In one painting I can do different styles.' In *Interior with a Picture* (fig.46),

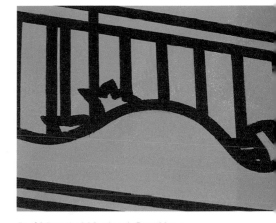

fig.44 Detail of *After Lunch*. Pencil lines from the initial drawing are just visible around the black paint lines.

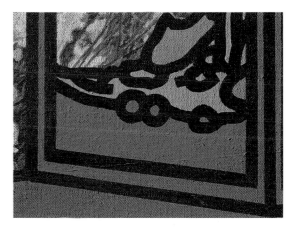

fig.45 Detail of *After Lunch* taken in partial raking light from the left, confirming evidence of Caulfield's use of masking tape.

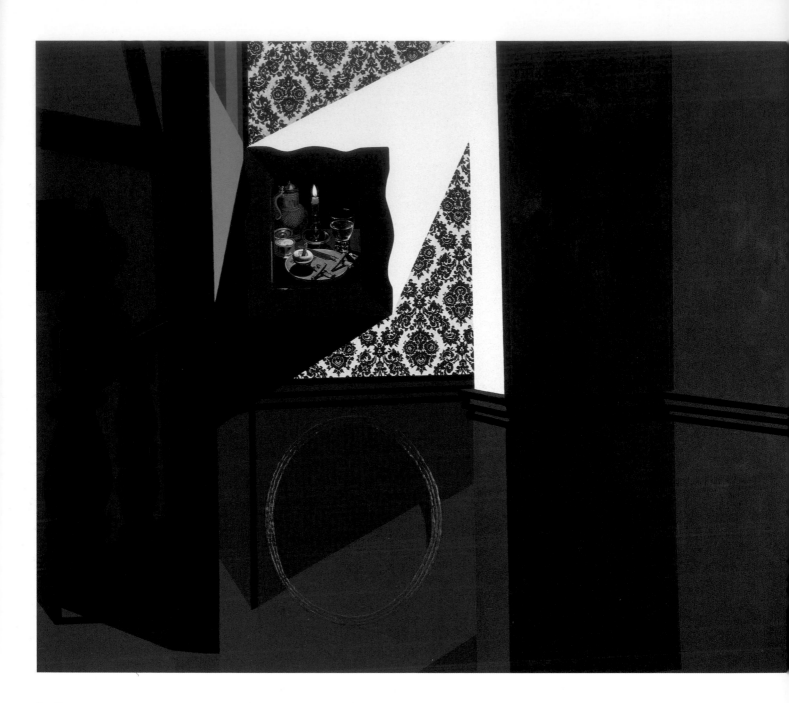

fig.46 *Interior with a Picture* 1985–6, acrylic emulsion on canvas 205.8 x 244.2 cm.

the background wallpaper mimics a flocked paper surface. 'I copied the wallpaper you see in Indian restaurants, and I bought a roll of it from a shop in Brewer Street.' The red pattern in the wallpaper is raised slightly by the small dabbed-on impastoes of colour, beneath which are occasional areas of blue and black. 'I wanted to give it a bit of a lift, without the blue [and black] I thought it would be too flat. With this underpainting, which I don't normally do, it gave it a richness.' The texture of the wallpaper and the adjacent pillar is evident in the raking-light detail (fig.47), contrasted with the flat paint application of the other surfaces. Despite this even quality, it seems that Caulfield made constant changes to the colour scheme. In several areas in the main red foreground, for example, an underlayer of purple paint is sometimes visible. However, the true extent of these colour changes only becomes apparent when a paint fragment taken from the lower-left corner is viewed in cross section (fig.48). The upper red colour is clearly visible at the top of the cross-section, beneath which lies the purple colour. Underneath these, several additional layers are seen, but the wide variety of colours probably corresponds to changes in composition as well as the overall colour scheme.

The painting in the image was copied from an illustration of *Meal by Candlelight* by Gotthardt de Wedig (1583–1641), which he found in a book called *Still Life*. The illustration was squared up using cotton thread and enlarged slightly onto the cotton canvas. The oval shape beneath the dado rail was made by squeezing white acrylic paint directly from the tube, following a line previously marked on the surface (fig.49). This was then painted over with colour after it had dried, 'which took a bit of time, usually overnight, because it was so thick'. Caulfield found that the thickly squeezed line of paint had to be done with the painting laid flat, 'and you have to work out if you can reach! It is very difficult to keep the pressure on the tube consistent'. Minor irregularities were clearly part of the effect: 'I don't mind it not being precise, as it's really representing plasterwork which chips – instant patina!'

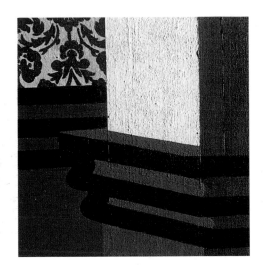

fig.47 Caulfield's technique and use of masking tape are visible in this detail of *Interior with a Picture*, taken in raking light from the right.

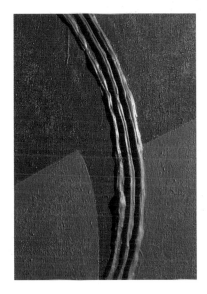

fig.48 (above) Detail of the three raised ovals in *Interior with a Picture*, taken in raking light from the right.

fig.49 (left) A cross-section of paint taken from the lower left corner of *Interior with a Picture* and photographed at 125 x magnification. The complex layering system of colours suggests that the composition, as well as the colour scheme, was changed in this area.

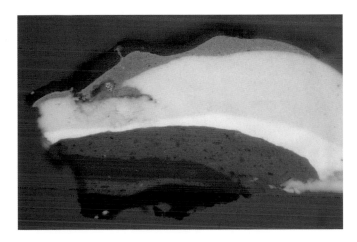

Caulfield has continued to paint in acrylic emulsion and his inclusion of three-dimensional form and textured paint has increased. In *Second Glass of Whisky* (fig.51) he used 'a piece of card that I cut teeth into' to make the semi-circular shapes. 'I like the idea of creating a rough surface and then trying to paint realistically on it. It gives you a kind of barrier'. In fig.50, the raking light reveals the combed effect of the paint on the surface over which Caulfield thinly painted the glass and its contents.

There is little doubt in Caulfield's mind that 'in hindsight I think I would have used acrylic' much earlier, certainly for the period when he was painting with the Bromel matt housepaint. Acrylic paint suited the direct method with which Caulfield chose to evoke the subject. 'It seems to me to be the most magic thing. I work slowly but I can think in the short term because acrylic dries quickly. I don't see the point in using oil colour, it has a richness but I don't use that element … it's driven in image rather than a surface. And you see I quite like the plastic surface of acrylic, which people think is one of its lesser attributes. I like it because it establishes itself … In one painting I can do different styles using acrylic.'

fig.50 Detail from *Second Glass of Whisky* taken in raking light (from the top), showing the texture created in the paint.

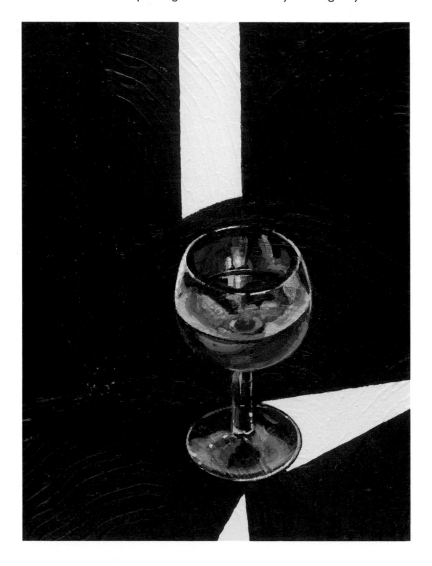

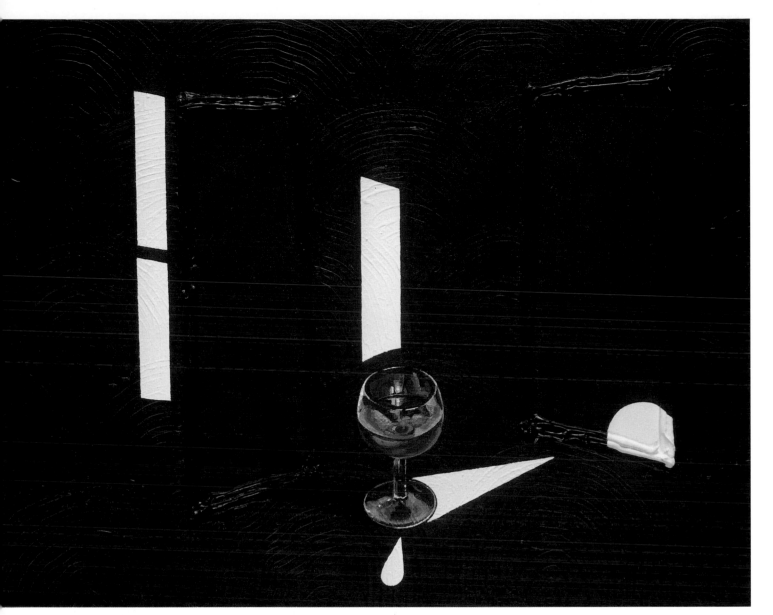

fig.51 *Second Glass of Whisky* 1992, acrylic emulsion on canvas 61 × 76.5 cm.

Richard Hamilton born 1922

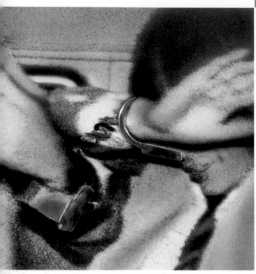

Richard Hamilton was a leading member of the Independent Group, established in 1952, which sought to embrace advances in technology in their art, particularly those resulting in mass-produced consumer goods. Hamilton, like other leading members of the group, such as Eduardo Paolozzi, Nigel Henderson and William Turnbull, not only took his subject matter from this area of popular culture, but also frequently incorporated materials associated with new technology into his work. He once said, 'fine art is the medium in which I work; the mass media is often the content of the painting'.[1] Integral to this idea was his use of household and industrial paints.[2] These were usually applied in his work alongside areas of 'best quality artists' oil paints', which had the effect of maximising the differences in gloss, texture and other optical properties between the various types of paint. His paintings also frequently incorporated collage and areas of relief, as further means of breaking down aesthetic restrictions. 'It's an old obsession of mine to see how conventions mix – I like the difference between a diagram and a photograph and a mark which is simply sensuous paint, even the addition of real objects. These relationships multiply the levels of meaning and ways of reading.'[3]

Hamilton's use of non-traditional painting materials was initiated during the previous decade while he was a student at the Royal Academy Schools in London. He remembers the advice of one of his lecturers, Professor A.P. Laurie, who suggested that 'if students could not afford canvas, the best thing was to buy masonite [hardboard]. He stretched it with scrim, a sort of cotton mesh, which was glued on with size and then painted with undercoat. This is what a lot of people worked on because it was easy and cheap to buy hardboard … I did this'. The hardboard was 'usually nailed to battening' to make it more rigid and the undercoat was a standard decorator's product that 'would have come from Woolworths. [I used] any cheap white undercoat'. The undercoat was usually applied in several layers (with sanding between each coat) and gave a very good surface on which to paint, despite sometimes being 'liable to crumble a bit around the edges'.

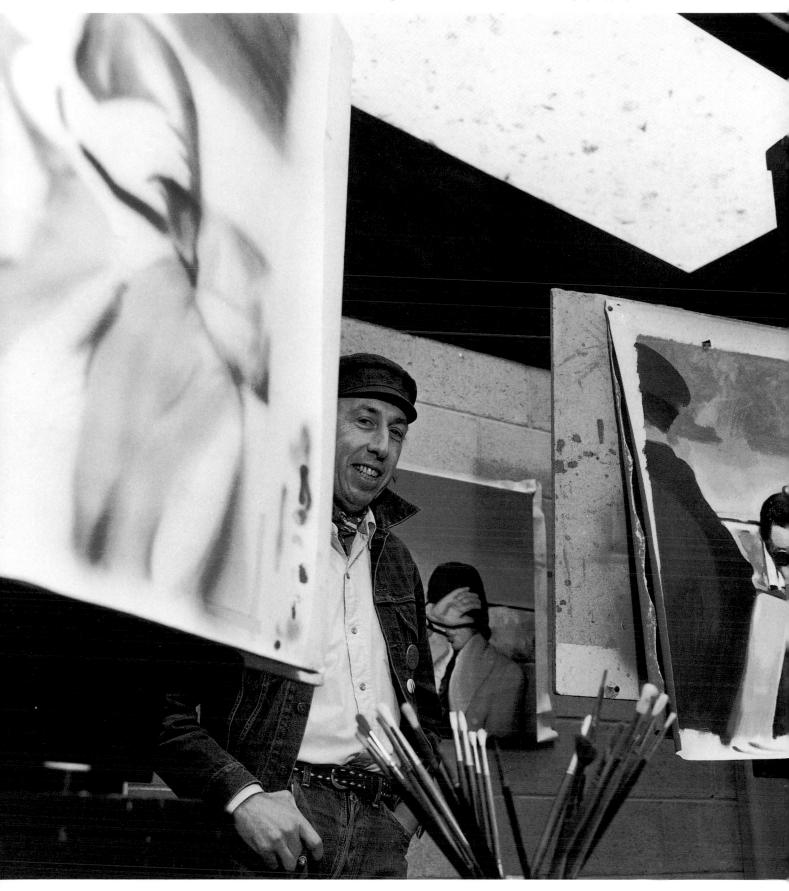

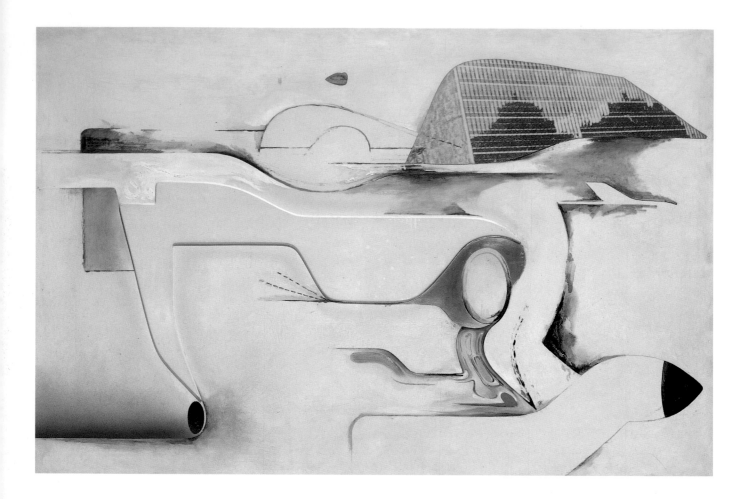

fig.53 *Hers is a lush situation* 1958,
oil-based undercoat, oil, nitro-cellulose and
collage on plywood 81 x 122 cm.
Private Collection, on loan to the Tate
Gallery

The decision to paint on a solid support soon ceased to be merely a financial consideration. A feature that Hamilton 'liked about board was that it has a smooth surface. I like to have something fairly smooth [to paint on], rather than something with the heavy grain of a canvas ... I didn't like that heavy tooth'. However, he soon found that the nails used to attach the hardboard to the battening 'rusted and when the panel flexed, the nails moved and the filling fell out ... [It was] not a very good system ... So I thought that maybe it would be more sensible to work on a rigid board'. He continued painting on rigid boards, such as plywood, chipboard and blockboard, until the mid-1960s. Another advantage of board became apparent when he started to use areas of relief on his paintings. 'I found that I could glue relief on it, or photographs, anything. [I could] use it as a collage surface and that was, I thought, very much more satisfactory.'

During the 1950s, Hamilton painted mainly in oil colour, which he often modified with a little varnish, turpentine and some additional linseed oil, although he 'always primed with Professor Laurie's recommended decorator's undercoat'.[4] The reasons for his choice of primer were 'ease of use and availability as much as cost', 'part of the conscious break away from the fine art tradition' and 'habit'. From 1957 onwards, there did not seem to be much of an alternative for priming blockboard'.

Towards the end of the decade he began to introduce a much wider range of materials into his work, including different types of paint and other 'ways of crafting the picture … I was prepared to incorporate into this aesthetic the idea of quotation and pastiche'.[5] In particular, he started to use nitro-cellulose paint – sometimes referred to simply as cellulose – which was the binder frequently used in car-spray paints. He recalls that 'the first time I used it was on *Hers is a lush situation*' (1958) (fig.53). He explains: 'the reason was that the [painting] has a cut-out panel on it, which represents the side of a car. It's all about cars and an elevational view of a car, and I thought it was appropriate to use cellulose since it was a representation of a car, even though it's rather abstract in a way'. In other words, 'I wanted the work to have as close a connection with the source as possible … Everything was directed not as representing the object but as symbolising it … It's meant to be a car, so I thought it was appropriate to use car colour'.

Hamilton's choice was also based on 'a feeling that car paints must be better' than artists' paints. 'A friend, an older artist, said to me (in 1939), "If manufacturers of paints put as much money into making artists' paints as they do car paints, then artists' paints would be better"'. He now accepts this to be 'one of those attractive myths, I'm afraid'. The nitro-cellulose paint was sprayed onto the piece of shallow hardboard relief, which gave the desired smooth and very flat finish that is characteristic of nitro-cellulose spray paints. He recalls that he 'would have put several layers of a grey nitro-cellulose primer on first to fill the [hardboard] grain and then put [on] enough white paint to get a smooth surface. Each [application] would be rubbed down with wet and dry [abrasive paper]'. Nitro-cellulose paints have certain handling properties that make spray applications very successful, but Hamilton claims he 'didn't think about the handling properties. I just used it [as a spray] because it was appropriate to the subject'.

The painting was primed with a standard type of decorator's under-coat in 'about ten coats, all brushed'. As with most of his work from this period, much of the undercoat remains visible in the finished painting and subsequently plays an important visual role in the final work. At this time, the undercoats were themselves based on drying oil, although they would certainly have exhibited very different handling and drying properties compared to an artists' quality paint. In particular, Hamilton observed the fairly rapid change in the colour of the commercial undercoat soon after application, and later remarked that it was something he began to utilise. 'I knew that it was going to change and I sometimes painted white on top of [the undercoat] knowing that the white I was putting on, the titanium white oil paint, would be whiter than the background, although when I painted it, it might not be very evident.'

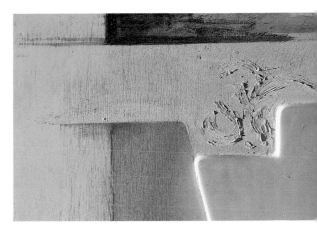

fig.54 Detail from *Hers is a lush situation* taken in raking light from the left, showing the different textures made using the various paint types.

fig.55 $he 1958–61, oil-based undercoat, nitro-cellulose and collage on plywood 121.9 x 81.3 cm.

This gradual discolouration of the undercoat with time became an important concept in Hamilton's work. He claims that by this time he 'was allowing for the changes. [The work] has several different kinds of paint on it. There's the background paint [the undercoat], there's oil paint and there's cellulose [paint], and they're all white, but quite different whites with different ageing rates. I was quite conscious of this'.

As well as colour, there are also visible differences in texture between the three types, which show up particularly well when viewed in raking light (fig.2). The extreme smoothness of the nitro-cellulose paint on the relief compared to the other types of paint is very apparent. It extends slightly beyond the edge of the relief shape in a few areas, for example over the pink paint to the left of the relief. 'I sprayed [the nitro-cellulose] on the panel and didn't mask it properly and so there's a fuzzy mix over the edge of the thing … I should have painted the background after I painted the cellulose … [as] I would like the wooden relief to be better defined by the change of colour.'

The textured white above the relief panel is oil paint, in which the brushstrokes are still clearly visible. For this area the paint was probably used straight from the tube; in other areas it has been thinned and applied as a flat coat. The surface of the undercoat is very scratched as a result of the sanding process used to prepare the panel. Often, the scratching becomes more apparent when a colour is applied on top of it, such as the thin pink paint seen in the detail (fig.54). What is particularly interesting about the surface of the undercoat is that in some areas the surface is remarkably smooth, whereas in others the scratches are numerous and somewhat severe. This lack of uniformity in the surface suggests that these differences were intentional. However, Hamilton does 'not remember putting scratches in deliberately' and feels that he 'was not particularly selective' about the surface qualities and colour of the primer at this time.

The idea of attaching areas of relief to the support had emerged from etchings he was doing at the time. 'A hole in the [etching] plate produces an area of raised relief in the print and the raised portion invariably looks whiter than the surrounding print. I simulated this effect on the painting by applying a raised panel to the surface, also heightening the whiteness by using a different kind of white [paint].'[7] This 'heightened whiteness' is most apparent in $he (fig.55), where the relief was sprayed with a pure white nitro-cellulose paint. In this work, Hamilton explored 'those commodities which affect most directly the individual way of life – consumer goods'.[8] Here the shaped shallow relief was used to resemble an apron to symbolise the 'relationship of woman and appliance [which] is a fundamental theme of our culture; as obsessive and archetypal as the western movie gun duel'.[9]

As with much of Hamilton's work, the composition was initially estab-

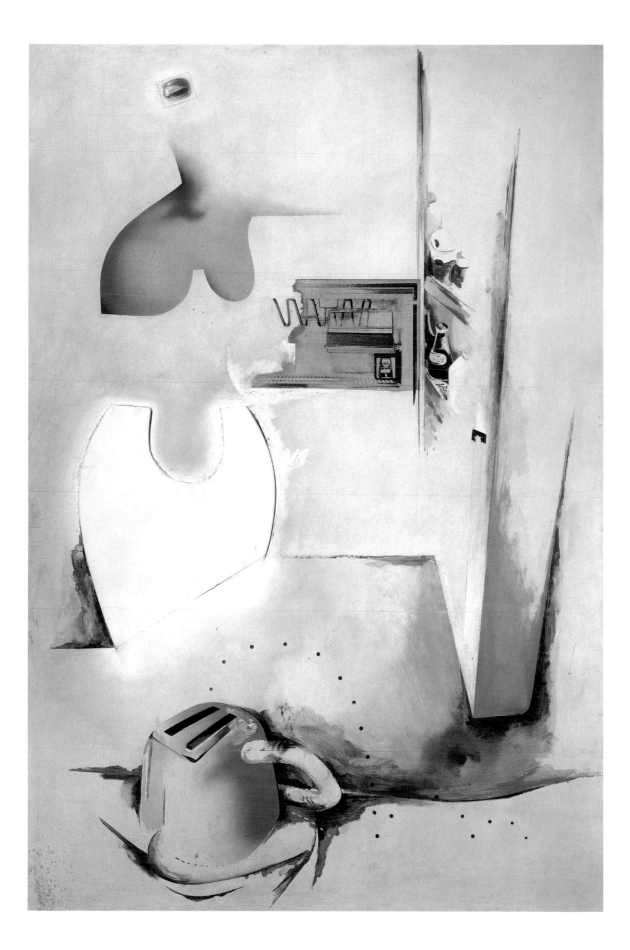

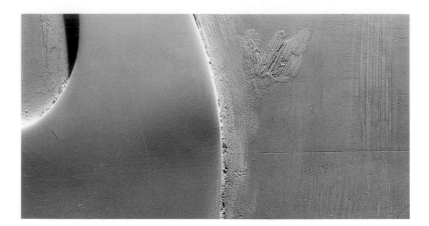

fig.56 Detail from $he taken in raking light from the right, showing part of the relief area and variations in the paint texture.

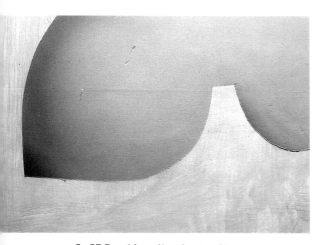

fig.57 Detail from $he taken in raking light from the right, revealing evidence of Hamilton's use of a scalpel and masking tape around the paint-sprayed areas.

lished with various preparatory studies, although it was not finalised by the time he started to paint.

I go on doing studies and then I feel that I'm able to start painting. But even then halfway through the painting I go back and try something out of a detail. Very often I have made a print in the middle [of executing a painting], which I find very fruitful – to rethink the whole thing in another medium. After I've done the print I always feel more confident with proceeding with the painting, so that print making has a purpose. I feel that if I've finished the painting then that subject is really at an end and there's not much point in making a print. Most of the prints I've made have been done during the course of the painting as part of this process of giving another jab in the arm of renewed vitality to the work I'm painting.

A detail of the region viewed in raking light (fig.56) again shows the differences in colour and texture between the three paint types. The undercoat has clearly yellowed and has a slightly streaky appearance. This may have been caused by an uneven application of priming, but is more likely to be the result of some additional painting that Hamilton had then removed by 'rubbing it off … with wet and dry paper'. He concedes that this process 'sometimes left a stain or some kind of change in the structure of the paint'.[10] In this picture, the relief area was properly masked so there is no nitro-cellulose paint around it. In fact, artists' oil paint was applied around the shape of the apron, which has produced further definition of the relief element against the slightly yellowed white of the primer. The flesh tones of the 'shoulders and breasts were lovingly sprayed with cellulose', again with masking tape placed around the area. The raised edges that are usually formed when masking tape is used are quite visible in raking light, especially along the bottom edges (fig.57).

In the image, 'sex is everywhere, symbolised in the glamour of mass-produced luxury – the interplay of fleshy plastic and smooth, fleshier metal'.[11] The metal paint used for the 'toastuum', the device in the foreground, compounded from a toaster and a vacuum cleaner, is an alu-

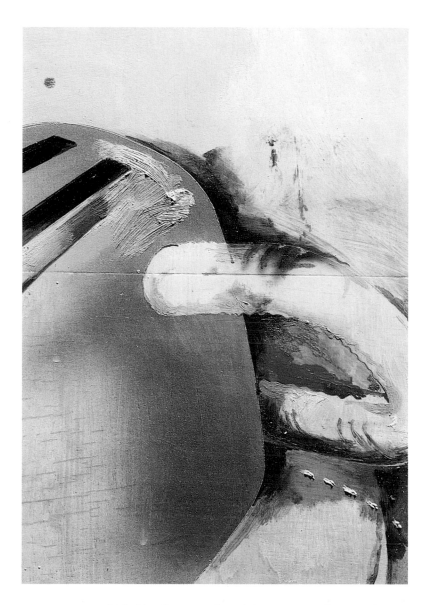

fig.58 Detail from *$he* taken in
partial raking light from the top.

minium paint, which Hamilton purchased from a specialist metal paint
manufacturer. The smooth metallic paint surface contrasts noticeably with
the effects created with oil colour around the toastuum, from very thin
transparent glazes used for some of the reds to a thick white, used over
the aluminium paint (fig.58). In addition, a few cracks in the veneer of the
plywood support panel have become apparent, for example in the main
body of the toastuum. However, Hamilton does not find this 'too disturb-
ing … I rather like it. I call it a patina. It doesn't worry me'. The collaged
area is an advert for an automatic defrosting system in a refrigerator,
which was photographed, blown up and then pasted onto the surface.

In *Towards a definitive statement on the coming trends in men's wear and
accessories (a) Together let us explore the stars* (fig.59), the intention of the
composition was 'to achieve a unity with disparate small elements of similar size and shape'.[12] The overall image was composed from photographs
of astronauts in orbit, incorporating elements of modern technology in

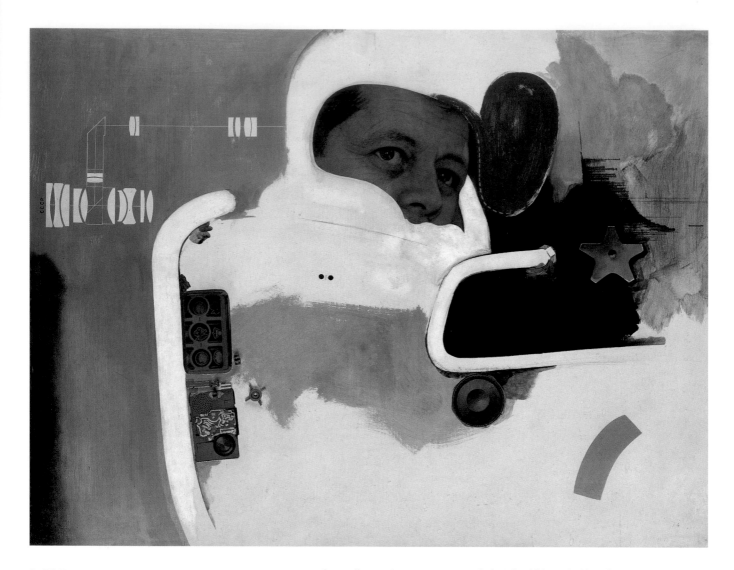

fig.59 *Towards a definitive statement on the coming trends in men's wear and accessories (a) Together let us explore the stars* 1962, oil, alkyd undercoat, blackboard paint, nitro-cellulose and collage on blockboard 61 x 81.3 cm.

the collage, plus some painted details. Although Hamilton was still using decorator's undercoat to prime his panels, the formulation of the undercoat had been altered since *$he*. By this time, most paint manufactures had started to use alkyd resins as opposed to a drying oil as a binder for undercoats. Compared to the pure oil-bound primers, these undercoats would have dried far more quickly and, if applied in the same manner, would be more likely to show brushstrokes in their surfaces. Such brushstrokes can be seen in the priming of this painting in raking light. In fig.60, for example, although the brushstrokes may appear to originate from the aluminium paint, they clearly extend into the white sections that correspond to the exposed priming.

The composition was roughly marked out in pencil before the painting began and many pencil lines are still visible around some of the forms (fig.62). Fig.60 also shows a detail of 'the reflex system of the Canon ciné camera'[13] which was 'copied from a diagram in a magazine' and then transcribed onto the surface using masking tape. The tape was applied directly to the undercoat, the outline of the system was 'transferred from a drawing with tracing paper' and then cuts were made to the tape following the drawn lines. The excess tape was subsequently removed so that only the shapes corresponding to the areas now seen as white were left. The alkyd-based aluminium paint was then brushed over the remaining tape, which was peeled off once the paint had dried. The cuts made by the scalpel to cut out the areas of unwanted tape are still visible, especially when they extend slightly beyond the shapes, for example at the bottom edge of the left-hand shape next to the 'CCCP' lettering.

Other non-traditional paints used on this work include the area of dark blue down the lower-left side of the picture, which was sprayed on to get the dry-looking surface (fig.60). This was nitro-cellulose paint, and was probably chosen to give the required opacity to this area, since oil paint that is sprayed has to be heavily diluted and therefore appears quite transparent. The area of very matt, flat-looking black paint to the lower

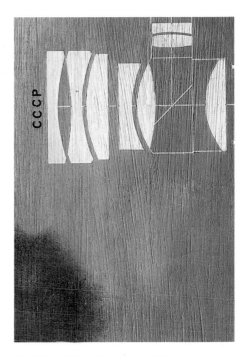

fig.60 Detail from *Towards a definitive statement …* taken in raking light from the left, showing brushmarks originating from the undercoat, and techniques used for the ciné camera.

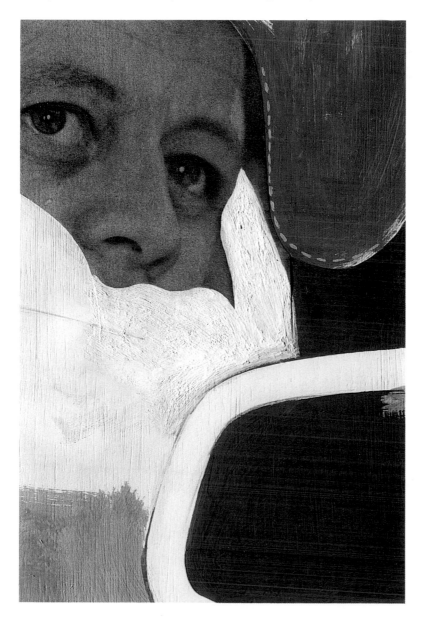

fig.61 (left) A second detail from *Towards a definitive statement …* taken in partial raking light from the left.

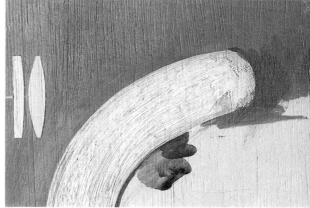

fig.62 (above) Pencil lines and variations in paint texture are visible in this partial raking-light detail (from the left) of *Towards a definitive statement …*

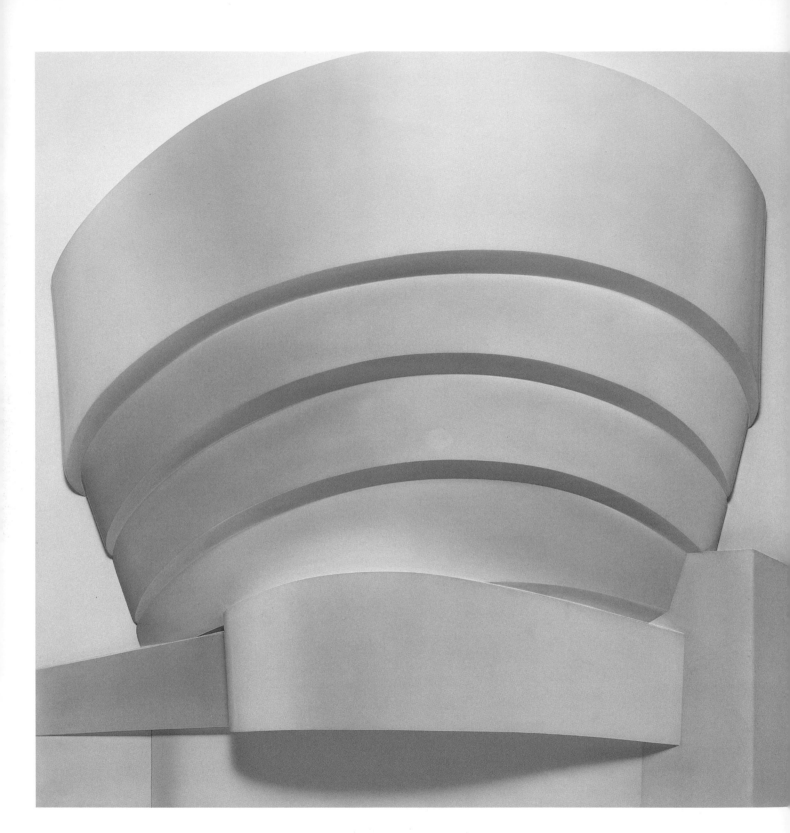

fig.63 *The Solomon R. Guggenheim (Neapolitan)* 1965–6, nitro-cellulose paint on fibreglass 121.9 x 121.9 x 17.8 cm.

right of President Kennedy's head (fig.61), is characteristic of blackboard paint. Although bound in a drying oil, this paint has an extremely high chalk content, which gives it this surface. Hamilton chose the paint because he 'liked different qualities of black as I liked different qualities of white'.[14] As before, he continued to use oil paint alongside the less traditional painting materials, applied using different techniques to produce a variety of transparencies and textures, for example the black washes in fig.62 and the red and textured white paints in fig.61.

In *The Solomon R. Guggenheim (Neapolitan)* (fig.63), the use of relief was significantly increased in depth. Hamilton describes it as a 'more sculptural extension of that projection of the picture into the spectator's space'.[15] It is one of six in a series of fibreglass relief works that were painted entirely in ICI nitro-cellulose car paint. He recalls that 'Roy Lichtenstein had made an exhibition of paintings of temples, and I'd seen paintings of buildings by Artschwager, and it occurred to me that I had never tackled this subject'.[16] The Guggenheim building was chosen not only because 'it is very much a work of art in its own right',[17] but also because 'it presented enormous technical problems from a perspective point of view. It is not the kind of building that is conducive to representation in perspective terms'.[18]

Hamilton had initially looked at coloured postcards of the museum, depicted in tinted colours that altered the original photograph of the building and suggested possibilities for modifying the architectural structure. He writes that *The Soloman R. Guggenheim* panel 'was an attempt to mirror the whole activity of architecture in the confines of a four-feet square panel'.[19] A layer of colour was applied to the fibreglass relief, in tones that simulated the modelled effect of the fall of light. This was achieved by placing the plain white painted relief under carefully staged lighting conditions, each stage photographed to record the pattern of light thrown across the surface. An application of cream spray paint preceded a coat of warm graduated pink, which reproduced the variation in tone and shadow captured in the photograph. The underside of the recessed bands of the relief was sprayed with a pale green. When the relief is lit from the side these colours are more easily seen (fig.64). The paint surface appears perfectly flat and masking tape has been used to produce the very sharp boundaries of each colour. However, Hamilton does not

think there's anything peculiar about my abilities as a spray man. I know there are hundreds of thousands of people who can rub down Rolls Royces and get a better finish than I could get on that painting … They do magical things with custom cars – far ahead, technically, of anything I could do with a spray gun … All I was concerned about was to get the best possible finish.

Hamilton continued to paint on the smooth surface of solid supports

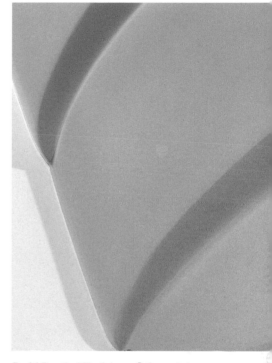

fig.64 Detail of *The Solomon R. Guggenheim (Neapolitan)* taken in partial raking light from the right, revealing the actual paint colours.

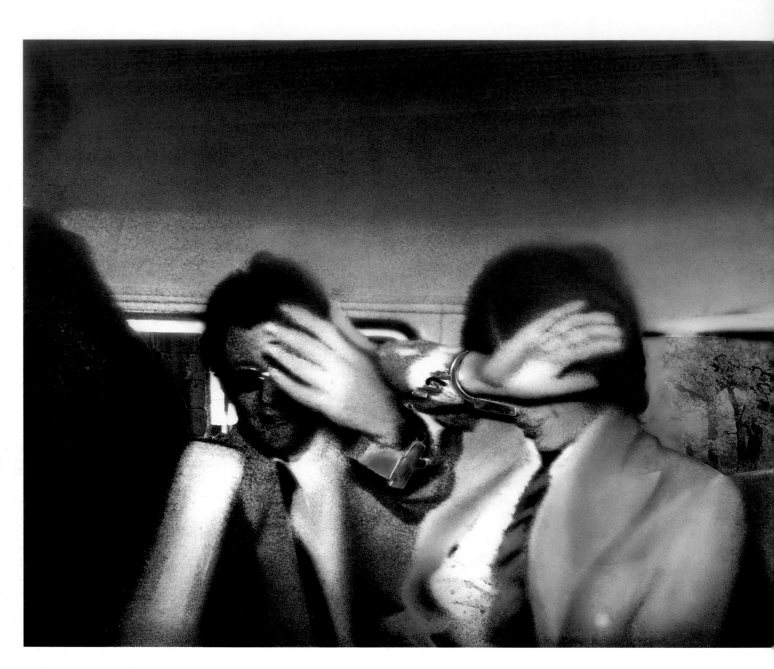

fig.65 *Swingeing London 67 (f)* , acrylic emulsion, silk-screen ink and collage on canvas 67.3 x 85.1 cm.

in preference to the heavy-toothed cotton canvas, 'until I realised that you didn't have to have the surface that I regarded as unpleasant if you put enough coats of primer on. Acrylic primer made that possible. It was the invention of acrylic gesso that enabled me to go back to canvas to get the kind of surface that I liked'. He started to use 'white acrylic primers when they became available' and recalls first becoming aware of the product when he 'saw it in an artists' shop in Highgate'. *Swingeing London 67 (f)* (fig.65), is one of a series of six paintings on cotton canvas. Although all the paintings in this series were primed with acrylic gesso, Hamilton varied their textures. This work is primed with a number of layers of acrylic gesso sanded to a smooth surface, 'so I could do something different on it [to] the things that were done on the ones with more canvas texture'. Compared to the undercoat primers he had been using, the acrylic gesso, which was 'probably Liquitex', also offered more permanency: 'If it was an American product made especially for artists I naively supposed it must be better – it felt better'.

The image is from a press photograph published in the *Daily Mail* of Mick Jagger and Hamilton's art dealer Robert Fraser, seen through the window of a police van before being convicted in court of possession of drugs in 1967. Hamilton first made a 'print, which was quite large, of the whole photograph'. He then retouched and cropped certain areas, 'removing the police van to get closer to its occupants'. The image was then transferred onto the primed canvas: 'all of the paintings were traced onto their canvases from the same drawing before painting ... I painted six versions because the many newspaper reports gave quite different descriptions of the event.' His colour scheme was fairly basic and based on these reports. As before, he applied his paint using different application techniques. 'I sprayed it and painted on it.' However, for this work he used acrylic emulsion paints. This is an unusual occurrence for him as in general he does not like acrylic paint 'because it dries too fast. I [only] use it if there is an advantage to be gained from the fast drying'. The light blue paint to the right of Jagger's head was clearly applied by spray (fig.66). 'Having worked for some time on the paintings, using different techniques (some were painted in a very academic way, and some were flat and posterised) [and] not feeling happy about them as paintings, I thought that it would be good to put the photograph on as a silk-screen ... All six paintings were screen-printed with Christopher Prater in an hour or so.' In some areas, such as around the tie, the image was silk-screened directly onto the acrylic priming (fig.67). However, Hamilton continued to make further applications of paint, some of which are also visible in this detail. The green stripes in the tie and some of the flesh tones are very thin applications of colour. These are distinguishable from the colour applied before the silk-screen by the reduced intensity of the black dots. In contrast, the raking light has picked up the raised brushmarks in the white

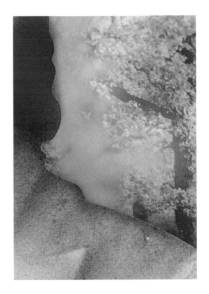

fig.66 Detail of an area of sprayed paint from *Swingeing London 67 (f)*.

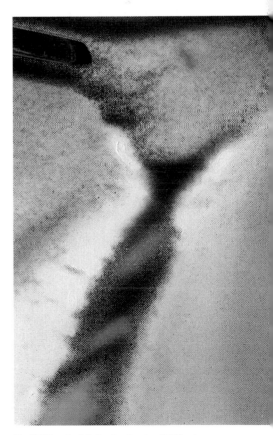

fig.67 Detail of *Swingeing London 67 (f)* taken in partial raking light from the left. It shows the sequence of paint and silk-screen application.

paint below the chin, characteristic of a much thicker application. This version was also the only one to contain collage (in the form of hand-cuffs), attached to the canvas at the final stage.

Hamilton has continued to work on canvas ever since, and has largely returned to using only artists' quality painting materials. 'Nowadays I feel much happier with a good canvas, primed with acrylic gesso, and using good paints, and not trying to be too ambitious in the way of sticking lots of wood on things.' *The Citizen* (fig.68), painted between 1981 and 1983, was executed in oil colour over a grey acrylic gesso ground on canvas. White acrylic gesso was tinted with black acrylic emulsion paint and applied initially in a thin layer to soak into the canvas, followed by twelve to fifteen coats, each one rubbed down with wet and dry paper. The whole preparation process took between two to three weeks. A rough pencil outline of the projected image was then made on the primed canvas surface, which for Hamilton was more satisfactory than squaring up. The underpainting was executed with diluted acrylic paint and the image was completed with slightly thinned oil paint, which was mainly brushed on, but with the occasional use of an airbrush.

Throughout his life, Hamilton has incorporated many different materials into his work. For the paintings from the late 1950s and early 1960s he recalls that

it was very important that they were built in a different kind of way from traditional painting. I tried … to represent the images in a way that was related to the source … Colour was seen symbolically rather than as representational. The same applied to materials – I could use cellulose and spray because it symbolised the object. So there was a level of colour, the philosophy, everything was directed not as representing it but as symbolising it … Also I thought there was something dishonest and stupid about copying something. I wanted the work to have as close a connection with the source as possible. So, [if] something had excited me, an image in a magazine, I tore [it] out [from] that magazine. If I painted it on the canvas or the board … it would have seemed to me rather perverse. Why do it the long way round when what I really want to do is stick it on? It can't be as good as seeing that thing stuck on there, so to redo it in a historically safer or more permanent way would have been a kind of cop out.

Hamilton views the deterioration of his earlier images made from unusual materials philosophically. 'It's an acceptable kind of hazard of using these cranky materials. That's one of the reasons I don't use them now. It's because I've realised that there are problems and I accept the problems and the results as a kind of patina. When I look at Duchamp or Picasso, I see the same problems occurring when they used funny materials.' He certainly has no regrets: 'otherwise everybody would paint with oil and nothing would ever change.'

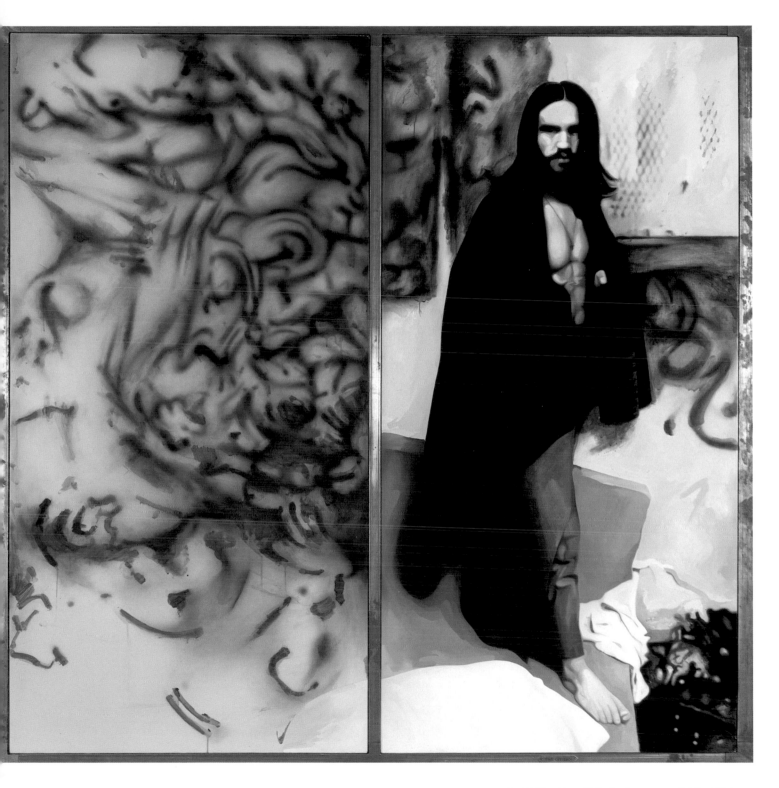

fig.68 *The citizen* 1981–3, oil on canvas 206.8 x 218.2 cm.

David Hockney born 1937

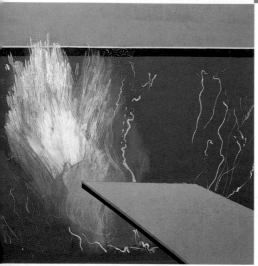

For much of the early part of his painting career David Hockney worked with oil colours. He had been 'taught to paint with oil paint in art school. They taught you quite a few things about it, what you could do with it; but you discover most of it yourself'. He found that 'you can put oil paint on and manipulate it on the canvas' to produce a wide variety of textures, a property that he exploited in much of his early work. He recalls that 'Dubuffet was the strong visual influence' at this time, in terms of the different textures that he created in his paint, his style and 'the kind of childish drawing he used'.[1] Hockney discovered that some of these surfaces had been created by modifying the paint itself, for example by adding sand to it, and soon began to recognise the significance of choosing the right materials with which to paint: 'the paint itself is interesting … and just as technique it's quite important'. The search for new textures also involved leaving some areas completely unpainted, allowing the surface of the canvas to play a much more prominent role. 'I left a great deal of the canvas bare to stop the spectator, who, seeing the bare canvas, senses little illusion or intrusion into its surface.'[2]

As a student of the Royal College of Art at the end of the 1950s, Hockney recalls 'that there were two groups of students there: a traditional group who simply carried on as they had done in art school, doing still life, life painting and figure compositions; and then what I thought of as the more adventurous, lively students, the brightest ones, who were more involved in the art of their time. They were doing big Abstract Expressionist paintings [with oil] on hardboard.' He was particularly interested in the ways in which the American Abstract Expressionist painters – whose work had by then been exhibited in London – had manipulated and modified their paints. One of the tutors at the Royal College was Sandra Blow. Hockney recounts that 'they got her in because she did big abstracts with sand in them, the sort of thing students were doing; she was brought in to control them!'

Tea Painting in an Illusionistic Style (fig.70) is the last of a series of three paintings in which Hockney represented a Typhoo Tea packet in a manner

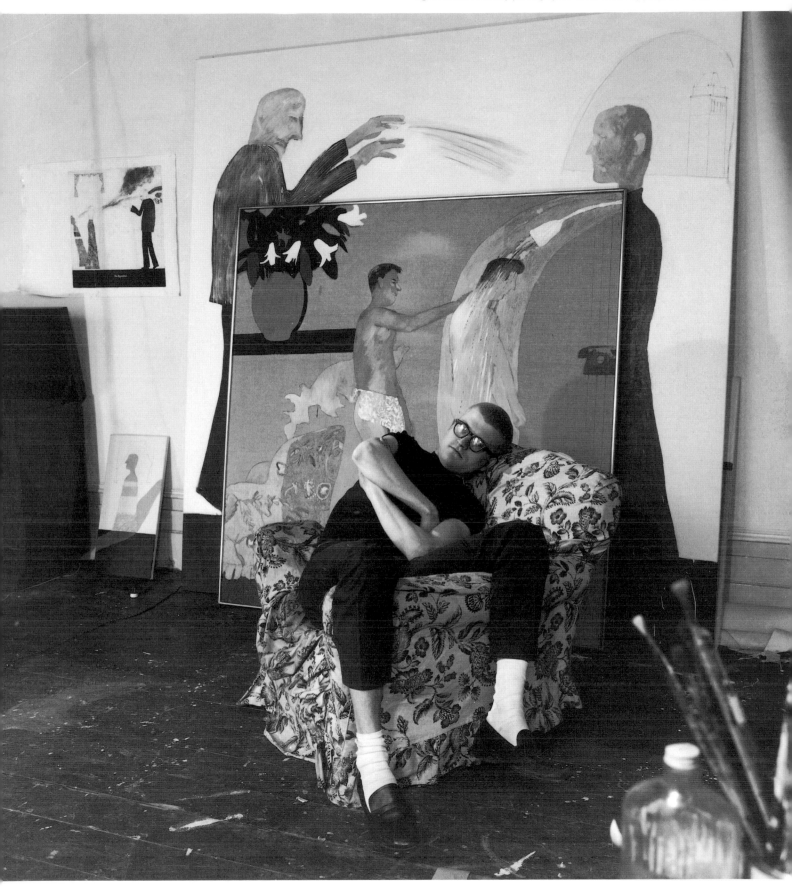

suggestive of 'an Abstract Expressionist painting with a strong reference to one strong visual – a very familiar sign'. According to Hockney, however, the painting 'is as close to Pop art as I ever came'. He remembers making tea for himself early in the morning at the Royal College. 'It was always Typhoo tea, my mother's favourite. The tea packets piled up with the cans and tubes of paint and they were lying around all the time and I just thought, in a way it's like still-life paintings for me … There was a packet of Typhoo tea, a very ordinary popular brand of tea, so I used it as a motif.'

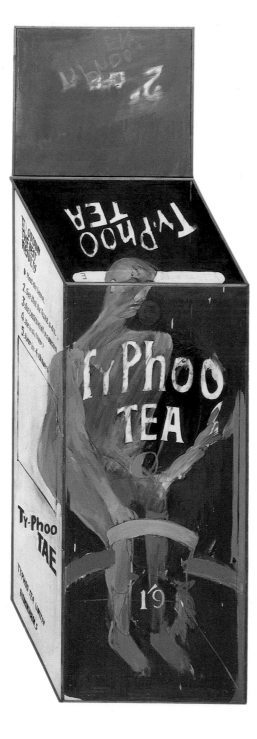

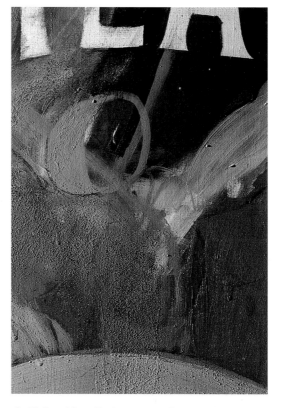

fig.71 Detail from *Tea Painting in an Illusionistic Style* taken in raking light from the left, showing variations in the paint texture.

fig.70 (left) *Tea Painting in an Illusionistic Style* 1961, oil on canvas 198.1 x 76.2 cm.

In common with much of his painting from the early 1960s, *Tea Painting in an Illusionistic Style* exhibits a range of different surfaces, varying from very thin coats of paint on unprimed linen canvas, where the canvas texture is evident, to areas in which sand was added to impart a granular surface to the oil paint. These textures are most apparent when the painting is viewed in raking light (fig.71). In this detail areas of oil paint in which sand was incorporated are clearly visible; other textures were achieved through brushstrokes and drips in the paint. The white letters of the word 'TEA' were made by leaving the commercial primer unpainted and the texture of the canvas weave is therefore most evident here. A slight ridge is visible around each letter, suggesting that Hockney used tape to mask off each letter during the application of most of the paint. However, the thin traces of pink and black paint that extend into the letters indicate that Hockney continued to paint after the tape had been removed.

An important aspect of the work was that the stretcher departed from the traditional rectangle. 'The idea that paintings should be rectangular or square was so fixed in every student's mind that even Italian paintings of the Crucifixion, constructed in the shape of the cross, still appeared in my memory as rectangular ... I can remember a precise moment when I realised that the shape of the picture gave it a great deal more power.' The support is made up of four individual stretchers, 'and I made the stretchers myself. It was quite difficult stretching them all up – the back is almost as complicated as the front; it took me five days. I don't think anybody had done shapes before. It meant that the blank canvas was itself already illusionistic and I could ignore the concept of illusionistic space and paint merrily in a flat style – people were always talking about flatness in painting in those days.'

Hockney uses his preoccupation with flatness to account for his misspelling of the word 'TEA' as 'TAE'. 'I spelt the word tea wrong on the left-hand section ... I am a bad speller, but to spell a three-letter word wrong! But it's drawn in perspective and it was quite difficult to do. I took so long planning it that in my concern for flatness or abstraction I spelt it wrong.' In fact he had originally spelt the word correctly. On close examination (fig.72) the original lettering (also painted in red) can be seen through the white background paint, which was applied over the first version before Hockney slightly re-positioned the two words. The detail also shows the battening that separates the two canvases. The paint can be seen to extend around the edges of each canvas, but not onto the battening, which suggests that much of it was applied when the four sections were in separate pieces. This was certainly the case with the top section: as the direction of paint drips around its top edge indicates that it was painted upside down (and thus the '2d OFF' would have been the right way up). However, in a few other areas the paint extends over the battening, indicating that some

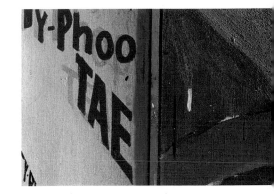

fig.72 Detail from *Tea Painting in an Illusionistic Style* taken in raking light from the right, revealing the original (and correct) spelling of 'TEA'.

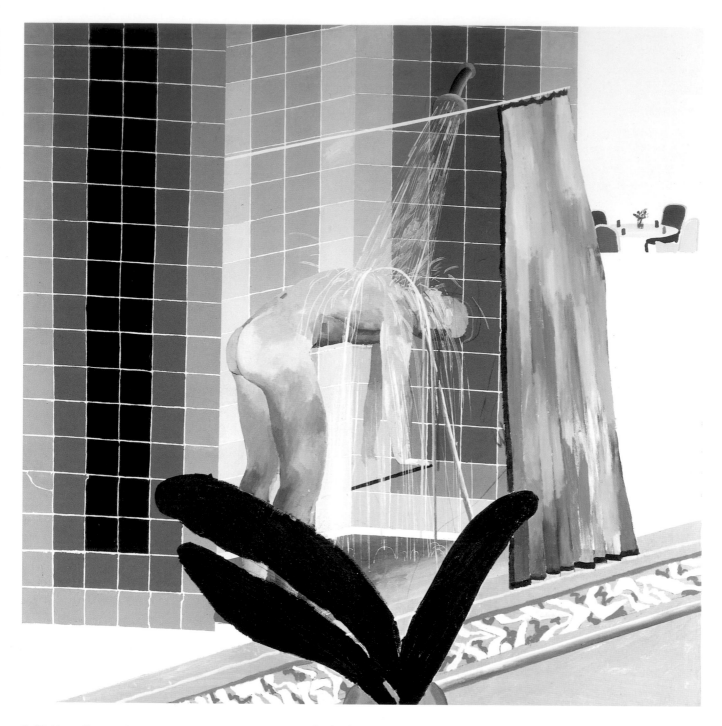

fig.73 *Man in Shower in Beverly Hills* 1964,
acrylic-vinyl emulsion on canvas 167.3 x 167 cm.

final adjustments were clearly made to the work once it had been fully assembled.

The major change in Hockney's choice of paint came towards the end of 1963 when he visited Los Angeles for the first time and started painting with acrylic emulsion paints. His use of this new medium coincided with a shift in emphasis in his work from texture to colour, and it has been noted that the matt, even quality and colour of acrylic paint evoked the flat, unworked surface of a photograph. 'I'd tried acrylic paint in England before and I hadn't liked it at all; [the] texture [and] colours weren't so very good. But the American ones I liked. It was superior paint. And so I started to use it.' This switch in medium resulted in an immediate change in his working method. 'You can work on one picture all the time because you never have to wait for it to dry, whereas you might work on two or three oil paintings at a time.'

Man in Shower in Beverly Hills (fig.73) was painted in 1964 during a six-week visit to Iowa. The composition was drawn onto the canvas in Los Angeles before he left, 'and I'd taken it off the stretcher and rolled it up and put it in the car'. His paintings at the time frequently depicted the relaxed Californian life he had found, and his images of showers and swimming pools evoke a world of physical sensuality. He continued to refer to his photographic material, which provided the source for much of the imagery.

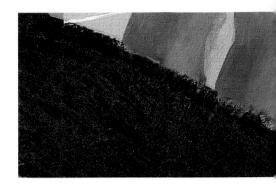

fig.74 Detail from *Man in Shower in Beverly Hills* taken in raking light from above.

Americans take showers all the time – I knew that from experience and physique magazines. For an artist, the interest of showers is obvious: the whole body is always in view and in movement … The figure and tiles … are painted from a photograph taken by the Athletic Model Guild, a group of Los Angeles photographers who do studies of the male nude. The idea of painting moving water in a very slow and careful manner was (and still is) very appealing to me.

Hockney used various brands of American acrylic emulsion paint. The paint in this work has been identified through analysis as a acrylic-vinyl emulsion paint, which is similar to pure acrylic but combines the components of PVA. The main brand of acrylic-vinyl paint was made by New Masters, a California-based company, and it is likely that he used it on this particular work. The New Masters paints had a slightly higher gloss and thicker consistency than the pure acrylic paints of the time. Both of these properties can be seen most clearly in a detail of the black plant when viewed in raking light (fig.74). Strong reflections of light are visible on the ridges of paint textured with a paintbrush. Although Hockney's preoccupation with texture had certainly diminished by this time, it was evidently still a feature that he used.

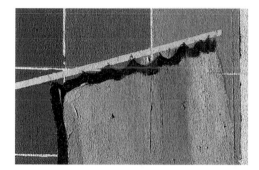

fig.74 Detail from *Man in Shower in Beverly Hills* taken in partial raking light (from left), showing evidence of Hockney's use of masking tape.

The first areas of paint to be applied to the primed cotton were the tiles of the shower, painted with the aid of masking tape. The raking-light detail in fig.75 reveals ridges of paint at the edges of each tile, which are typically formed when strips of tape are removed, and they can be clearly seen to extend beneath the shower curtain. The vertical edges are particularly pronounced, because the image is lit from the left, casting shadows to the right of each ridge. The width of each shadow gives an indication of the relative height of the paint. A slightly different effect is seen along the lower edge of the shower curtain rail. Here, thin drips of residue paint have been pulled away from the curtain rail, indicating that the cream paint was not completely dry when the tape was removed. It can be seen from its texture that the paint used for the curtain rail was applied fairly thickly, and this would have resulted in a slightly longer drying time.

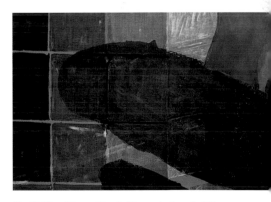

fig.76 Detail from *Man in Shower in Beverly Hills* taken under UV illumination. The tiles clearly extend beneath the plant and a diagonal line starting from the lower left corner is also visible.

When the painting is viewed under ultraviolet (UV) illumination, as in the detail in fig.76, the surface of the tiles fluoresce slightly in a light green colour. The fluorescence shows up the brushwork of this layer very clearly and is strong enough to shine through most of the paint above it. This method of examination therefore also confirms that the tiles extend beneath the black paint of the plant. In addition, UV illumination exposes a diagonal line that extends beneath the painted tiles. Part of this line is seen in fig.76, running from the lower-left corner to about halfway up the right side, but it extends all the way from the left edge of the painting up to just beneath the man's right hand. At this point the line has been painted over in black and is visible in the finished work (fig.73). This line probably corresponds to the edge of a bath, which may have been depicted in an earlier composition. However, since the tiles were painted over it (and they seem to lie beneath all other areas of paint) Hockney clearly abandoned this idea at an early stage.

One of the changes that Hockney had to make to his working methods when using emulsion paint was to undertake a greater degree of pre-planning of the composition. Because the acrylic (and acrylic-vinyl) paint dried more quickly than oil paint, it was more difficult to remove.

I began increasingly to draw first before painting. It might have had to do with using acrylic paint; with acrylic paint you must plan a little bit because you can't scrape it off as you can oil paint. At the end of the day, if you didn't like it, you'd have to start with a completely new canvas. But once you start bits of the painting you decide to keep [them], and you've painted a section, and you think it's going quite well … it makes you slightly more cautious in other areas. There's no need to be like that with oil paint. You can remove any section of it; you can remove it quite a while afterwards, two months afterwards, with solvent. Acrylic conditions the process; it's limiting in a way.

In this painting, much of the drawing seems to have occurred after the tiles had been painted. Graphite and charcoal drawing is clearly visible roughly outlining several areas of the image, such as around the figure's head and the plant's leaves.

The figure, shower, carpet and plant were subsequently painted in turn using varied techniques. For example, the stream of water coming out of the showerhead and bouncing off the figure's back was painted precisely with a small brush. The rapid-drying nature of the acrylic-based emulsion paint would have enabled Hockney to complete this part of the painting reasonably quickly and minimised the risk of smudging. In contrast, the paint used for the shower curtain and figure was applied with a larger brush and in a much looser technique. Here, the rapid-drying qualities of the paint prevented any blending of adjacent areas of colour into one another. Hockney painted the plant last. He recalls: 'I had great difficulty in painting the figure's feet and, although the plant in the foreground was a

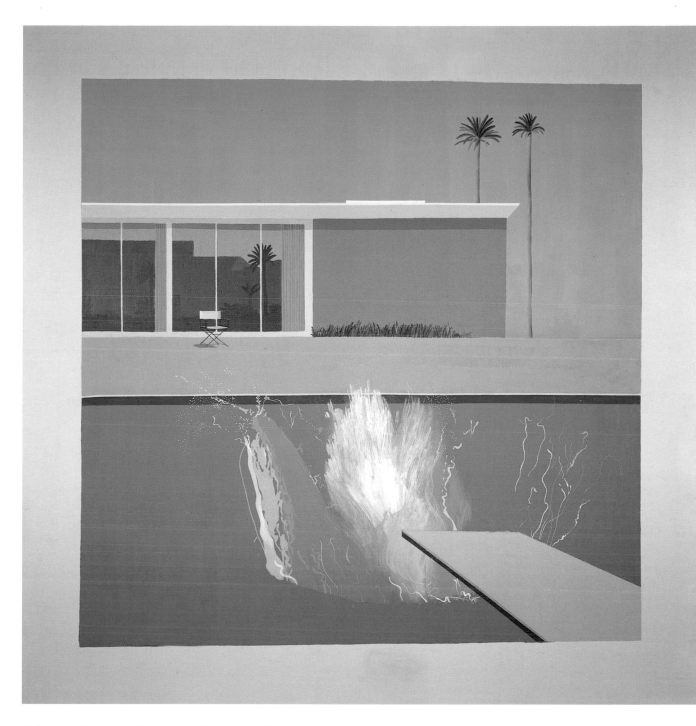

definite early part of the composition, I did take a rather easy way out by bending the leaves to cover his feet.'

A Bigger Splash (fig.77) was painted three years later, in 1967, and Hockney describes it as 'a balanced composition; it's worked out that way, very consciously'. For this work he used pure acrylic emulsion paint on a piece of cotton canvas that was 'stapled to [the] wall of [the] studio'[3] and stretched after completion of the paint application. 'I think the painting technique used here is very simple … The clear light of California suggested simple techniques.'[4] Although the canvas was not prepared with a

fig.77 *A Bigger Splash* 1967, acrylic emulsion on canvas 242.6 x 243.8 cm.

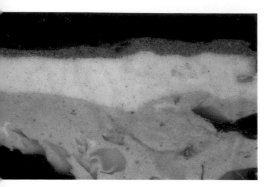

fig.78 Cross-section of paint taken from the left border of the left windowpane in *A Bigger Splash*, showing the presence of a blue (and white) layer beneath the grey (photographed at 200 x magnification).

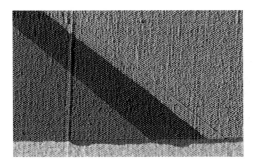

fig.79 Detail from *A Bigger Splash* taken in raking light from the left, revealing canvas weave and bleed from the first layer of blue paint.

conventional size or primed layer, Hockney applied a diluted coat of Liquitex matt medium prior to painting the image inside the canvas border. 'I used borders around an image a lot, from about 1964 to 1967 ... It makes the picture look more like a painting (you're even less likely to trip up and fall into the pool).'[5]

The first areas of paint to have been applied were the blue sections. 'The large areas of flat colour were rolled on', and a small proportion of acrylic gel medium was added to the paint to adjust the consistency for application by a paint roller. Hockney also observed that 'the gel medium helps the flatness'.[6] These blue areas extend beneath most of the other painted areas, as is evident around many of the edges. For example, the blue used for the sky extends beneath the entire building and was initially a blue rectangle (the right edge of this rectangle was never painted over and therefore shows the original dimensions at this side). The pink layer representing the paving does not appear to have any blue beneath it, but a second large, slightly darker blue rectangle was applied to the bottom half of the painting as the base coat for the water in the pool. Hockney recalls that at one point the work would have been 'just about a striped painting'. A fragment of paint taken from the left border of the left windowpane in the building and viewed as a cross-section (fig.78) clearly shows this initial (and relatively thick) blue paint layer. The next layer to be applied in this area was actually a white layer, which in the finished work is visible as the white window frame. However, this white layer lies beneath the grey paint used for the window, so Hockney's painting process clearly incorporated a considerable amount of 'blocking in' of areas before he incorporated more detail into the image. All of these blocks of colour were applied with the appropriate area masked by tape to produce a smooth edge. However, the paint was sometimes sufficiently fluid to bleed slightly under the tape edges. This is seen mostly in the various blue colours extending slightly into the border around the main painted area, such as the blue along the bottom edge of the detail shown in fig.79 (taken in raking light). This detail also reveals the slightly raised edges of the paint borders in the diving board (indicating the use of masking tape), and a raised, oversized, vertical thread in the canvas, which actually runs up the entire height of the painting.

After these areas had been painted, Hockney used delicate brushwork, in contrast to the rolled-on paint areas, to paint the details such as the splash, chair and foliage. The rapid drying time of the acrylic emulsion paint enabled Hockney, within a relatively short period, to apply the brushstrokes over other brushstrokes that had dried completely. This technique becomes apparent when these areas are magnified, such as part of the splash shown in fig.80.

[The] splash itself was painted with small brushes and little lines; it took me about two weeks to paint the splash. I loved the idea of painting this thing that lasts for two seconds; it takes me two weeks to paint this event that lasts for two seconds ... The painting took much longer to make than the splash existed for, so it has a very different effect on the viewer.

Although in some places the use of masking tape and the build-up of paint layers has resulted in a certain thickness, in many areas the paint is

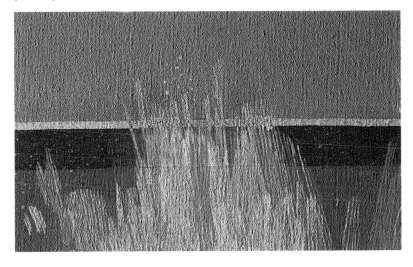

fig.80 Detail from *A Bigger Splash* taken in partial raking light from the left.

extremely thin, leaving the texture of the canvas weave visible underneath (apparent in both fig.79 and fig.80). The acrylic emulsion paint was diluted with a large proportion of water. Hockney found this paint – particularly the American brands – to be a versatile medium, well suited to staining bare canvas. Soon after the painting was finished, he exploited the staining technique further.

There is another technique with acrylic paint that I began to use in 1967 or 1968. It is a technique that was used a lot by American painters – Helen Frankenthaler and then, later, by Morris Louis [and] Kenneth Noland. Acrylic paint is diluted with water. If you put a little detergent in this diluted paint, then paint onto unprimed raw cotton duck, the detergent has the effect of breaking up the oil in the cotton, making it much more absorbent, as though you're painting on blotting paper. The paint spreads and stains right into the canvas, literally staining the canvas and not resting on its surface. You have some control over it. You learn how much detergent to put in; if you put in too much it just goes everywhere, but if you put in too little it's very slow. I learned this technique through Lenny Bocour, in New York, who manufactured acrylic paint, and I realised it was a possible technique for me to use. I really used it on water paintings, literally to paint water with kind of watercolour effects.

Hockney continued to be interested in the surface of the paint. 'I ... liked the idea that the eye could sense the difference between this watery effect of the acrylic paint with detergent in it and the effect of acrylic paint painted onto gesso ground. In a sense, this is using texture;

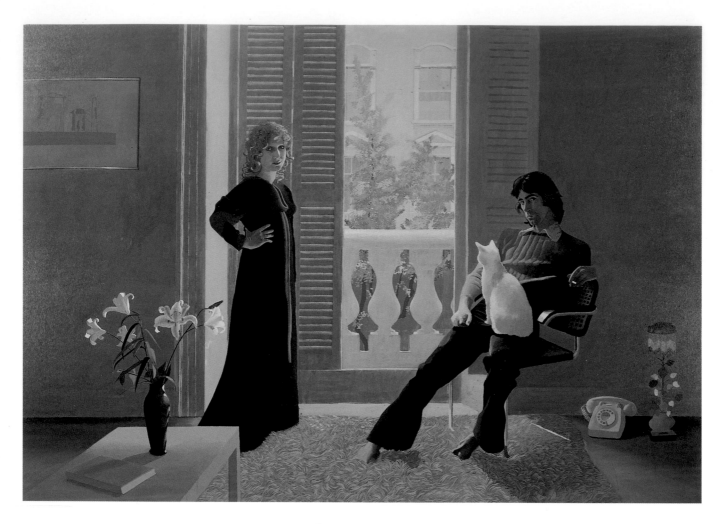

fig.81 *Mr and Mrs Clark and Percy* 1970–1,
acrylic emulsion on canvas 213.4 x 304.8 cm.

the eye can tell there are two distinct textures on the paintings, two very, very distinct things. I'm not sure that's completely possible with oil paint; I don't think you can quite get these effects'.

Mr and Mrs Clark and Percy (fig.81), executed between 1970 and 1971, was also painted in acrylic emulsion paint and for Hockney 'is the painting that comes closest to naturalism'. His preparatory work for the painting involved 'taking photographs, making drawings, trying to work out a composition; for these big paintings I worked out the composition before I began, although I didn't draw them out totally. They're often drawn with a brush.' One of the sketches for the work is shown in fig.82 (Study for *Mr and Mrs Clark and Percy*), in which the main features of the composition had already been established and Hockney had started to fill in some areas with colour. It is also squared up, ready for the transfer over to canvas. A larger grid in pencil was drawn onto the primed cotton canvas, which would have facilitated the correct proportioning of figures on the final work. As Hockney recalls: 'The figures [in the painting] are nearly life size; it's difficult painting figures like that, and it was quite a struggle'.

Although Hockney continued to use acrylic emulsion paint for this work, he used it in a very different way from the two earlier acrylic paint-

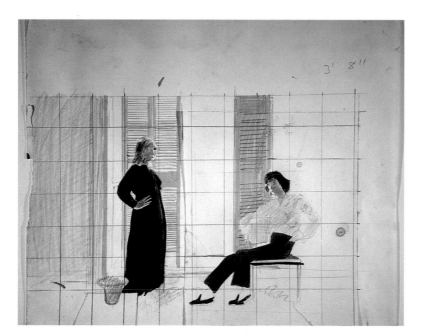

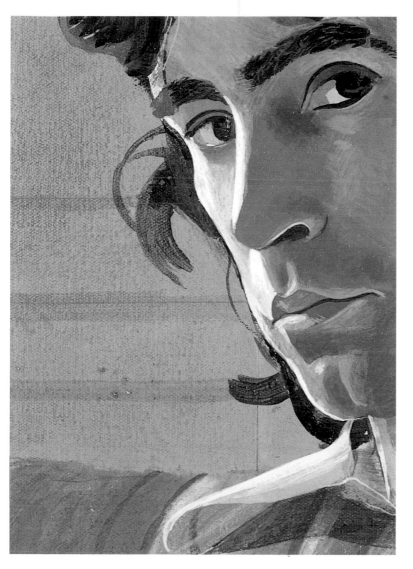

fig.82 Study for *Mr and Mrs Clark and Percy* 1970, pencil and coloured pencil on paper 27 x 40.3 cm.

fig.83 Detail from *Mr and Mrs Clark and Percy*, showing Hockney's use of paint glazes and the pencil grid to square up the composition.

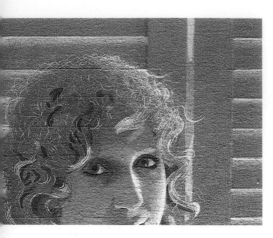

fig.84 Detail from *Mr and Mrs Clark and Percy* taken in partial raking light from below, revealing the presence of shutters extending beneath Mrs Clark's head.

ings described above. He replaced his use of a 'simple technique' that had seemed appropriate to California with 'more complicated glazing techniques … The light in a London room suggested an older chiaroscuro technique'.[7] In many areas, the acrylic emulsion paint was diluted with appreciable quantities of water to produce thin washes of colour. Hockney found the acrylic paint perfectly suited to this method of working. 'The great way to use acrylics is the very old-fashioned method of glazing with washes, which you can do with acrylics of course, marvellously. The glaze dries in ten minutes and then you can put another on so it's just adapting it.'[8] Thin glazes of coloured wash are apparent all over the painting, especially over the walls and shutters (see fig.81). In the shutters, for example, a warm brown glaze is apparent over most areas of the cooler light-blue base coat. The thin brown glaze was applied in a loose, uneven manner, resulting in an overall patchy appearance in which broad brushstrokes are clearly visible.

In addition to this warm brown glaze over the shutters, many other glazes are discernible in the detail of Ossie Clark's face and collar (shown in fig.83), such as the curls of his hair, some of the flesh tones in the neck and the shadow beneath the collar. The detail also shows that Hockney used a thin black glaze to depict the space between the shutter slats. In addition, pencil lines can be seen, one running beneath the middle of these three horizontal lines and the other running vertically from the middle of the collar wing. These lines are part of the grid used to transfer the composition from the sketch to the canvas. In other areas of the detail, much finer brushwork can also be seen, for example in the lips and eyebrows. Hockney recalls that the figure of Ossie Clark was worked on extensively: 'I probably painted the head alone twelve times – drawn and painted and then completely removed, and then put in again, and again'.

Even thinner brush lines are scattered through Celia's hair (fig.84). This detail was taken in a raking light from below and reveals the ridged paint lines of the shutters, indicating that Hockney continued to use masking tape. The shutters can be seen to extend beneath the head and hair, but even in these areas, the texture of the canvas weave is still apparent in raking light, which again highlights the thinness of the paint layers.

Although Hockney has suggested that 'all the technical problems were caused because my main aim was to paint the relationship between these two people', many more were caused by the fast-drying quality of the acrylic emulsion, especially for such a large picture. 'It's very difficult with acrylic paint to grade one colour into another … you've got to keep going and doing it at such speed!' In contrast, he found blending oil colours to be 'very easy because it's wet all the time, but with acrylic it becomes very difficult actually to do, [so] I … keep it wet constantly by spraying water on it.' An acrylic-based varnish was also selectively sprayed on during the painting process to keep the gloss of the surface reasonably high. Fig.85 shows Hockney spraying this varnish onto the painting's surface. The varnish was very fluid, as evidenced by the many dribbles on the painting's surface, for example, running from the top edge of the detail shown in fig.86. Another consequence of spraying an emulsion varnish is that the process can cause the formation of small air bubbles. A number of these are evident in the lower-right corner of the detail. The detail also shows that not all areas of paint were applied as thin glazes and scumbles. The horizontal brushstrokes seen in the top of the balustrade are characteristic of a much thicker paint, with a consistency closer to that of an acrylic paint used straight from the tube.

In the mid-1970s, when Hockney switched back to painting in oil, it became immediately apparent how much his technique had changed through using acrylic. He recalls that 'the first four paintings I started in oils I abandoned completely, partly because I was a little rusty, and it only slowly came back to me'. His decision to use acrylic emulsion paint for most of the 1960s had primarily been an aesthetic choice. During this time

I was using acrylic paint; texture interested me very little. In the earlier oil pictures it had. It interests me more now because I'm painting with oil again, although the only reason I went back to oil was that I got frustrated with acrylic colours. That was partly because of the naturalism. I wanted things to be more naturalistic and acrylic is not really the best medium [for that]. When you use simple and bold colours, acrylic is a fine medium; the colours are very intense and they stay intense, they don't alter much. I probably will do some acrylic painting again; it's not that I've abandoned it.

Hockney also acknowledges another reason to explain his use of acrylic emulsion for such a significant period of time. 'The reason I kept up with them [acrylics] was people said they were very safe to use – permanent and everything. I didn't know anything about oil paint; I thought well, if people have paid £200 [then approximately $400] for paintings, then that's an awful lot of money. I should try to make sure that they don't fall to bits after six months.

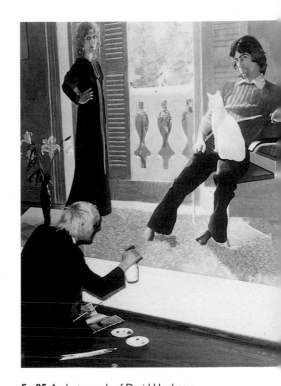

fig.85 A photograph of David Hockney taken in 1971, applying local areas of varnish during the final stage of painting *Mr and Mrs Clark and Percy*.

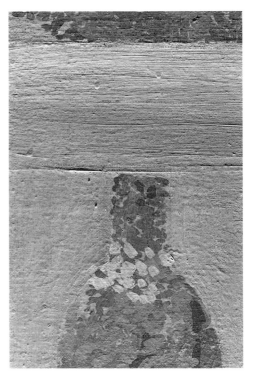

fig.86 Detail from *Mr and Mrs Clark and Percy* taken in raking light from below. There are drips in the varnish and air bubbles in the thicker passages of paint.

John Hoyland born 1934

Although John Hoyland's paintings are frequently described as 'abstract', he claims to have 'never liked that word', preferring the term 'non-figurative'. As he explains, 'I don't think you would call [them] abstract paintings if you really looked at them ... [They are] allowing a slight opening of the curtain to nature, to the natural world'. His paintings are often highly coloured and usually characterised by great variation in the thickness, texture and gloss of the paint. As his friend Patrick Caulfield recounts, 'he uses paint like it's just been invented. It's splashed on. He just puts on paint like nobody's done before'.

Hoyland has 'always worked in kind of series ... but [with] each [painting] trying to be a different animal ... I could never repeat the same thing over and over again. I still can't, I find it too boring ... I didn't want to go through the kind of serial process that say, Bridget Riley goes through. I found it emotionally too restricting, not only emotionally but technically as well. I wanted more responsibility, more spontaneity, more feeling, less logic.' However, many aspects of his paintings are carefully controlled, albeit often taking 'advantage of controlled accident'. He tends to 'do masses and masses of drawings of different possibilities and variations' before the actual painting begins, so that 'the concept would [be] fixed' and has remarked that in fact 'there's nothing spontaneous about [my] paintings except the colours and the way they're resolved.'

The process of paint application has always been under careful control.

You stretch up a blank canvas and for a while it's like shadow boxing ... hitting an opponent who doesn't hit back. Slowly the painting starts to impose itself. When it dictates where it wants to go, and I let it, it never works. I've got to be slightly on top of the painting. But you can't get heavy with a painting. You have to watch it out of the corner of your eye. It has to be allowed to go its own way to some extent; it's a compromise.[1]

In terms of Hoyland's choice of paint, there has only been one major change throughout his entire career, and that was his move from oil to acrylic emulsion paint in 1963, the year that these paints first became

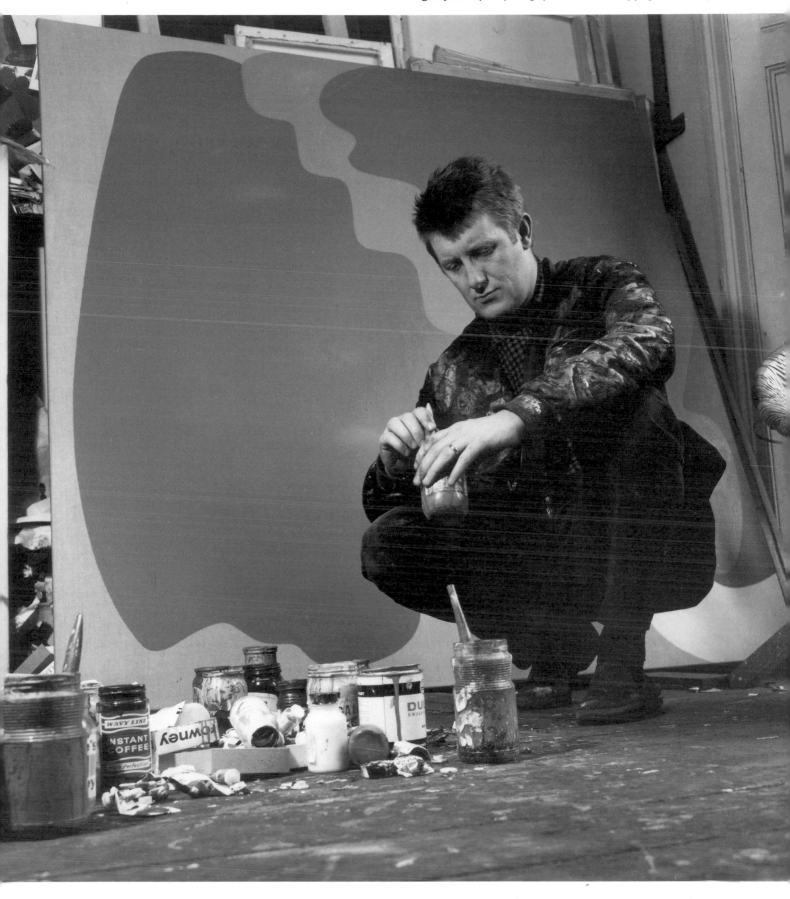

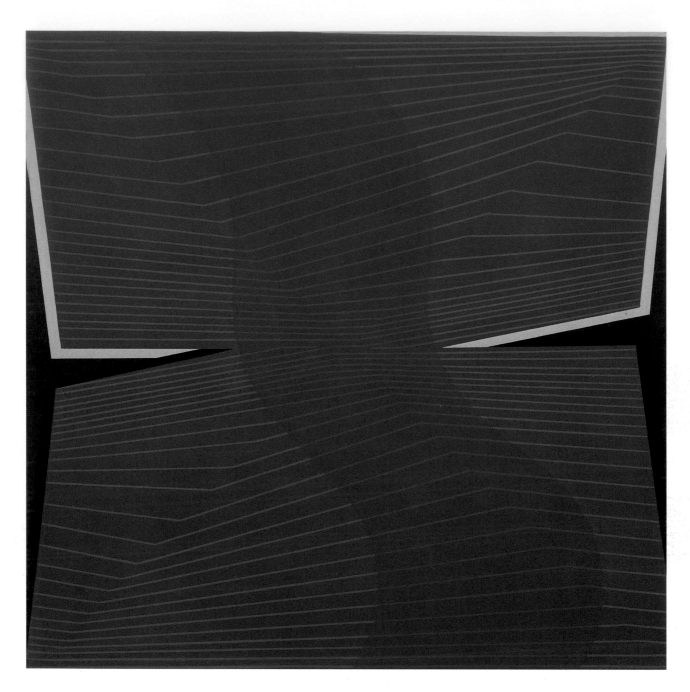

fig.88 *No. 22, 20. 2. 62* 1962,
oil on canvas 172.7 x 172.7 cm.

available in the UK. In the few years leading up to 1963, he used 'good [quality oil] paint … I was aware that it was necessary to use the best materials that were available'. *No. 22, 20. 2. 62* (fig.88) was painted at a time when Hoyland expressly wanted 'to break up this all-over painting thing that everyone was doing and introduce more illusionistic space, [to] get away from the flat … it was one way of creating space through lines'.

By this time, Hoyland had seen the work of Morris Louis, Kenneth Noland and Mark Rothko exhibited in London. He recalls thinking that Rothko's paintings 'looked like a kind of denial of paint. It really wasn't, but at the time, compared to de Kooning, it was something different … Rothko was my hero'. However, he was particularly struck by the stained surfaces that Louis and Noland were creating and quickly found out that they had used Magna acrylic paint to achieve them.

I remember the first Nolands I saw were some of those Target pictures ... which I thought, and still think, were the best things Noland ever did, and they were done in this acrylic. They were like the cutting edge of painting. [Noland was] ten years older than me and it just seemed like the most exciting thing around. And it broke with nature, it was a new sort of urban art.

By aligning himself with what he saw as the most advanced painting of the day, Hoyland was keen to adopt the same binding medium. 'Noland used to say to me ... "you've got to get these acrylics, they're brilliant".' However, Magna 'wasn't available over here. This guy Bocour used to test it on [American painters], so they used to get all the paint for nothing, which I was very envious of ... We couldn't even get a discount.'

As a result, Hoyland had to use oil paint to achieve a similar surface, which was clearly 'oil trying to look like acrylic'. The oil paint used for the background red colour in *No. 22, 20. 2. 62* was heavily thinned with turpentine, so that despite being 'put on in quite a lot of layers' it is no more than a wash of colour. The raking-light detail (fig.89) shows evidence of a green layer beneath the black, to give 'an optical buzz' to the black. The cotton canvas texture remained apparent through the surface of this stain layer and provided the surface onto which the thin lines were then drawn, using only a mahlstick to position them.

Hoyland remembers eagerly awaiting the arrival of acrylic paint in the UK, and when in 1963 Rowney introduced their Cryla acrylic emulsion range he began painting with it immediately.

It seemed something different. People talked vaguely about how significant changes had taken place historically: techniques had changed, materials had changed, and that [acrylic] seemed to be like the new material. I mean I didn't really think it out, I was just sort of following the general rush.

Although this suggests a certain degree of ambivalence in his decision to try acrylic paints, he was alert to what others were saying about how they differed from oil.

I remember reading articles in magazines. They talked about the radiance of it and the fluidity of it, that kind of thing ... and that it would never yellow ... It seemed exciting in the way people got excited about the use of plastics, aluminium ... and other industrial materials. It wasn't very clear cut. I was a student looking to see where to go and that seemed like a good idea at the time.

Although the change to acrylic emulsion may appear to have prompted a general increase in size in his paintings, Hoyland insists this was simply 'to do with getting a bigger studio, because the bigger the studio, the bigger you went'.

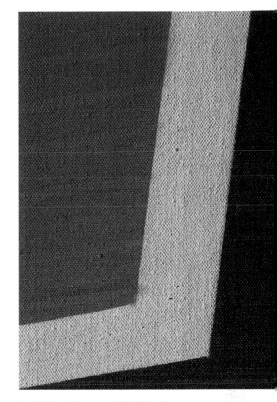

fig.89 Detail from *No. 22, 20. 2. 62* taken in partial raking light from the left, revealing the thinness of the paint.

fig.90 *28. 5. 66* 1966, acrylic emulsion on canvas 198.1 x 365.8 cm.

When he first started to paint with acrylic, Hoyland continued to aim for a thin paint surface, which paradoxically he associated by this time with oils: 'I liked to get the quality of oil paint'. The acrylic emulsion paint used for *28. 5. 66* (fig.90) was thinned with so much water that it behaved almost 'like a watercolour' and he felt 'able to get the [effect of] watercolour and oil paint in the same picture'. The painting was made during a period when he believed that 'painting wasn't doing any-thing' and when he felt more influenced by English sculpture, particu-larly that of Anthony Caro and William Tucker, whom he believed had found a freedom to make sculpture out of invented form. He describes *28. 5. 66* as 'suggestive of sculpture … more about imagined form, imag-ined conceptualised space'.

The feathered edges of the floating forms that 'soften the so-called geometry', are incorporated as a 'device to enmesh the so-called figure into the ground'. The paint was applied using a roller directly onto the cotton canvas. The red was the first colour to be applied, around the bands reserved for the areas of green and grey. These other colours were applied (also by roller) immediately after the red, but in a slightly thicker consistency. 'I thought at the time I was making quite a distinction between the forms and the ground, but as the years go by it wasn't as thick as I thought it was.' By rolling the paint wet-into-wet in several applications, Hoyland prompted the bleeding of the green and red bor-ders into one another (fig.91). Although the grey and purple bands were also worked wet-into-wet, the smoother edges were 'reinforced without going right to the edge. I'd leave the bleeding and then firm up the form'. He refers to the drips of paint that emanate from the lower edge of the green block as 'ties', which are frequently used as 'ways of pulling the eye to the edge [of the painting] because everything relates to the edge'.

In preparing his works at this time, Hoyland would first stretch the canvas onto a stretcher, leaving it unprimed, 'to keep the fabric of the surface and get as much contrast as possible'. He found he couldn't work with the canvas in the way some of the American artists at the time preferred, whereby they determined the precise dimensions of the work after its completion. 'They'd use this thing called cropping, where they actually would take the best bit. I remember Barnett Newman saying, "cropping, that's photography", because he always painted on a canvas with an edge.' The paintings were worked on 'flat a lot of the time but I always have to look at them vertically, my decisions are always made on the vertical.'

As his work began to increase in scale, Hoyland recalls a frustration with the locally available acrylic emulsion paints. 'The thing that was infuriating was [that] all the art suppliers in London were always based on the amateur market so you could only get these farting little tubes of it … whereas in America you could buy tubs of it, huge quantities of it and get stuck in'. However, 'this guy from Spectrum started making it' in the mid-1960s in containers that were often quart-sized. When he first began to use Spectrum's acrylic emulsion formula in the late 1960s, Hoyland recalls that supplies of it were brought into central London regularly on a Friday night, to a café in Soho. 'There'd be all these sinister figures sitting alone who you didn't know, and they were artists waiting' to collect their orders from the back of 'an old station wagon'. This assignation became known among those artists as 'the drop'.

Towards the end of the 1960s, Hoyland's work started to move in a different direction. He remembers arriving at the realisation that in his 'interest in optics and spatial games, I'd forgotten about the beauty of paint … It seemed to me the next thing to incorporate into my work was … the magic of what paint can do by taking advantage of the way paint behaves naturally.' He soon discovered the versatility of acrylic emulsion paint and started to exploit this property to create a whole range of effects. By the time Hoyland painted 25. 4. 69 (fig.92), he had seen his first Hans Hofmann painting:

only a little one, and I really liked them because I had already decided that American painting by now … was just a kind of dead end. Somehow he'd taken European art and made something new out of it in California, in a different light. And it seemed to have influences of Cubism, the Fauves, Van Gogh and Matisse … but it had this kind of expanded quality that America had given it.

Hofmann's richly applied layers of oil paint in the stirred-up surfaces were made by the 'push and pull', a term he originated for the effect of flatness and depth simultaneously created on the surface with paint. 'Only

fig.91 Detail from *28. 5. 66* taken in raking light from the right, showing the feathered edge between the red and green paint.

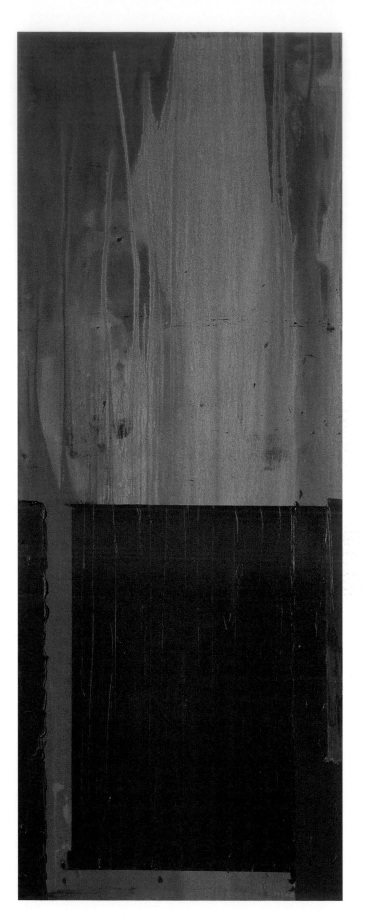

fig.92 *25. 4. 69* 1969, acrylic emulsion on canvas 243.8 x 91.4 cm.

the varied counterplay of push and pull, and from its variation in intensities, will plastic creation result.'[2] This approach inspired Hoyland to consider his paint in a different light. He began 'to examine surface more and try to get the maximum out of acrylic' by exploring its capacity to be used as a thick, buttery material that could sustain high impasto, contrasting this with its staining ability when used in a heavily diluted form. 'The pouring came from Louis and the blocks came from Hofmann, except Hofmann never did a block like that.'

The first paint layers of the background were rolled onto the surface in a variety of colours that had been mixed in trays to a thin consistency. 'I would have different colours and drop the roller into it, even putting flicks of paint on to it', as seen in the raking-light detail, fig.93. The cotton canvas was then propped against the wall and the heavily diluted yellow and orange paint was poured down the surface, helped with brushes or

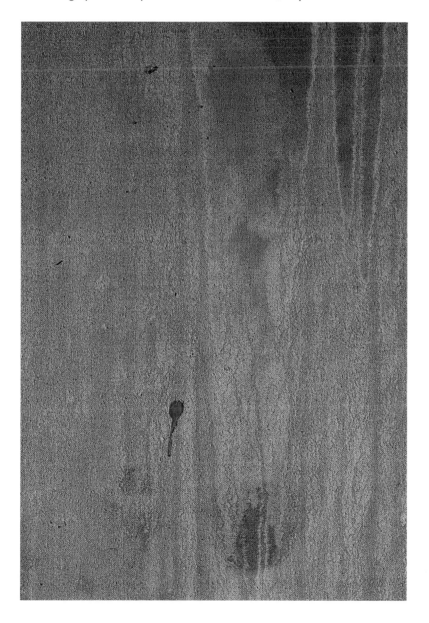

fig.93 The effects of excessive dilution in acrylic emulsion paint are shown in this raking-light detail (from the left) of 25.4.69.

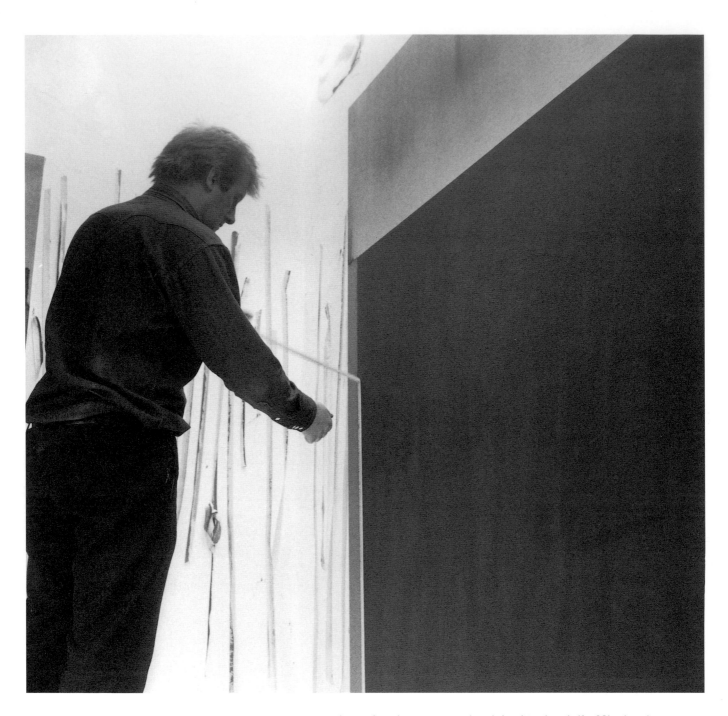

fig.94 John Hoyland at work in his studio in 1968. He is removing a strip of masking tape after the paint has been applied, ensuring a straight edge to that part of the painting. Photograph by Jorge Lewinski.

anything else that came to hand. In this detail (fig.93), the thin consistency of the paint is apparent in the fine cracking pattern caused by the pigment–medium separation when the paint was diluted with water. The painting was often turned during this process, as can be seen by the drips of yellow stain running up the canvas. The paint was thinned to such an extent that sometimes pigment particles clumped together on the paint surface. Hoyland recalls, 'I just saw it happen and then I would go on further and induce it in other pictures'. The acrylic stain created a shimmering veil of colour that was then interrupted by 'this kind of opposing block put in afterwards', plastered on in thick applications with the painting knife. 'I was aware of the limitations of acrylic; this was done to get maximum contrast from the material.' The slightly raw, straight edges of the blocks were initially made using 'masking tape [fig.94], but I used it in such a way that it didn't look as though I'd used masking tape. I'd let the knife go and fudge it a bit, otherwise it came out hard-edgy and horrible.' The ridged line of paint, formed by painting up to the masking tape line is visible in the raking light detail (fig.95), which is then broken in the black area of paint where the knife was used to continue the block, softening the edge. The fudged edges represented Hoyland's attempt to return to drawing with paint and colour, at a time when many of his contemporaries preferred to eradicate the approach. 'When I tried to introduce shape back into painting, I remember Noland saying to me once, "that's old-fashioned geometric European painting, a figure and ground".'

From 1969 to 1973, Hoyland lived and worked between New York and London and therefore painted with both American and British brands of acrylic emulsion paint. He became concerned with 'making a more complex, physical, tactile surface'[3] and found that the slightly thicker viscosity of the British brands was more suitable for areas of impasto. 'You could

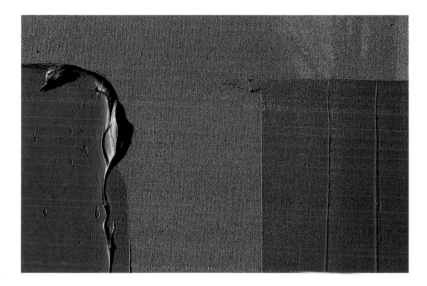

fig.95 A second raking-light detail (from the left) of 25. 4. 69 shows Hoyland's use of masking tape and a painting knife.

always just take it out of the can and butter it because it tried to imitate oil paint here, which suits me better really', whereas the American brands required the addition of gels to 'beef up' the paint for areas of impasto. It was at the start of this period that Hoyland began to blend colour on his canvases. 'I was putting myself in the position, quite consciously, of using colours that didn't come very easily to me. I made myself use all kinds of strange, high-key colour relationships. I didn't know the hell how to mix them or what to do with them.'[4] Hoyland's preoccupation had always been 'with shape, where to locate colours, what kind of shapes to use, and so on. This was all in the wake of Rothko, etc. – it was trying to come

fig.96 *Saracen* 1977, acrylic emulsion on canvas
243.8 x 22.8.6 cm.

to terms with those paintings of his but knowing that one couldn't go on making them that simple.'[5] In *Saracen* (fig.96), Hoyland varied the size of the blocks in the foreground that were made with 'freer marks', and he attempted to impose an overall colour radiance, reminiscent of the work of the Fauves and Van Gogh across the surface. 'I didn't want them to be limited to being read as anything in particular but they could be landscapes, they could be houses, they could be portraits.'

As with *25. 4. 69*, a stain was initially applied over the entire surface of *Saracen* using diluted washes of colour that were applied by roller and then poured down the cotton canvas, which was tilted in different directions. Then 'I put a whole lot of different colours on and then tried to pull them all together without getting grey, while at the same time trying to keep the surface very vital because you know this stuff [acrylic paint] can look like lino if you don't know how to use it'. Hoyland worked with large cans of paint from which he scooped out each colour with a painting knife, and slathered it onto the canvas. The thin stain of paint revealing the texture of the canvas in the raking-light detail (fig.97), is set against thickly knifed-on paint with raised impasto. 'I've always liked the idea of colours coming through from behind other colours, which I've done in the pourings. So this is a way of breaking down the geometry effect, first of all stressing the edges … and putting colour on in such a way that colour would come through from behind. It's like mixing colour on the painting.' In the main area of colour, consisting of red, yellow and blue paint blended together, he was 'working wet-into-wet, trying to keep the surface vital, with energy in the marks' (fig.98). This process had to occur very rapidly (Hoyland recalls these periods as 'panic stations') to ensure that the acrylic paint would not start to dry before the next colour was applied. Occasionally, drips from the thin under-painting were allowed to occur, again functioning as 'ties' to unify areas and break up the geometry (fig.99). He insists that, as with most of the paint he applied, the drips are 'pretty contrived, it doesn't just happen out of clumsiness'.

In other works from this period, Hoyland practised the mixing of ranges of colour on his surface 'that shouldn't necessarily operate together'. This was part of an exercise to broaden his range of colour, which would eventually enable him to use black and white in a painting. 'Anyone can paint a grey picture or a chromatic picture but trying to get the whole chromatic scale in one picture, that's always something that's interested me.'

In *Gadal 10.11.86* (fig.100) painted in the following decade black and grey are dominant, but 'with suppressed explosions' of vivid colour erupting in localised areas. Hoyland made many preparatory drawings for the work because with the organic form in the centre of the painting he wanted to avoid allusion to any kind of recognisable shape, such as a figure. An important feature of this painting was the use of wet paint filled with lumps and flecks of dried paint, which were obtained by 'scraping the bottom of the [paint] can' and then 'throwing them on' to the wet paint surface. The technique was adopted 'because I knew that when they dry up they'll produce additional galaxies behind the main galaxy'. The raking-light detail (fig.101) shows the dried aggregates of paint firmly stuck to the thin, stained background, adjacent to a swirling application of black

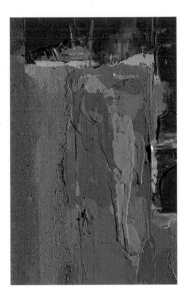

fig.97 Detail from *Saracen* taken in raking light from the right, showing Hoyland's layering technique and variations in the paint texture.

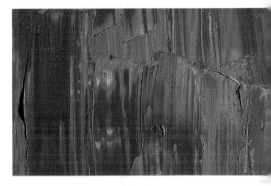

fig.98 Hoyland's wet-in-wet working of the three acrylic colours with a painting knife is clearly visible in this raking-light detail (from the right) of *Saracen*.

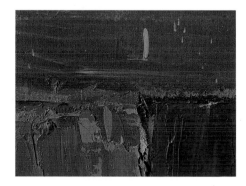

fig.99 A third detail from *Saracen* taken in raking light from the left.

fig.100 *Gadal 10.11.86* 1986, acrylic emulsion on canvas 254 x 254 cm.

paint that had been vigorously mixed to a fluid consistency, as revealed by the drips and tiny pitted bubbles in the surface.

The underpainting was worked over a longer period of time than in previous compositions. The cotton canvas was laid down flat as the initial stain was applied in black acrylic with a pale grey veil washed over it. The canvas was then turned and tipped up in all directions, as indicated by the thinned splashes and drips of the stain that run into each other before reaching the edges in fig.102. The surface is crowded with textures in the paint, introduced 'to keep vitality throughout the painting and make it look as though it all just happened in one go'. As observed earlier, Hoyland found it advantageous to work on a stretcher because 'you can tip it up and then I hit the painting to force the paint to move. Then I can turn the canvas over and hit it [again] so it can go and make another strand of structure in another direction. Then you can arrest it. You can lay it on the floor and arrest it, when you've got what you want. So you've got a lot more control on the canvas.' He also cut the vertical stretcher bars so that the canvas could be folded, thereby allowing access to the middle of the painting by walking over the canvas. The stretcher was later reinforced with metal plates. The painting was executed over a period of four or five sessions. 'I've never done a painting in less than five shots. It would probably be five days, maybe a couple of days drawing out each time.' This was longer than the 'American … one-shot painters', like Frankenthaler and Noland, who would 'have to get the intensity in one go; there was no redefining, no revision in their work'.

Hoyland has continued to use acrylic emulsion paints and is always willing to try out the latest developments in this medium, such as his recent incorporation of 'pearlescent' colours into his images, which has provided him with yet 'another dimension to acrylic paint'. He has continued to use a black background, 'because I like this black undercoat coming through the stain. I like the way it affects the colour, even if I put a yellow on it, it comes out … and gives it that additional radiance.' However, he now uses a brand of acrylic that is supplied in a plastic bottle and can be dispensed through its nozzle, thus enabling him to 'draw with them on a larger scale, which you couldn't do with a brush … I can tell from the viscosity if it's too loose and if it's going to flow all over the place, or too thick and won't do what I want … It's a nice way of drawing.' He sees this technique as very similar to that of 'Pollock [who] made holes in his cans so he could get that extended line, because you could never get a brush to hold that amount of paint'.

For Hoyland, therefore, the introduction of acrylic emulsion paint has been crucial to the development of his painting. His work provides a particularly good example of the enormous range of different surface effects that can be achieved with the paint, in terms of colour, texture and gloss. Once he had tried acrylic emulsion paint, he never returned to oil and remembers finding the renunciation of oil very easy: 'the future was new materials, synthetic materials in everything, nylon, clothes, etc. Oil paint smacked of garrets and starving artists and [acrylic paint] was like *Brave New World*'. But he also cites practical reasons for his preference: 'As much as I like the smell of oil, to me the advantages of acrylic outweigh the disadvantages of oil … Acrylic was a more vivid colour, a brighter, stronger colour and of course it had the benefit of being quick drying, which, when you painted pictures that size, was a factor … Imagine [the large paintings with thick impasto] in oil, how long they would take to dry … If I'd painted in oil I'd be doing about as many as Howard Hodgkin; I could date them over five years.'

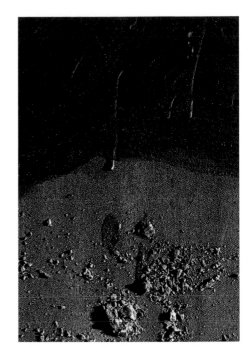

fig.101 Detail from *Gadal 10.11.86* taken in raking light from the right.

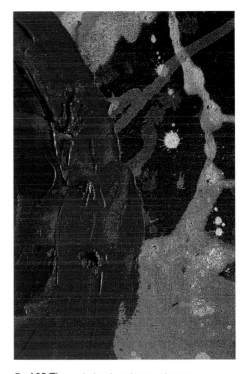

fig.102 The variation in paint consistency and application is visible in this second raking-light detail (from the right) of *Gadal 10.11.86*.

Roy Lichtenstein 1923–1997

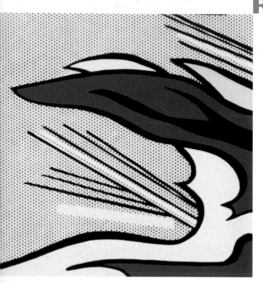

Roy Lichtenstein began to paint his comic-book images in 1961. They were painted in a style that imitated the visual effect of the processes used in commercial printing, with none of the lively brushwork employed by many Abstract Expressionist painters at that time. Cartoon figures had appeared in his abstract work before this date in 'the way de Kooning might do a woman, [but] then it occurred to me to do it by mimicking the cartoon without the paint texture, calligraphic line, modulation – all the things involved in expressionism.'[1]

Comic books initially provided not only his subject matter, but were also a source for the technique he used to produce his paintings. One of the most visible aspects of this was his characteristic use of Ben Day dots, which were borrowed directly from the techniques of mechanical printing. It became important that the surface of these paintings should 'become an industrialised texture rather than what we're familiar with as a paint texture ... the kind of texture I would use would be the commercial texture of half-tone dots and flat printed areas.'[2] Lichtenstein's method of painting was developed with this 'industrialised texture' in mind. He used a methodical procedure for paint application and in an attempt to prevent the emergence of any illusory space he frequently turned his paintings so that they stood on different edges as he worked on them. 'Once I am involved with the [act of] painting I think of it as an abstraction. Half the time they are upside down anyway.'[3] Lichtenstein even designed a rotating easel to facilitate this process for his smaller paintings.

Whaam! (fig.104) was painted in 1963, 'in Brunswick, New Jersey, in my garage ... I remember I didn't have an easel big enough to paint it so I could rotate it. But I probably turned it around anyway.' The image was derived from a picture found in the comic *All-American Men of War* (fig.105). Lichtenstein first made a detailed preliminary drawing on paper (fig.106), in which much of the composition for the final painting was worked out. Despite being clearly based on the comic strip image, it was not a straight copy. It is unlikely that he would have referred to the comic

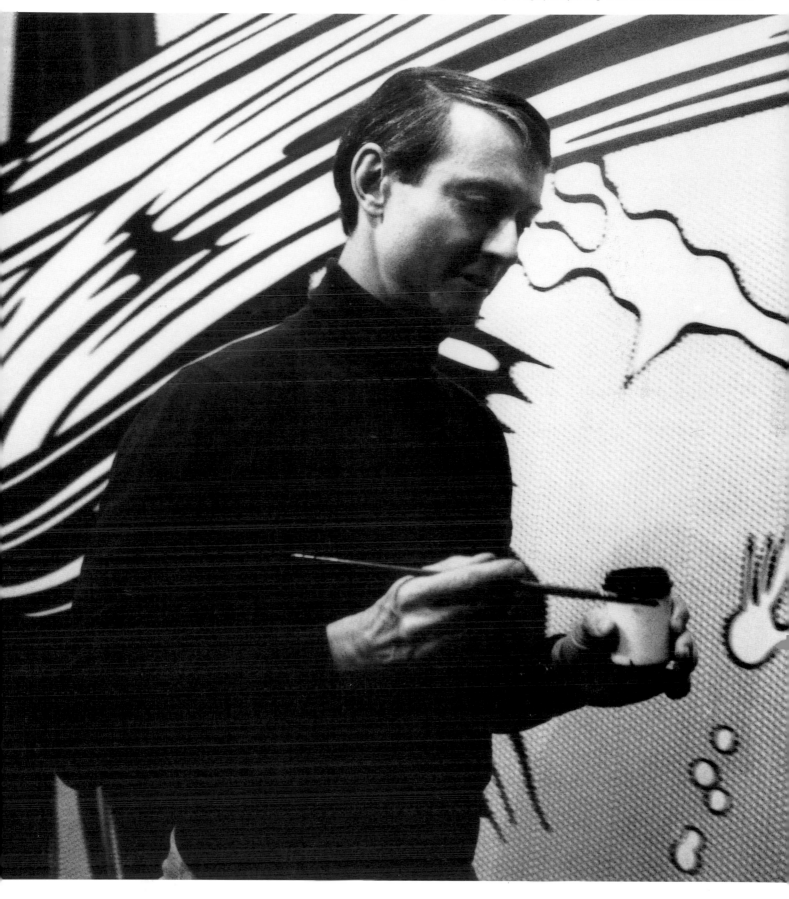

fig.103 Roy Lichtenstein photographed painting *Yellow and Green Brushstrokes*, 1966.

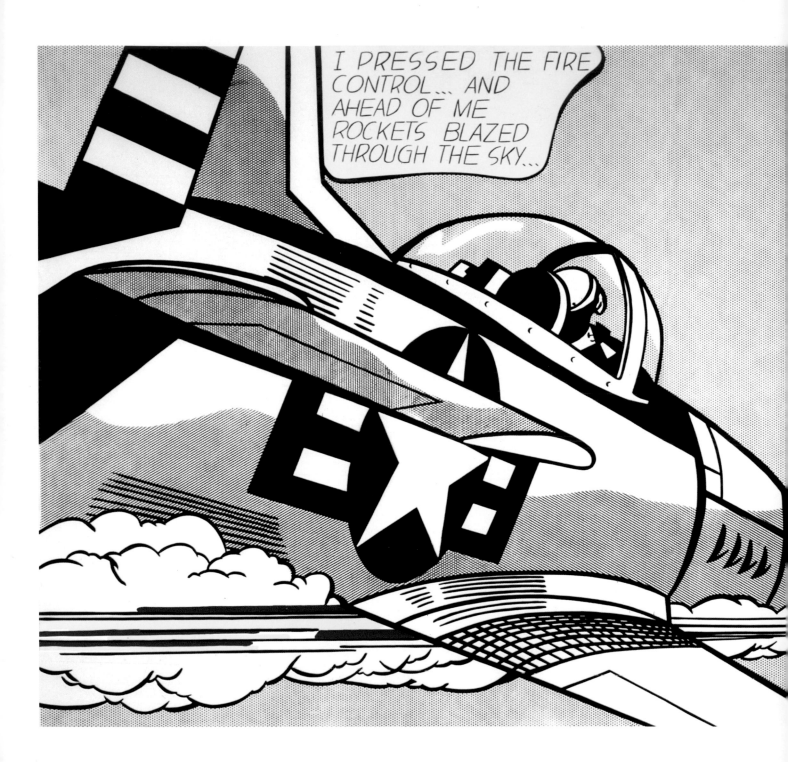

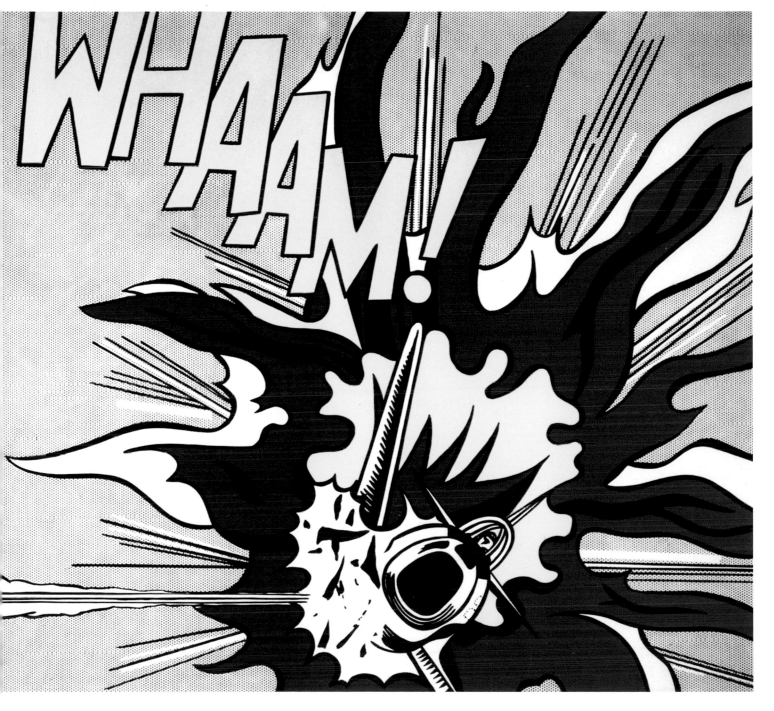

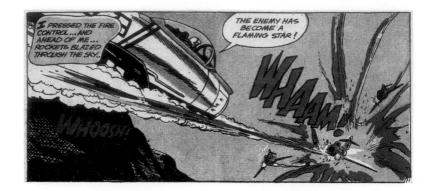

fig.105 A panel from 'Star Jockey' in *All American Men of War*, 89 (January–February 1962). Drawing by Irv Novick, lettering by Gaspar Saladino. Tate Gallery Archive

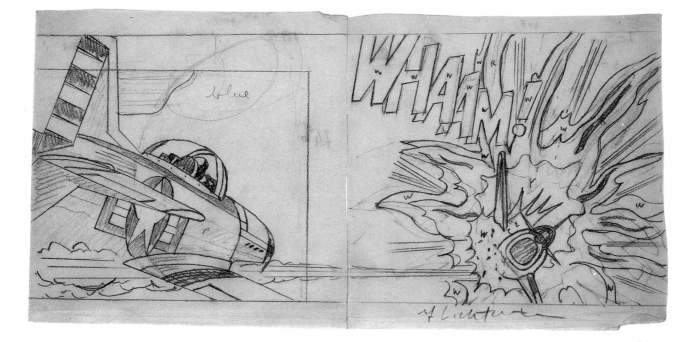

fig.106 Drawing for *Whaam!*, pencil on paper 14.9 x 30.5 cm.

strip again once he had drawn this version of the image.[4] Although more than one drawing was frequently used for other paintings, sometimes including coloured versions, Lichtenstein recalled that for *Whaam!* this drawing 'was probably the first and only'. The 'W' that can be seen in many areas stands for 'white' and shows that Lichtenstein had already started to consider which colours to use. However, all parts of the composition and intended colouring were still open to alteration, and it was not white but yellow that was finally used for the lettering of 'WHAAM!' 'I used to mark what I thought the thing might be but it didn't come out that way. It might have been white but I thought "that doesn't really look too wonderful" … I just decided it should be yellow as it was up there, painted'. It is also evident that initially the fighter plane was smaller in comparison to the explosion; in the painting it was increased in size proportionally by cropping the area around it. The lines drawn around the plane indicate the composition to be used in the painting.

Once the final composition of the image was established, the drawing was projected onto the commercially prepared and pre-stretched cotton canvas with an opaque projector. Lichtenstein would draw directly onto the outline in pencil, 'in pretty much the way it is. I did it quickly and lightly and then I re-did it', so it could be erased easily later.[5] However, many lines remained visible after the work's completion, in particular at the boundaries of dots that have no black outline, such as the area of red and blue dots shown in fig.107. 'I would tend to erase any pencil lines that were still showing after it was painted but you can always see something there. I don't mind that they show really'. One of the main decisions taken at this stage was to paint the image on two separate canvases. As Lichtenstein recalled, 'I think I did them separately; both canvases were connected – it's supposed to be one painting. When I projected I shifted [the image] around and made compositions out of them ... I thought it would be funny to shoot from one canvas to another. There was no particular reason to make it into two, but they both sort of make compositions'. It is interesting to note that the decision to paint the work on two separate canvases only came at this stage, even though the drawing is also on two pieces of paper.

With the image transferred, Lichtenstein could then start to paint. All the solid areas of colour and the black outlines were painted in solvent-based Magna acrylic. Lichtenstein had been aware that Kenneth Noland and Morris Louis were painting with Magna and began to use it himself just prior to this. He especially liked its fast-drying nature (compared to oil) and its ability to produce areas of flat and uniform colour. It was clearly important to him that the painting retained an impersonal surface and it seems likely that he associated the expressive brushwork that characterised much of his abstract work of the 1950s with the oil paint that he had used at that time. As he put it, 'to express this thing in a painterly style would dilute it'.[6]

He had also tried acrylic emulsion paints, in particular the first brand, Liquitex, but he preferred the optical properties of Magna:

I liked the colour quality better than I liked Liquitex. Somehow the [Magna] medium is very transparent; it doesn't look yolky ... When I was working out things for murals ... I tried [them] out in Liquitex, [but] it would get milky in a way where you couldn't really see what the colour was ... So the clarity of the [Magna] medium was interesting to me.

However, he still used oil colour for the areas of paint intended to mimic Ben Day dots, although this choice was made for a purely practical reason and had nothing to do with the different visual properties of the two types of paint. '[The dots] are oil because you can't do it [with Magna paint]. It dries too quickly ... so I had to use oil paint'. The blue and red dots were the first areas to be painted. The oil paint was rolled onto a

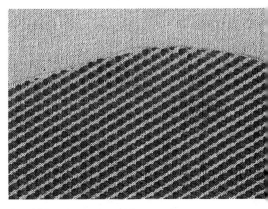

fig.107 Pencil lines are visible around the area of Ben Day dots in this detail from *Whaam!* taken in partial raking light from the left.

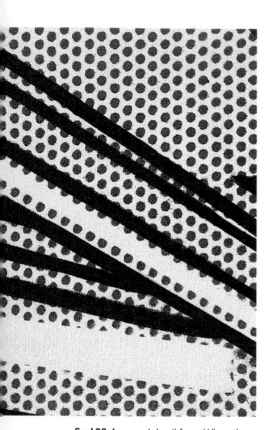

fig.108 A second detail from *Whaam!* shows the slight irregularity of some of the Ben Day dots.

stencil and then brushed through the perforations onto the canvas. They were painted before any of the areas of solid colour because he used an aluminium stencil at this time, 'which was fairly heavy and had to be taped on to the painting and it would just scrape [any] other paint'. This screen provided another reason for not using Magna for the dots: Lichtenstein had discovered earlier that Magna paint would adhere so strongly to it that it was almost impossible to remove it after use without also removing the paint.

To ensure that the holes in the stencil were regular in shape and position, Lichtenstein 'put a piece of graph paper on top and drilled'. He recalled that before he could use the stencil 'it had to be sprayed with enamel because it oxidises. So if you're trying to put red on you get a kind of brown. Black works alright but I still didn't use it that way and the yellow, well, yellow didn't work at all'. The use of a stencil was a significant development in Lichtenstein's technique and resulted in dots with a high degree of sharpness and consistency (as seen in fig.107). However, occasionally the oil paint would smudge or bleed slightly under the stencil – minor irregularities that become apparent on close inspection (see fig.108).

The Ben Day dots were allowed to dry before the rest of the image was built up with Magna acrylic paint, beginning with the lightest colours and finishing with the black lines. When viewed in strong lighting, the dots and solid colours are often still visible beneath the black lines, especially where the black paint is a little thinner. In the detail shown in fig.108, the blue Ben Day dots are visible in many areas through the black lines that were painted over them. The detail also shows that the white lines in the picture were not made by painting over the dots, but are areas that were masked with tape before the dots were applied. In fact, masking tape was not generally used to define the lines in the composition because Lichtenstein preferred to draw them in by hand, resulting in lines of varying thickness and size. A detail of the solid red and yellow colours is shown in fig.109, which shows the general order in which the colours were painted before finishing with the black lines. The red paint can be clearly seen through the black lines and in some areas it extends through to the other side of the line, for example at the top of the white area in this detail. At the right edge of the yellow area the white colour of the canvas priming is still visible, indicating that Lichtenstein left gaps between the solid coloured areas for the black lines to fill.

However, Lichtenstein admitted the order was not always strictly followed. 'It never works out quite the way I plan it, because I always end up erasing half of the painting, re-doing it and re-dotting it. I work in Magna colour because it's soluble in turpentine. This enables me to get the paint off completely whenever I want so there is no record of the changes I have made'. The areas that needed to be re-worked were masked off with tape and the paint removed to the ground layer with a rag, soaked in turpentine, or a brush.

Lichtenstein's colours needed to be strongly schematic in order to assert a flat, commercial quality to the image. 'I picked out four contrasting colours that would work together in a certain way. I wanted each one as complete in its own way as it could be – a purplish blue, a lemon-

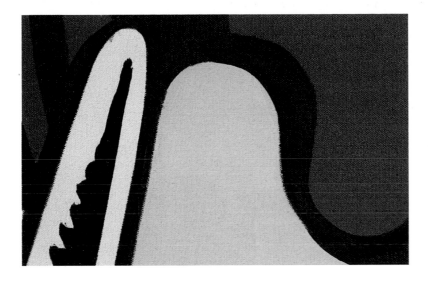

fig.109 Detail from *Whaam!* taken in partial raking light from the right, confirming the black outline as the final application of paint.

yellow, a green between the red and the blue in value ... a medium-standard red and, of course, black and white'.[7] Lichtenstein often mixed the Magna colours to achieve the value and intensity required:

Some of the earlier yellow I mixed green into to make it more lemony. I don't know if I was doing it at the time of *Whaam!* ... I don't mix the cadmium reds with anything – Magna has such a deep cadmium red medium. I mix the ultramarine blue with a little white. I mix the yellow with a little green. The yellow on *Whaam!* is probably just straight yellow Magna.

The Magna paint was brushed on in two to three thin layers, depending on how well the colour covered the white ground.

Although Lichtenstein worked with paint on cotton canvas for most of his career, he also occasionally created three-dimensional pieces with enamelled steel or, as he describes them, 'semi-3D, just like real life'. *Wall Explosion II* (fig.110) was one of a limited edition ('I think I may have done three editions in different colours') made on sixteen-gauge steel in 1965 by fabricators at a factory called Architectural Porcelain, New Jersey, which produced bodies for 'refrigerators and that sort of thing'. Although he was not opposed to using quasi-industrial processes in his art, Lichtenstein stressed that they had to leave him something to do. For *Wall Explosion II*, he first made a drawing of the outline for the fabricators, indicating the colours he wanted and their position. 'I'd show them a side view so they could see what lay behind what, and a front view that showed where

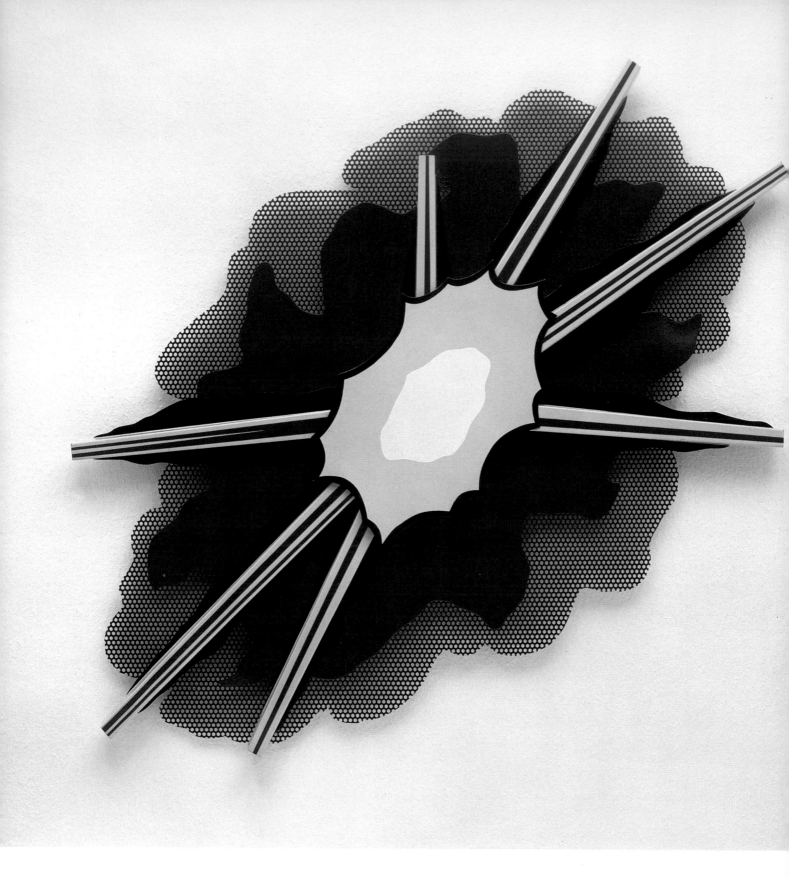

fig.110 *Wall Explosion II* 1965, industrial enamel paint on steel 170.2 × 188 × 10.2 cm.

the colours went, and they would simply make their masks from my drawing'. Each metal piece was first sprayed with porcelain enamel of the designated colour.

I'd give them swatches of colour, and they'd give me swatches of their colours … they could only do certain colours … [but] I didn't have much of a range myself then. Almost everything they did was either black or white, but they were also able to get certain colours, but they all had to be fired at the same temperature, which is a kind of a limitation.

A detail taken in raking light is shown in fig.111. The gloss is uniformly high in all colours, clearly shown by the strong reflection of the yellow piece in the surface of the black enamel paint. The paint is characterised by an extreme flatness, apart from a slightly raised area along most of the edges of the various metal pieces. This is particularly apparent in this detail in the red paint. The positioning and production of the red lines on the yellow pieces were achieved through a stencil that had been made from the original drawing. This was laid on top of each relevant piece and instead of spraying the colour through the stencil, the enamel was removed from the surface using abrasive methods in the areas not covered by the stencil. 'It's almost the reverse of printing, or silk-screen'. The enamelled perforated mesh at the rear of the work and to which the other pieces are attached, 'is the material we used to make the stencils for the Ben Day dots'.

Lichtenstein made few modifications to his painting technique over the following three decades. However, one of these occurred soon after the completion of *Whaam!* when 'I realised that I could have paper skins [i.e. stencils] made easily' as an alternative to the heavy metal ones. This was around the time that he took on his first assistant, James de Pasquale, who was employed initially to cut the stencils. 'I don't think I had any assistants until I moved to New York [in 1964]'. The paper stencils offered a number of advantages over the metal ones: 'the paper's much cleaner and the whole thing is just easier. The dots are undoubtedly more round and more exacting'. The paper did not scratch any areas of paint that had already been applied, so he was no longer tied to painting the stencilled areas first. And by carefully peeling back the stencil after the paint had been applied, he found it was possible to use Magna acrylic for this part of the painting too, thereby entirely eliminating the need for oil paint. As well as cutting the stencils, de Pasquale also painted the dots onto the canvases. This took time because the Magna had to be applied very precisely with a stencil brush, to ensure that no paint extended over the borders of the circles in the paper stencil. If this was allowed to happen, they found that the paper would readily absorb the paint and, on its removal, would tend to pull off more paint than was intended.

Another modification occurred in the mid-1960s when Lichtenstein

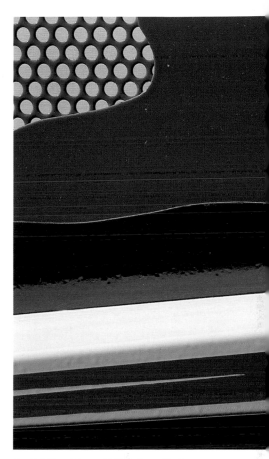

fig.111 Detail from *Wall Explosion II* taken in raking light from the upper left showing the surface character of the industrial enamel paint.

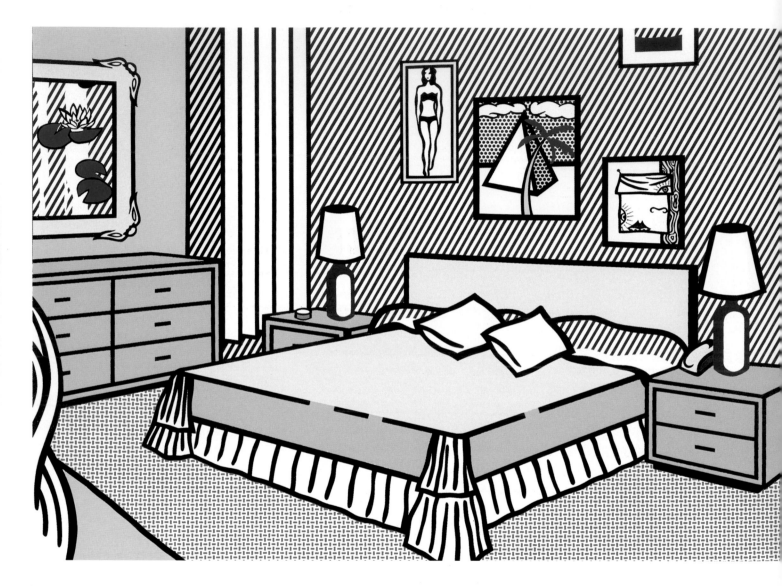

fig.112 *Interior with Waterlilies* 1991, acrylic solution paint on canvas 320.9 x 455.3 cm.

began to apply his own priming layers to the canvas support. At first he would apply a layer of white paint (Magna 'Underpainting' white) over the commercial priming already on the canvas. By choosing the nature of the top layer of ground, Lichtenstein found he could control the absorbency, texture and whiteness of the support far more effectively. 'I thought the canvas might change colour in time and also it's easier to make corrections when I paint on my own white'. But after 1970 he only purchased unprimed cotton canvas to which his assistants applied all the priming layers. The support and ground used for *Interior with Waterlilies* (fig.112), painted in 1991, is typical of those used after 1970. It consists of a heavy grade (10oz) cotton canvas, which was first primed with two thin coats of acrylic gesso emulsion and then with two layers of white Magna paint. In addition, the first layer of white Magna was sealed with a varnish in order to prevent the second layer from dissolving it on application. Using this priming, he found that the dots 'stencil on better. I guess they partly dissolve [the priming]'. Lichtenstein always preferred cotton canvas to linen. Although he has tried primed linen canvas as a support, he found that 'trying to erase on linen canvas proved difficult', because if he erased through the priming layers he 'would usually get a dark mark. If I go that far on the cotton duck, it still looks white and you can't tell the difference'.

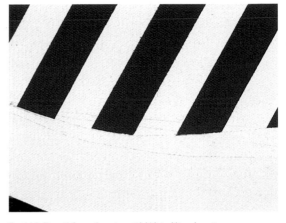

fig.113 Detail from *Interior with Waterlilies* showing the presence of pencil lines beneath the paint.

Interior with Waterlilies is one of a series of paintings of interiors done in the early 1990s and demonstrates a number of ways in which his technique had evolved. An initial drawing of the image was first projected onto the wall 'to get a feel of how big [it was] going to be'[8] and to determine the proportions of the life-size interior. By now, Lichtenstein's preparatory techniques had become more complicated, involving the making of a 'maquette' between the drawing and painting stage. This was essentially a collage of pieces of painted paper that could be moved around the picture plane, thereby enabling him to visualise a great number of variations in the composition of a work.

I can change things constantly and get shape and colour at the same time … As it develops I can see that [for example] it could use something more daring in the colour over here, or this could be pushed a little bit up there, and maybe the sizes of the areas aren't right. So I can easily make changes.[9]

The entire finished collage was then projected onto the piece of primed canvas and 'redrawn in the same way, except I just try to pin it down a little better. Nothing is really in the same place as it is in the collage, but it's not significantly different'. The painted collage was positioned alongside the canvas as the painting progressed, although the composition remained 'open to change at any point'. The pencil lines were drawn in lightly on the canvas so they could be erased – Lichtenstein removed them more thoroughly than he had on earlier paintings. However, he remained unconcerned that some evidence of drawing would be visible on the surface: 'the more meticulous you get to be the more you have to be. You get more and more compulsive'. Pencil lines are still visible in a few areas, for example along the top boundary of the area of blue diagonal lines used for the sheet (fig.113).

Lichtenstein's palette also expanded dramatically from the four con-

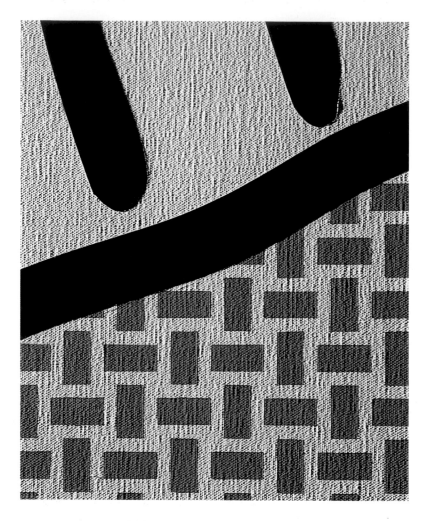

fig.114 Lichtenstein's use of stencils and masking tape is seen in this raking-light detail (from the left) of *Interior with Waterlilies*.

trasting colours and black delineation around each shape that he had used for much of his work until well into the 1970s, to almost thirty colours, some of which were now also used for the lines. This extensive range was made possible in part by Golden Artist Colors, an American paint company, which began to custom-make his paints after the Magna paint formulation was discontinued. These colours are known as MSA (Mineral Spirit Acrylics) paints and are based on a formulation similar to Magna. 'We are sort of trying to mix the same colours as we had before but we also use [Golden's]. Now I have maybe four different light yellows instead of one'. The paint was generally mixed in jars with roughly the same amount of turpentine, to a slightly thinner consistency than Magna paint.

Lichtenstein's paper stencils became far more elaborate in design, with many other shapes being used in addition to dots, such as the series of green rectangles (orientated in alternate directions) used to represent the carpet in *Interior with Waterlilies*. Fig.114 shows a detail of the green carpet pattern viewed in a raking light. The edges of the rectangles are extremely precise and slightly raised, unlike the frequently smudged outline of the Ben Day dots in *Whaam!* The solid areas of colour were next applied, before the black outlines, the last part of the process, were painted on. These, however, were no longer painted in freehand but with the use of masking tape. Fig.114 shows that in many areas their edges are more noticeably raised than in the stencilled areas, especially the lower right section of the near-vertical black line seen in the top right corner of the detail. One problem with masking tape was that it often left residues of the adhesive on the white priming. However, in most areas this was painted out with additional white paint and is now almost entirely hidden.

Lichtenstein also started to vary the numbers of paint layers applied, which resulted in slightly different transparencies and surface gloss in certain colours. Generally, two to three layers of paint were used, but for areas that required a little more prominence, Lichtenstein added 'two more coats of paint, so it's a little shinier'. The number of paint layers also varied depending on the inherent transparency of a particular colour. 'Yellow tends to cover easily, while with the ultramarine blue, I may even use four layers with Magna varnish in between'. The detail in fig.115 shows the edge of the blue vase, which consists of additional coats of blue compared to the diagonal stripes. This has resulted in a more opaque and slightly more glossy blue in the lamp, compared to a more transparent and less glossy blue in the stripes.

Although Lichtenstein made several modifications to his painting technique at various points in his career, the basic method of applying thin applications of a solvent-borne acrylic paint using brushes and stencils remained remarkably consistent throughout his life. When asked about his work in an interview in 1982, he remarked that 'almost everything I'm doing, I did in the 'sixties'.[10] This held true for his materials and techniques for the rest of his life.

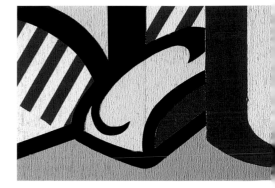

fig.115 A second raking-light detail (also from the left) of *Interior with Waterlilies* showing variations in the number of paint layers used in areas of the blue.

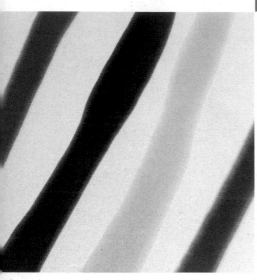

Morris Louis 1912–1962

Morris Louis spent the majority of his painting career working in isolation in his home/studio. Access to the studio was denied to virtually everyone while he was working and as a result, his methods of painting are largely unrecorded and have been the cause of much speculation since his early death in 1962. His wife, Marcella Brenner, was 'rarely invited'[1] into the studio, which she found 'difficult, but I respected his need not to be bothered, annoyed, pestered. And I knew that he did not want to have to explain'.[2]

In the early part of his career, Louis primarily used oil paint, although he did spend a brief period at David Alfaro Siqueiros's experimental workshop in New York during 1936 where he came into contact with a number of synthetic painting materials and diverse application techniques. In 1953, he and his friend Kenneth Noland made a visit to Helen Frankenthaler's studio that was to initiate a significant transformation in their working methods. Both artists admired the effects that Frankenthaler was achieving with her paint, in particular her use of very thin washes that made her colours almost at 'one with the fabric – a stain instead of a discrete covering coat'.[3] Louis was especially intrigued by the possibilities offered by staining unprepared canvas. As Noland put it, 'we were afraid of using oil, stained into canvas, because it rotted the canvas'.[4] Recognising the role played by a liberated attitude to materials and methods in Frankenthaler's achievement, Louis and Noland embarked on a period of intense experimentation with different paints and application techniques in an attempt to 'break down their previous assumptions … to break open painting'.[5] They referred to these sessions as 'jam painting',[6] working closely together for a short time, sometimes even on the same canvas.

One of the paints they tried was Magna acrylic, samples of which had been sent to Louis in the late 1940s by Leonard Bocour, the paint maker, whom he had previously met in New York. He soon realised that the paint entirely suited the effects he now sought. In particular, the paint retained colour intensity even when considerably thinned. After 1954,

fig.116 Morris Louis.

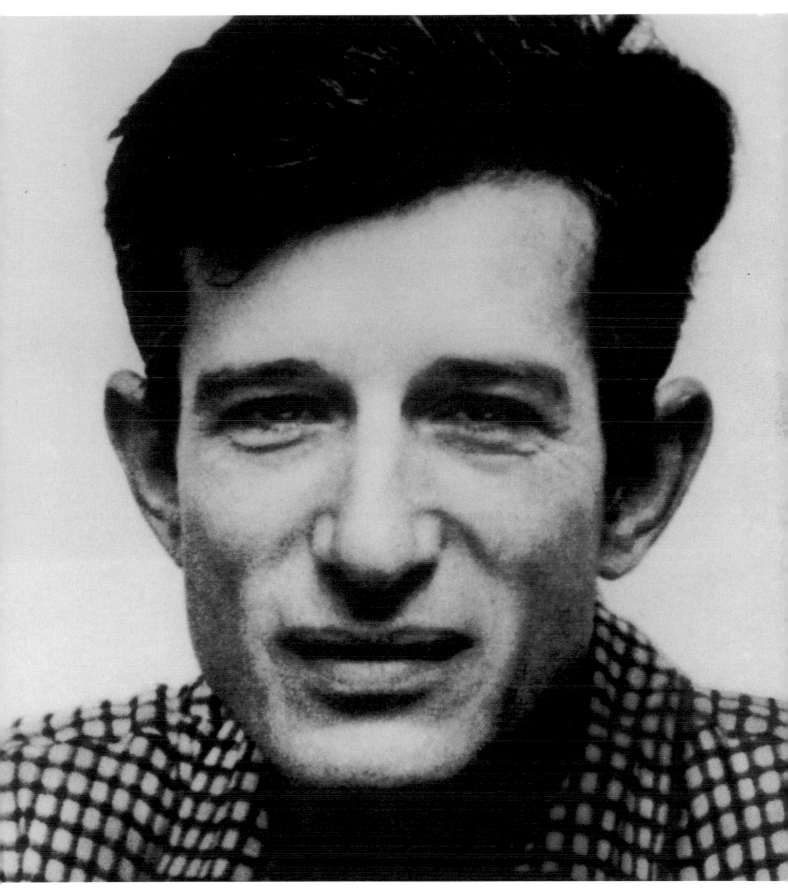

fig.117 *Beth Kuf* 1958, acrylic solution on canvas 232.4 x 339.1 cm. On loan to the Tate Gallery from Mrs Marcella Louis Brenner, the artist's widow.

Louis never used any other type of paint. It allowed him to broaden his experimental approach, taking the advice he had given to his students: 'find a formula and follow it. [Then] risk everything'.[7] It is doubtful whether Louis could have achieved many of his effects with any other type of paint. Bocour certainly understood this: 'A lot of fellows said "I tried [Magna] and it's no good". Morris on the other hand tried it and he found himself … When he discovered Magna, it was when he really began to blossom. It was unbelievable. His work took on a whole dynamic quality that he never had before'.[8]

Beth Kuf (fig.117) was painted in 1958 and is from the second series of paintings known as the 'Veils',[9] which explored the fluidity of the paint and transparency of staining. Prior to any paint application, the cotton canvas was prepared with a thin layer of transparent animal glue size and was then partially stretched around a working stretcher, certainly along the top edge and probably down the sides as well. The working stretcher was reinforced with two vertical cross-members presumably to strengthen it so that it could support the heavy canvas, which increased in weight as it became impregnated with paint. Although it is now attached to a different stretcher, the positions of the cross-members from the original working stretcher are still visible in the completed work, in particular the more central member, when viewed in a slightly raking light (fig.118). Also visible in this detail are four holes in the bright green paint, typical of those made by staples, which were probably used to attach the canvas onto this working stretcher. The second cross-member is further to the right. Lines made by the two vertical cross-members are seen in fifty-seven of the Veil paintings, indicating that he reused the same working stretcher for all of these works.[10] The dimensions of his studio have been measured as 14' x 12' 2".[11] Given that the working stretcher was about 8' x 12', it seems unlikely that he would have worked on any more than one canvas at a time.

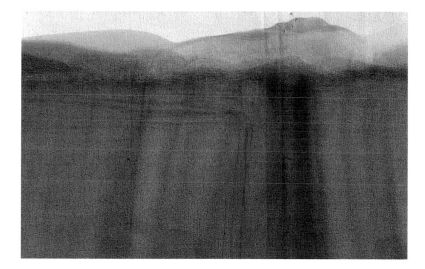

fig.118 Detail from *Beth Kuf* taken in partial raking light from the left.

For these works, Louis used large quantities of Magna paint that had been diluted to such an extent that it stained the canvas 'in the same way as dye'.[12] Its consistency was such that it could easily be poured down the tilted canvas face. The paint could be thinned either with additional acrylic binding medium (a resin called Acryloid F10),[11] or with turpentine. Louis would probably have used both, but the extreme dryness and presence of small cracks in the paint surface, are typical effects in a paint extremely low in binder content, in this case through extensive additions of turpentine. Noland recalls that the viscosity of Magna 'was soupy, [but] it was very easy to thin with turpentine and you could get it to just about the consistency [of] water'.[14] Noland points out that what was so impressive about Magna acrylic was that even at this dilution the paint 'held its intensity … The colours stayed brilliant and thin, and with turpentine in it, it would soak into the fibres of the cotton canvas'.[15] From Louis's receipts for painting supplies in 1958 it has been calculated that for each painting he would have used about nine tubes of paint and four and a half US gallons (3.75 UK gallons) of thinner.[16] His wife remembers the smell of turpentine that pervaded the whole house. She recalls being collected one morning for work. 'The young teacher who picked me up said, "My goodness, you do set us an example". I was her principal. "You polish your shoes every morning. I can smell it".'[17]

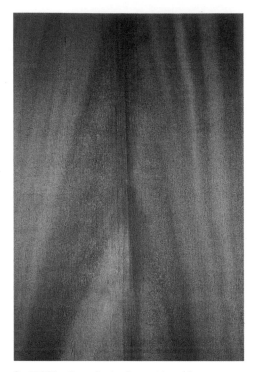

fig.119 The flow of paint down either side of the vertical cross-bar is evident in this partial raking-light detail (from the left) of *Beth Kuf.*

The paint was poured from just below the top edge of the canvas in numerous individual thin applications of bright colour. This can be seen along the top margin of the Veil shape, where single paint layers are still visible, such as the orange, yellow and green colours in fig.118. However, the extreme thinness of the resulting film of mixed colours could only have been achieved if the poured paint were assisted down the canvas face in some way, with, for example, wide brushes, sponges, or a long swab stick. Brenner does not recall having ever seen Louis with a brush, but a long stick, wound at the end with cheesecloth, was found in Louis's studio after his death. The dragging of this type of implement through the wet paint would have assisted the formation of the long, narrow, vertical bands that characterise the delicate variations of colour (figs.118 and 119). In contrast, the lines visible to the right of the top of the centre cross-member (fig.118) have the appearance of those that would be formed at the edge of an area of paint that had been moved around with a slightly different implement. Their shape suggests that Louis used a stiff brush or a piece of card to push the paint across the canvas from right to left and then suddenly down in a fairly sharp right angle as he reached the right edge of the cross-member.

The overall shape of the painted area, gently tapering at each side to leave exposed margins of canvas around it, is characteristic of all the Veil paintings. The art critic Clement Greenberg noted that staining permitted Louis 'to describe a firm and regular edge without having it become a cutting one as it would on a non-absorbent surface: the slight, hardly visible bleed left by soaking serves to deprive an edge or contour of sharpness but not necessarily of clarity or firmness'.[19] Variations to this shape could be made by tilting the stretcher to varying degrees or adjusting the tension of the canvas. As more paint was applied, the increase in weight in the canvas would naturally cause it to sag between the working stretcher bars, resulting in the later layers being more likely to flow into narrower channels, on either side of the off-centre vertical member (fig.119). Each paint application was allowed to flow down to the bottom of the canvas where the excess collected in a fairly thick pool, the top of which is visible along the bottom of the Veil; the remainder has been folded around the bottom stretcher bar. In some areas this pooling has resulted in an uncharacteristically thick area of paint, but it is perhaps most apparent in the overall image at the two lower corners. Fig.120 shows a detail of the lower-left corner; the sharp deviation to the vertical edge of the paint shows the upper limit of this pooling effect. Also seen in this detail is a large area of the sized canvas with the various paint layers subtly bleeding into it, giving it a delicate, feathered edge.

As with all the Veil paintings, the technique used in *Beth Kuf* relied on the unique properties of Magna acrylic paint. Magna dries quickly, allowing the subsequent application of sequential layers that would still run down the canvas. The drying of the paint film on the canvas was accelerated with large fans in the studio,[20] which meant that Louis could view the painting as a whole before the canvas was rolled up and put away at the end of a painting session. As the acrylic could be re-dissolved by the same solvent in which it was initially diluted, subsequent layers could be blended to produce a very thin final paint layer with all the previous layers mixed together.

In 1958, Louis was still using Magna paint in tubes. Bocour recalled that he 'would get these tubes and squeeze it into a little can or something and thin it down'.[21] Bocour had recently developed a new formula for Magna colours, which contained a small proportion of beeswax. The wax improved the stability of the paints by binding the pigment and binder more firmly together, but it also resulted in a thicker consistency. Noland believes the reason for this change was 'to make it more like oil paint, so that it was more commercial ... A lot of artists were working with thick paints. The kind of de Kooning type of painting'.[22] Louis, however, found these new colours difficult to dilute down to the appropriate viscosity without affecting the colour intensity. In letters to Bocour, dated 1958, he complained of being 'not too happy with the present Magna since it doesn't particularly lend itself to my purposes, tho' I suppose all other artists are grateful now that you pack so much solid pigment into a tube',[23] and requested that Bocour send him any supplies of the old stock which was bound more loosely. 'My hands get worn out from trying to grind the recent beeswax stuff into a more liquid state'.[24]

In 1960, Bocour suggested making a special formula of Magna for Louis and Noland. 'Morris ... loved the paint but he didn't like the viscosity. He wanted something that was very soft and very liquidy ... So I would say to him ... I'll make you your paint ... a gallon at a time ... and put it in a can'.[25] Bocour therefore began to custom-make Louis's paint in which he omitted the beeswax and simply dispersed the pigment in equal amounts of Acryloid F-10 and turpentine. It was supplied in US one-gallon (0.83 UK gallon) quantities of Louis's palette of twenty different colours, to which he added two more the following year. The omission of beeswax eased the thinning considerably, but its absence also caused the pigment and binder to become more prone to separating out. Bocour suggested a simple remedy to Louis: 'a possible solution to stop the hardening of the paint at the bottom of the can, that you keep turning [it] upside down every week'.[26] But it also had ramifications for the paint on the canvases. The strong capillary action of the canvas fibres could draw the acrylic binder away from a painted area and result in a bleed of medium around it.

This is clearly visible in *VAV*, a Veil painting from 1960 (fig.121). A detail of the separation is shown in fig.122. The cream-coloured area between the white of the bare cotton canvas on the left and the red pigmented

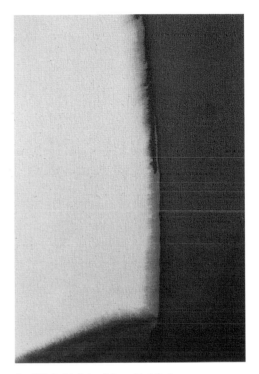

fig.120 A third detail from *Beth Kuf*, taken in partial raking light (from the right), shows the bleed of the acrylic paint into the canvas.

fig.121 *VAV* 1960, acrylic solution on canvas 260.3 x 359.4 cm.

area on the right is the acrylic medium that has separated out from the Magna paint. Another factor that may have exacerbated the extent of the separation between pigment and binder was that the canvas used for this painting was not sized. Unlike oil paint, Magna acrylic does not degrade the cotton-canvas fibres, so it can be applied directly to the fabric without the need for a preparatory size layer. The absence of size allowed the colour to penetrate the canvas more effectively, but probably also assisted in the bleed of the acrylic medium away from the pigment through capillary action. Although he would certainly have seen it occur almost immediately after paint application, it seems unlikely that Louis either intended or could really control this effect. Nevertheless, the resulting separation produced a number of subtle variations on the edges of the painted shape in *VAV*, including a far 'softer' feathering of the pigment and a very faint but quite distinct fringe of red colour just outside the main painted area (fig.122).

As with *Beth Kuf*, individual colours are visible along the top edge of the painting, but here the paint film is so thin that in some places the colour of the canvas is apparent through the paint layers (fig.123). Again a swab stick, such as the one found in Louis's studio, was probably used to direct the flow of paint down the canvas and to ensure that the individual paint layers became thoroughly mixed. However, when the painting is viewed *into* a raking light, a different type of mark can be seen in the paint

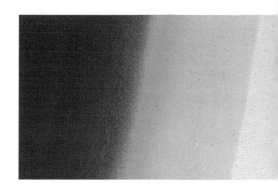

fig.122 Detail from *VAV* showing the edge of the painted shape.

fig.123 The extreme thinness of the paint is evident in this detail from *VAV*, taken in partial raking light from the left. The cream colour is the cotton canvas.

fig.124 Detail from *VAV* taken *into* a raking light from the left. Evidence of Louis's use of a card to spread the paint around is visible.

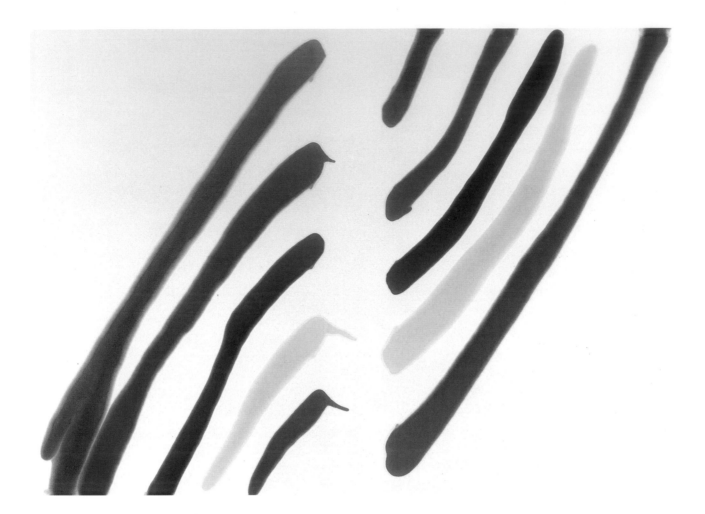

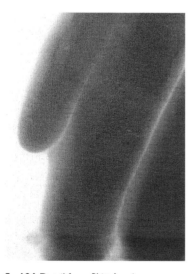

fig.126 Detail from *Phi* taken in partial raking light from the left, showing the thinness of the paint.

surface (fig.124). The edges of these marks are definite and straight, formed through using an implement with a square edge, such as a piece of card.

In the summer of 1960, Louis started a new series of paintings, now known as the 'Unfurleds', which used pure colour rather than mixing it on the canvas. *Phi*, painted between 1960 and 1961 (fig.125), is typical of the early paintings from this series, in which the paint is still diluted with extensive amounts of thinner. These works are characterised by their pale colours, appearing stain-like on the unprimed cotton canvas. The colours were presumably similar in appearance to the initial individual layers used in the Veils. Fig.126 shows a detail of the purple and blue bands at the lower edge of the painting. The thinness of the paint is indicated by the visibility of the canvas texture through the colours. Also evident in this detail are clumps of a red pigment at the centre of the purple band of colour, which indicates that this colour contains a mixture of pigments and that the red pigment has partially separated out from the others. At the lower edge of the detail is a horizontal band of slightly more saturated colour in both blue and purple, which corresponds to the presence of a stretcher bar behind this part of the canvas during the application of paint. This suggests that the entire canvas was stretched for this painting, unlike the Veil paintings which may only have been attached along their top edges.

Louis soon modified the image to the format for which he is now best known, as exemplified by *Alpha-Phi* (fig.129 overleaf). These paintings have caused the greatest amount of conjecture as to how they were made. The paint appears to have been poured diagonally across the cotton canvas, beginning at the side members of the stretcher and directed inward. Each resulting band of colour was probably formed by a single application. The canvas must have been stretched fairly taut so that Louis could control the path taken by each band of colour as it ran down the canvas by changing the direction of tilt of the stretched canvas. It is possible that he gathered and pleated the canvas first, creating channels for the paint to flow down, but the absence of any visible creases in the canvas makes this unlikely.

The paint was certainly used in a much thicker consistency than in the Veils, often resulting in an opaque covering of colour sometimes masking the canvas-weave texture. The consistency of the paint was crucial to the effect. If it was too thin, the bands of colour would have soaked into the canvas and widened. If it was too thick, it would not have poured freely down the canvas. In *Alpha-Phi*, Louis has been able to prevent most of the streams of colour from overlapping by careful pouring, although occasionally adjacent bands bled into each other at intervals, such as the orange into the yellow (fig.128). The proportion of resin or turpentine thinner could be varied according to the colour intensity and matt or gloss surface required. Louis does not seem to have inter-mixed the colours for this series of paintings and his concern about their quality was reflected in a letter to Bocour, requesting that he 'see to it that the colours are made fresh each time ...' Another important matter which I've hollered about before is that the machine is hardly cleaned between the different colours'.[27] A striking feature of this painting is that the degree of fringing appears to be dependent on the colour of the Magna acrylic. In the orange band, for example, the bleed of medium has extended a considerable distance out of the colour, unlike the band of yellow, which has remained completely bound (fig.128). In some parts of the orange band, two forms of fringing have occurred. The first is the broad transparent bleed from the initial separation between pigment and medium. The painting then appears to have been positioned upright before the orange paint had dried completely, causing the paint to collect at the bottom of the band; it is visible as a raised area of paint. In a few places where this build-up of paint became particularly heavy, it dripped into the yellow band beneath. These individual drips then appear to have themselves undergone a further pigment-medium separation. In fact, there are visible differences between

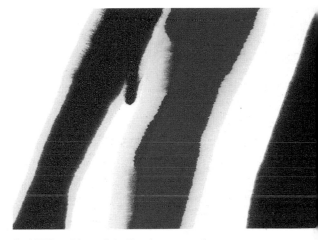

fig.125 *Phi* 1960–1, acrylic solution on canvas 265 x 362 cm. On loan to the Tate Gallery from Mrs Marcella Louis Brenner, the artist's widow.

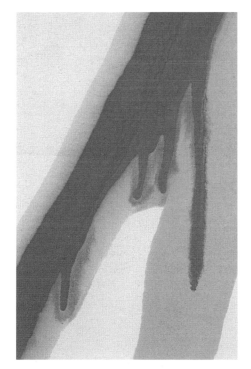

fig.127 Detail from *Alpha-Phi* taken in partial raking light from the left.

fig.128 The difference between paint surfaces of various acrylic colours is evident in this detail from *Alpha-Phi*.

fig.129 *Alpha-Phi* 1961, acrylic solution on canvas 259.1 x 459.7 cm.

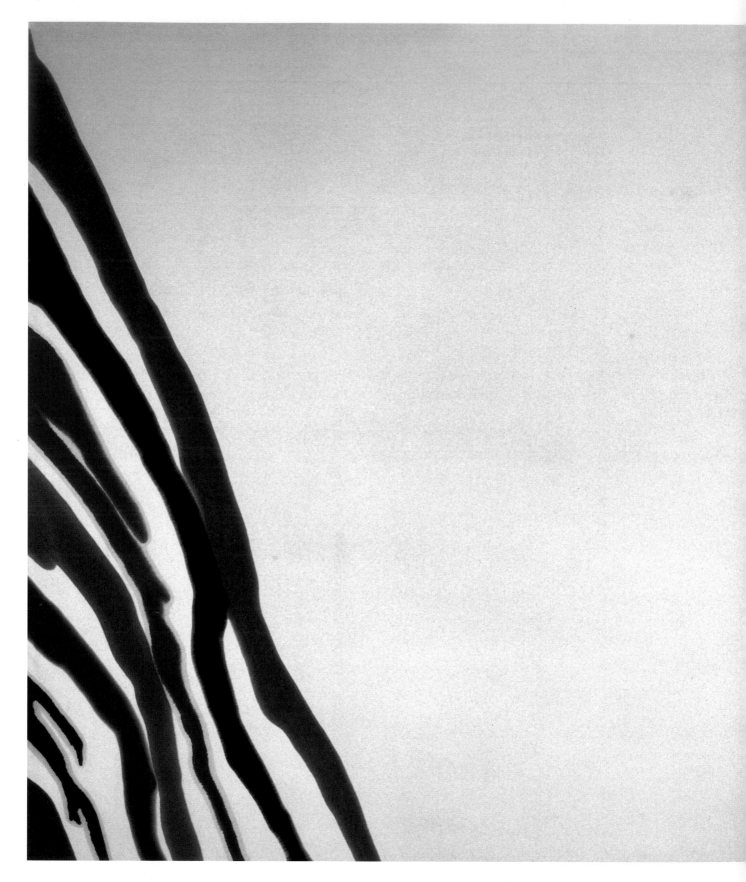

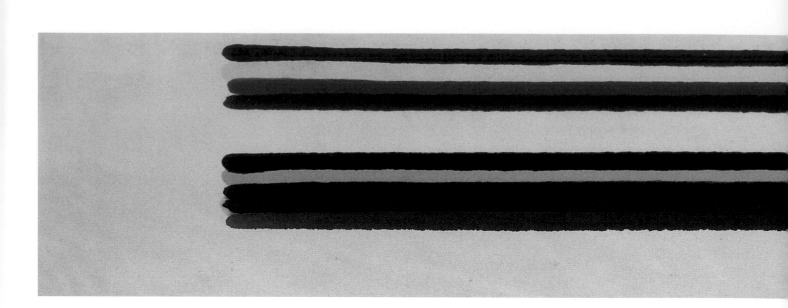

fig.130 *Partition* 1962, acrylic solution on canvas 259.7 x 44.5 cm.

fig.15 Detail from *Partition* showing the precision of Louis's technique.

most of the bands of colour, either in the amount of binding medium separation or in their surfaces. For example, in fig.127 three different surfaces are visible in the dark blue, brown and dark green bands. The pigment and acrylic binder in the green band have remained almost totally mixed. Although there is a slight degree of separation at the very edge of this band, the medium in these areas has retained a small amount of pigmentation. The brown band, on the other hand, exhibits a significant amount of separation and the coloured area appears uniformly matt and flat. The binder in the blue band has also separated from the pigmented part, but within its coloured area, further separation has occurred. Some parts of the band are no more than a thin blue stain, whereas in others the surface seems somewhat granular due to the build-up of pigment. Light is reflected from these areas in such a way that a degree of crystallinity is suggested.

The larger scale of the Unfurleds, compared to the Veils, meant that Louis had to sometimes extend his studio into the 'living-dining room … We had put two rooms together' with the wall taken out.[28] Marcella Brenner remembers him working in this bigger area. 'But then by the time I came back everything was back in place and everything rolled up, and you never would have known that he worked there. … In other instances he worked by folding the canvas and actually stayed in the studio'.[29]

In early 1961, Louis stopped painting Unfurleds and began a series of

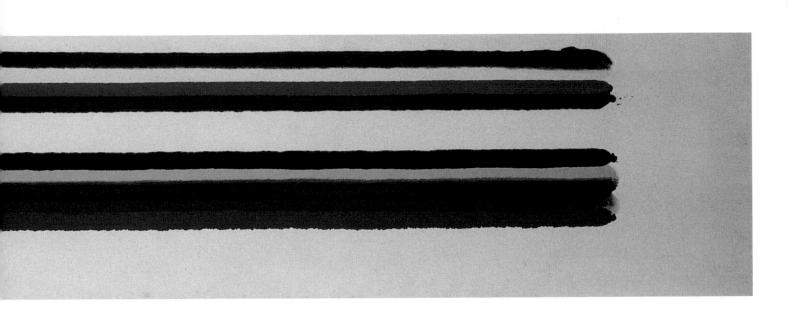

'Stripe' paintings consisting of parallel bands of colour. The early works appear to have been produced in a similar technique to that employed for the Unfurleds with the paint poured down the cotton canvas. However, by the time he painted *Partition* (fig.130) in 1962, the bands had become characterised by a higher degree of regularity, a more even colour intensity and carefully controlled ends, all of which suggest that they were now being 'drawn' rather than poured. Such an effect would have been produced if Louis had used a swab stick to draw the bands, with the canvas placed flat. Fig.131 shows a detail of one end of the stripes. It can be seen that the pigment-medium separation has almost been eliminated, with only the occasional occurrence of two adjacent bands bleeding into each other.

In certain respects, the later Stripe paintings would have been less complicated to make than those from the preceding series. They are painted on a much smaller scale and the technique of drawing the lines with the swab stick avoided the physical effort of tipping the canvas. However, in other respects they represent a significant development in his technique just before his sudden death in 1962. The fact that the lines of paint are now so closely aligned as to be touching one another, and that the amount of bleeding between two adjacent lines is almost non-existent, suggests that Louis now had full control over his technique, and had abandoned the elements of chance that had existed in the Unfurleds.

Bridget Riley born 1931

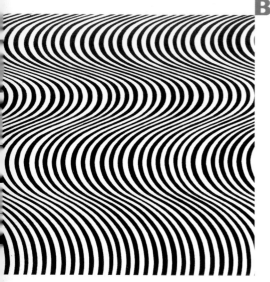

Bridget Riley thinks of her compositions as structures. Although her work has often been described in terms of the illusion of movement, she believes that 'abstract art does not deal with illusions. As with Mondrian, I was using the reality of perception. What you perceive is real in terms of the painting. The concept of illusion is quite wrong'. To explore this 'perceptual world', in each painting Riley first establishes 'a constant, to which variations are related'. The 'constant' can be regarded as a reference point within the overall structure of the image. She views it as 'regular, repeatable and stable', and it often consists of some sort of regular division of the painting surface. The 'variations' can be changes in colour, form, proportion or direction, which occur across the painting in relation to the constant.

In all Riley's paintings the relationships between constant and variation have first been explored through detailed and often full-size preparatory studies, which are then refined into the tightly balanced structure of the painting itself. Riley realised that in applying the paint it was important that 'any sort of distraction should be avoided'. This would include anything 'that was not integral to the duality (of constant and variant)', such as reflections in the paint's surface or variations in its thickness. 'I do not want to interfere with the experience of what can be seen ... personal handling, thick or thin paint applications, these are in themselves statements and irrelevant for my purpose. My painting has to be devoid of such incidentals'. Riley recalls that she 'reacted against the gesture and touch of rank and file Abstract Expressionism' and notes that 'Pollock never touched his best paintings'. She also remembers reading a passage by the nineteenth-century French art critic Felix Fénéon, who in writing about the technique of Georges Seurat, described *Un Dimanche d'été à l'Ile de la Grande Jatte* (1884–5) as the 'kind of painting in which ... "stylish handling" [is] quite pointless. There is no room in it for the bravura piece. The hand may go numb, but the eye must remain agile, learned and perspicacious'. For Riley, these words 'struck a powerful echo — and this attitude became part of my credo'.

Riley was, and she quotes Matisse, 'trying to eliminate the suggestive-

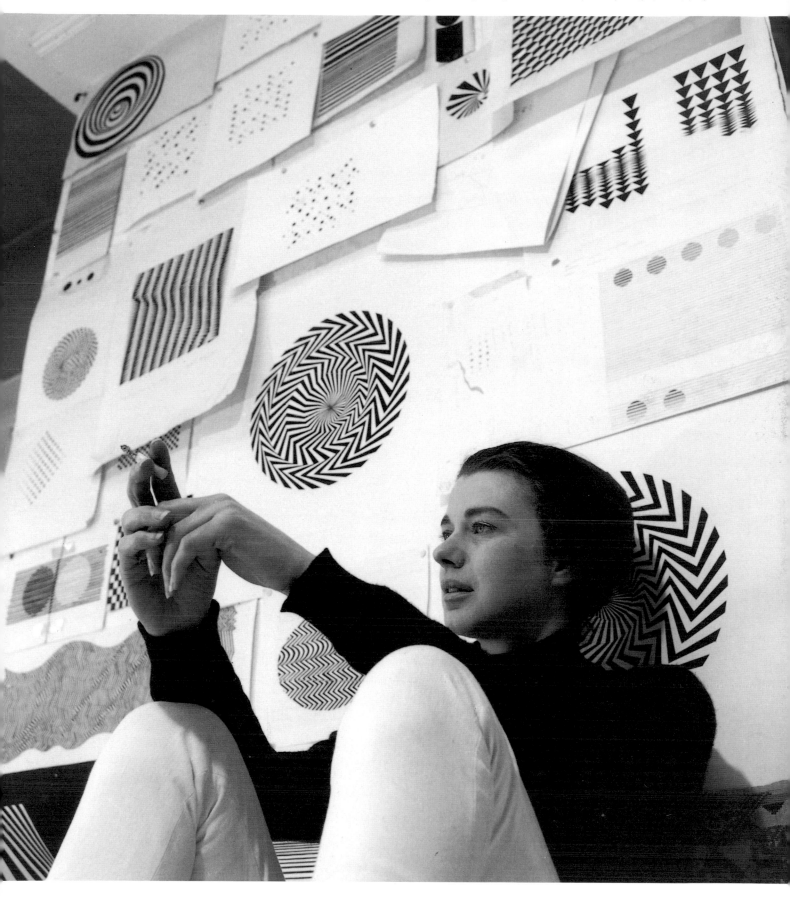

fig.133 *Fall* 1963, PVA emulsion housepaint on hardboard 141 x 140.3 cm.

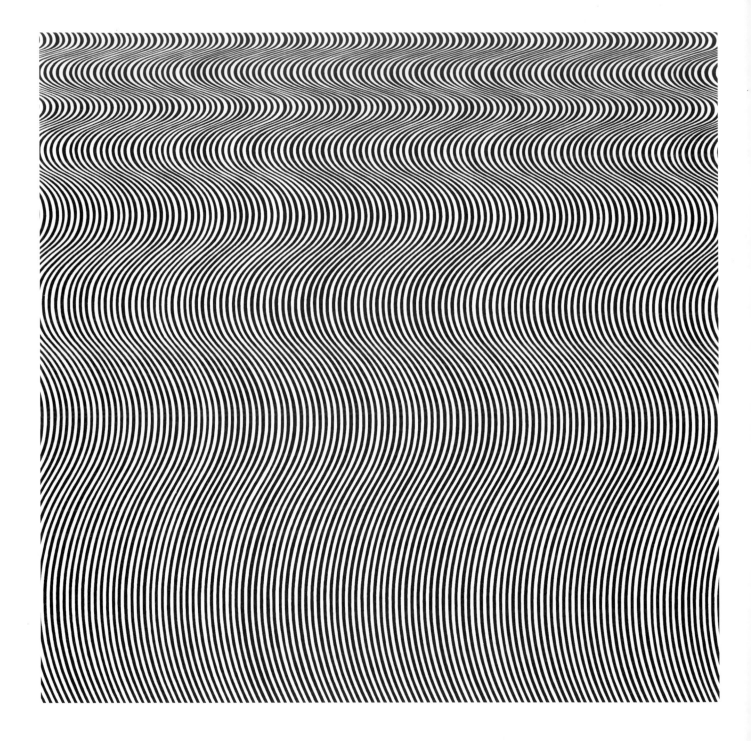

ness of paint'. She soon discovered that all of 'these distractions could be minimised through using a matt paint, built up in successive layers to a uniform density'. The resulting surface concealed most of the signs of brushwork and was 'less suggestive and more stable'. The use of assistants carried this further. 'The work should aim to be objective and go as far as possible beyond personal subjectivity'.

Riley began to use studio assistants in the early 1960s. She views technique as much more than just the actual process of applying paint to a support. Technique 'is an intellectual ordering, a putting of the mind into a series of actions which are necessary … It is necessary to plan, to work, to study, to endure, to conserve, all that is part of making something – and the physical aspect of a painting technique is only one part of this intellectual framework.'

The works by which Riley became internationally known are the black and white paintings from the early 1960s, such as *Fall* (fig.133) and *Hesitate* (fig.136 overleaf). Before 1963, acrylic paints were not available in the UK. Riley had discovered that oil paints could not produce the matt uniform finish she required, and had turned to household emulsion paint. Andrew Smith, an assistant since 1971, recalls 'the only matt paints available were in the commercial sector … it was the only thing there was to do that job and to flow well enough'. He also points out that 'if oil had been used, each layer would have taken days to be touch dry, and much longer if overpainting was needed'.

For her work in the early 1960s, Riley needed 'the strongest contrast obtainable between black and white'. Eventually, she chose her paint from two different manufacturers. Each paint 'had to be opaque, a good colour. Della Robbia was a very, very good white … [and] Ripolin was a splendid black'. She had learned of their use by other artists, in particular that of Ripolin by Picasso: 'if he had used it then it was probably the best around'. These two brands were easily obtainable and were both regarded as 'high quality household paint'. Smith explains: 'the problem with using pure white is always covering power; it is surprisingly difficult to overpaint with white to create a completely pure surface, particularly if the other colour is black'. The properties of the paint used were perfectly suited to the painting technique adopted for these early works. In particular, Riley recalls 'their rapid drying and the way that it flowed onto the hardboard. It would just flow on and dry … It had a surface tension to it' and she remembers that 'the paint would form a slightly convex surface on the hardboard, which meant that a single coat would be thicker than would otherwise be the case'.

In both *Fall* and *Hesitate*, Riley painted on a hardboard support backed with a timber frame; in *Hesitate* a second sheet of hardboard was attached to the back, sandwiching the frame. She admits that 'there was an element of doing something that was not Beaux Art' in her choice of

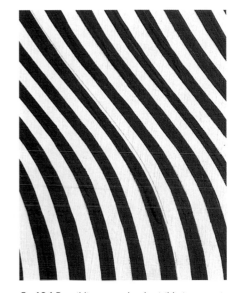

fig.134 Pencil lines are clearly visible in this detail from *Fall*, taken in partial raking light from the left.

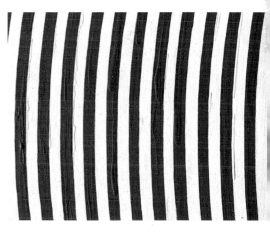

fig.135 Detail from *Fall* taken in raking light from the left. There is evidence of retouching by the artist in both the black and the white areas.

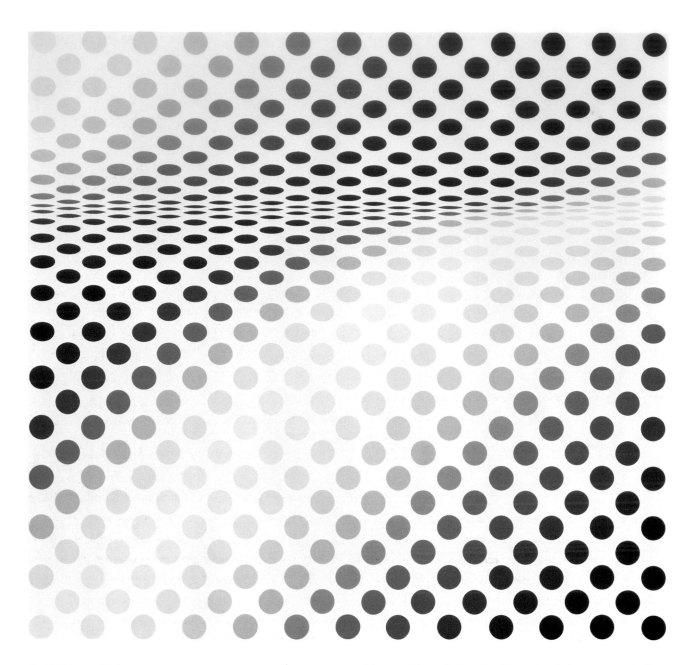

fig.136 *Hesitate* 1964,
PVA emulsion housepaint on hardboard
106.7 x 112.4 cm.

these commercial materials and also that 'the cult of the amateur in English art was objectionable'. The hardboard surface was prepared with the white Della Robbia paint in several layers (the initial layers were diluted with water) to achieve opacity, then sanded to a smooth finish. The compositional structures were 'developed through drawing'. For *Fall* Riley 'drew a curve and cut a template out of hardboard. The curve was not a pre-existing mathematical form', but one that Riley constructed herself. 'The final criterion was made by eye'. By moving this template across the surface of the painted hardboard panel in measured intervals, 'a regular field of curves' was established in pencil. Using these lines as a guide, the black emulsion paint was then applied with the hardboard support laid flat on a table. It was found that the flow of paint could be better controlled in this position, and it also prevented drips from forming. When the painting is examined in closer detail (fig.134) it can be seen that the black lines vary slightly in width and opacity, having been 'painted by hand, without much interest in perfection'. In contrast, vertical brushstrokes, which are characteristic of a much wider paintbrush, can be seen in the surface of the white paint. Also visible in this detail are some of the curved pencil lines, particularly where the application of black paint deviated slightly from the drawing. Although a certain amount of variation in terms of opacity and smoothness of curve was inevitable, where these were considered too much they were retouched locally. When the paint surface is viewed in a strong raking light (fig.135) these retouchings become more apparent and it can be seen that they were applied in both black and white areas.

For *Hesitate* (fig.136) Riley recalls that in order to establish the positioning of the circles and ovals she referred to preparatory studies. 'No grid was drawn on the priming. The centres of the ovals and circles were marked with a piece of adhesive tape. The position was marked on the tape rather than on the priming'. She then 'used a compass for the circles, and templates for the ovals', although 'the very narrow ovals in the centre could only be done freehand'. The ovals and circles were then painted in sequential tones of grey with mixtures of the black and white emulsion paint. 'The first was a "just visible" grey, nearly white, then there were a number of gradations to black. I could shorten the number [of gradations] to make faster movements or increase them for slower movements. It is impossible to mix the greys by using quantified amounts of each colour; they always have to be adjusted visually'.

All the forms were painted freehand apart from the circles, whose outlines were applied using a spring compass filled with paint. When viewed in raking light, the circles are seen to have the precise and slightly raised edges characteristic of paint applied in this way (fig.137). In addition, the small indent made by the point of the compass remains just visible at the centre of each circle. By contrast, in the ovals far more distinct brushstrokes can be seen, typical of a freehand application.

A severe restriction to using these commercial paints was the limited range of available colours. In 1967, when Riley began to use pure colours, it was inevitable that she would require a different kind of paint. Although artists' acrylic emulsion paints were on the market in the UK by this time and she had certainly used Cryla, Rowney's range of acrylic colours, by 1965, she recalls that none of the brands she tried had very strong or pure colours. 'They tended to have a pale, greyish quality'. Instead, she started to mix her own colours by grinding dry pigments directly into a polyvinyl acetate (PVA) emulsion medium. She recalls being given a sample of the unpigmented emulsion by Brian Rogerson at Spectrum Oil Colours, 'I think it was a little treat he gave me'. The advantage of this

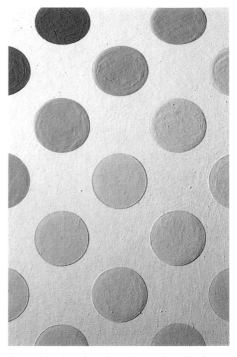

fig.137 A raking-light detail (from the left) of *Hesitate* shows the differences in Riley's technique for painting the circles and the ovals.

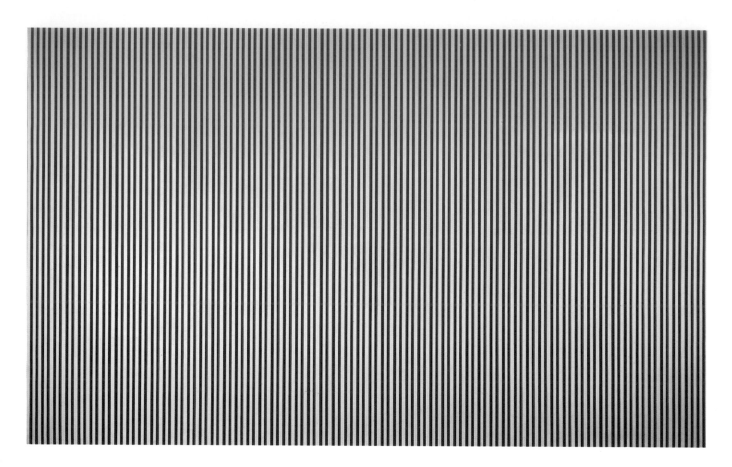

fig.138 *Late Morning* 1967–8, dry pigment
mixed into PVA emulsion medium on canvas
226.1 x 359.4 cm.

system was that it gave her far more control over creating the colours and intensities she wanted. However, she recalls 'I had to grind away with a pestle and mortar for hours and hours, and that was a real problem because it was very difficult to get the pigment into the medium. But there was no alternative, there were no strong colours in the household emulsion paints then'. The paints produced were not only extremely quick-drying but would also dry to the required matt finish. By this time, Rowney had also started to market an unpigmented artists' PVA emulsion binding medium, but Riley does not recall being aware of this as she already had her own supply. 'One didn't know that there were all these wonderful resins, the whole thing was a brand new field'.

The paintings from this period involve pairs, triads or larger groups of colour, which are organised in simple stripes or curves. 'Colour energies need a virtually neutral vehicle if they are to develop uninhibited. The repeated stripe seems to meet these conditions'. For *Late Morning*, painted in 1967–8 (fig.138) 'the constants are the white and red lines and the variants are the modulations in the blues and greens. There are ten stages of blue to green – a very extended movement'. The colour order was established by 'making many sequence studies using shorter colour bands'. Fig.139 shows Riley comparing a colour swatch to a series of the sequence studies on the studio wall behind her (although these are not the actual studies for *Late Morning*). One of the problems addressed in these studies was the 'difference in energy of the different colours', in particular the 'colour spreading effect' of the red. As Riley explains, 'if bands of the same width were used for all three colours, then the red would appear wider because of its greater expansive power'. Or, put another way, 'if it was made the same it wouldn't look the same'. To compensate for this, the red bands were made slightly narrower, as is appar-

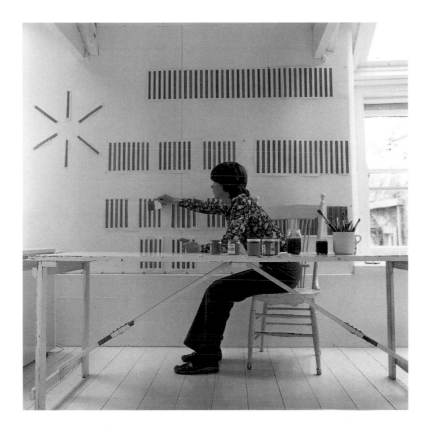

fig.139 Bridget Riley working in her studio in 1973, photographed by Jorge Lewinski.

ent on close inspection (fig.140). The PVA colours were used at full strength to get the intensity of hue, but Riley found the paint 'granular in application', certainly compared to the fluidity of the commercial paints, because the pigment hadn't been milled into the PVA medium. Riley 'even made enquiries at Rowney's about buying a small mill, but it was prohibitively expensive'. The granular quality resulted in some minor inconsistencies in the paint film: 'if you look at the surface you will see unwanted thicks and thins'. These variations and the slightly granular character of the paint become apparent in raking light (fig.140). It is often assumed that Riley must have used masking tape to achieve her straight lines, but 'in fact it has never been used as it leaves an unsightly ridge on the edge of the band and creates a mechanical effect'. No such ridges are apparent in this raking light detail and it can be seen that the colour is hand-painted up to a line.

By the time Riley began painting *Cantus Firmus* (fig.141) in 1972, she was using Rowney Cryla acrylic paint, considering it a 'real breakthrough

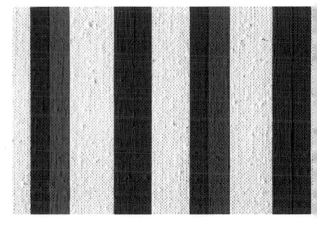

fig.140 Detail from *Late Morning* taken in raking light from the left, showing the granular nature of the paint and the difference in width between the blue and red bands.

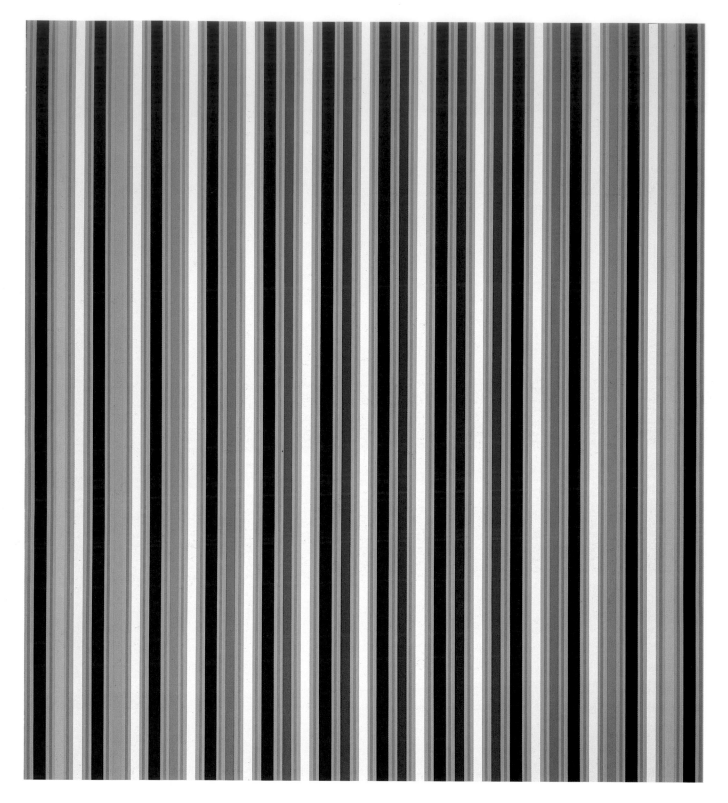

fig.141 *Cantus Firmus* 1972–3, acrylic emulsion on canvas 241.3 x 215.9 cm.

when the paint manufacturers changed from PVA to acrylic resin'. She started working with acrylic emulsion medium in the late 1960s when her range of colour 'began to incorporate more greys and coloured greys'. She realised that her paintings could now 'accommodate the colours that acrylic emulsions could yield'. She also found that the acrylic paint 'had a more durable surface than PVA and was less brittle'. Examination of *Cantus Firmus* shows the more uniform surface and colour of the acrylic (fig.142). 'Its smooth consistency made it much easier to hand paint up to a line than the homemade granular PVA-bound paint' she used earlier. By this time, Riley would make 'a final full-size study of the image, in gouache on paper; a cartoon in the traditional sense. If that works then the painting is made from it, or if necessary, it will be revised'.

In 1976, Riley started to use Aqua-tec, an American brand of acrylic paint that was by then marketed in the UK. It was generally more transparent than Cryla and took more coats to achieve a similar opacity, but the final result had a more intense colour. It also 'had good flowing properties on application. It was invented by Bocour and was fundamentally a paint for the American stain-painters. So although the colour range was good, it wasn't necessarily exactly what was required.' Its transparency meant that it was necessary to apply a succession of thin coats to the primed canvas, the required intensity only being achieved after the seventh or eighth layer. 'It was like glazing, virtually'. She also recalls another problem that was peculiar to the brand: 'Aqua-tec did look like the best at the time, the only problem was its shine … it built up to a rather glossy sheen'. This was difficult to control and an effective way of reducing it was never found.

To a Summer's Day 2 (fig.143 overleaf), painted in 1980, is one of a series of paintings using 'twisted curves or crossovers'. Riley explains:

these are complex in appearance but simple in principle, with one colour crossing in turn over the other two and also crossing from one side of a curved band to the other, with the resulting interaction of colour giving rise to the appearance of colours not actually painted. In this way different colour relationships could be established, not just across the painting (or up and down) but in both directions.

As with *Cantus Firmus*, the structure was worked out in a series of smaller drawings followed by a full-size gouache cartoon. The stretcher was ordered using the dimensions of the cartoon and the linen canvas was then stretched. After the edges had been masked with tape, 'to provide a firm edge to draw from', it was primed and then removed from the stretcher to be laid flat on the table for the drawing. Horizontal lines were drawn and diagonals established in relation to them. These were marked with a series of measurements and a long hardboard template was used to draw a field of curves on a diagonal. Then

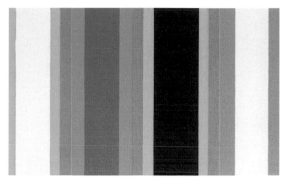

fig.142 Detail from *Cantus Firmus* taken in partial raking light from the left. The bands are precise and the texture of the acrylic emulsion paint is smooth.

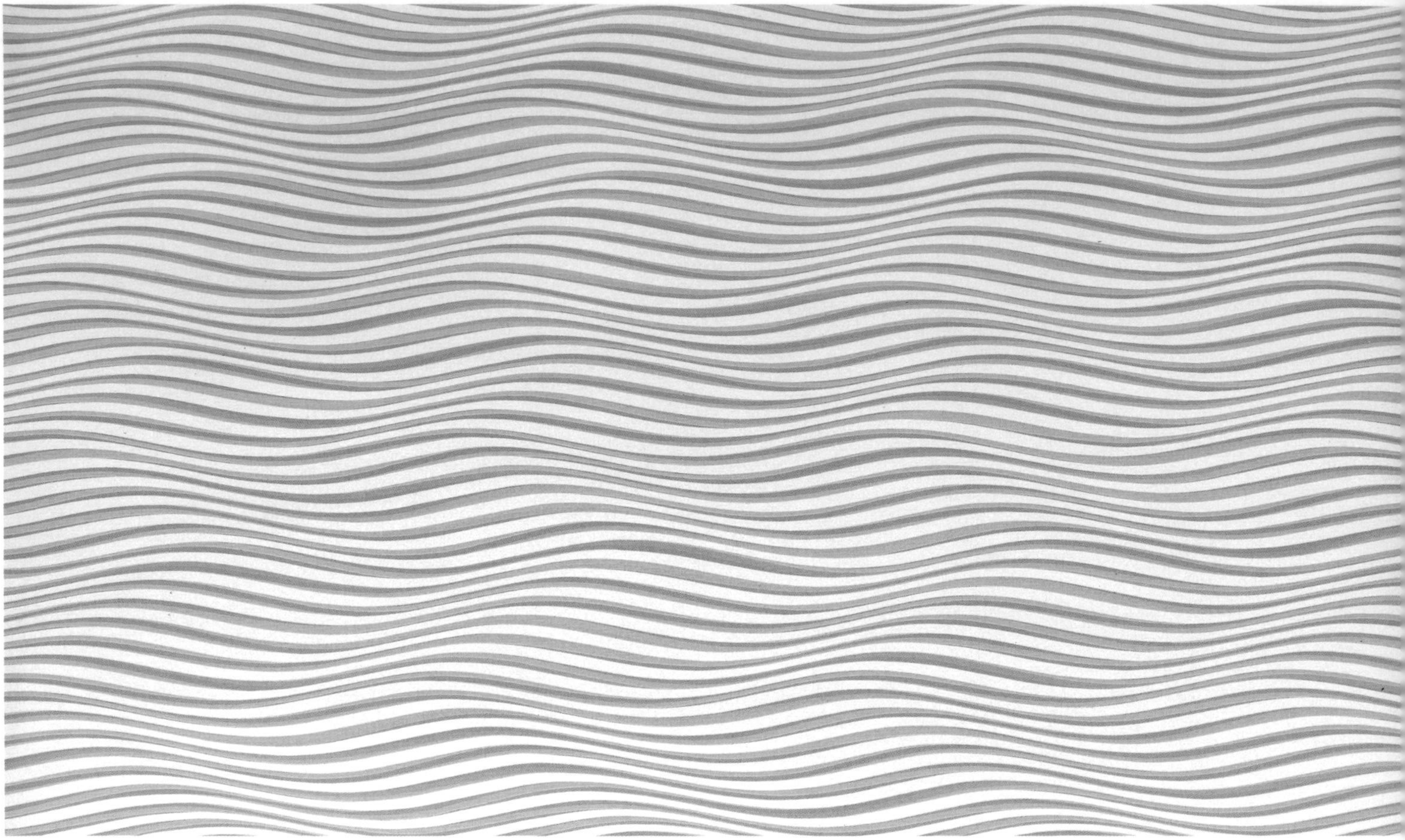

fig.143 *To a Summer's Day* 1980, acrylic
emulsion paint on canvas 115.5 x 281 cm.

two shorter hardboard templates were used to draw the 'crossover' bands inside the first set of curves. 'They are handmade and they are not always exact'. The lines could not always be made with precise measurements and sometimes alterations were made to the structure. For example, the distance between the curves was slightly reduced as the curve approached the edge, a detail that could only be judged by eye. For Riley, it was always the visual effect that remained crucial. The canvas was then re-stretched, and the painting was executed in an upright position against the wall. The colours – blue, violet, pink and ochre – were mixtures using Aqua-tec acrylic emulsion paints. The colour was ruled along the pencil lines using a ruling pen. 'The consistency of the paint is critical. If you have heavy, thick paint it is hard to control with a small brush, but if it's thinner it is easier to apply; it will just glide along'. Even when the surface is observed in raking light (fig.144) the paint surface exhibits only a minimal amount of texture, with just the occasional build-up of paint at the edge of a curve.

In 1980, having returned from a visit to Egypt, Riley introduced a new palette of more intense colour to her painting. She continued working with acrylic emulsion, but discovered that applying a final coat of oil colour over an acrylic base created greater colour intensity. The oil paint

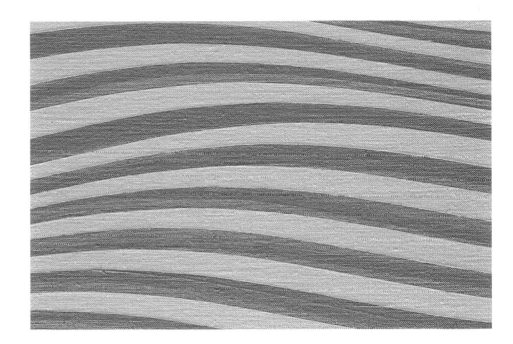

fig.144 Detail from *To a Summer's Day* taken in raking light from above, showing the consistency of the paint.

was thinned with an oil medium so that it could be applied in one thin, even layer. 'Oil paint has a transparency. So in order to give it the density that had been achieved with acrylic, I used an acrylic base'. She recounts making two versions of a painting, *Ka1* (1980), one with acrylic emulsion only, and the other with the top coat of oil, which 'permitted a direct comparison. You could see quite clearly that the oil was more intense in colour. So there was no question'.

The technique of using oil colour over acrylic underpainting was employed for all Riley's subsequent paintings, although in the early 1980s she again changed brands of acrylic emulsion. 'I met a painter in Germany who was using the Swiss Lascaux acrylic paints. They were not available in England, so I ordered them direct from Switzerland myself'. Because the brand has a higher opacity, fewer layers were needed. *Nataraja* (fig.145), painted in 1993, is an example of this working method and also of the preparatory process that she still employs. The compositional structures differ slightly from previous ones in that she allows for 'a wider range of possibilities, an open palette. And the colour interaction, whilst still very much there, is no longer the primary role of the colour'. The basic composition is established with coloured, rhomboid-shaped paper cut-outs, with which she explores various colour configurations by actually placing them

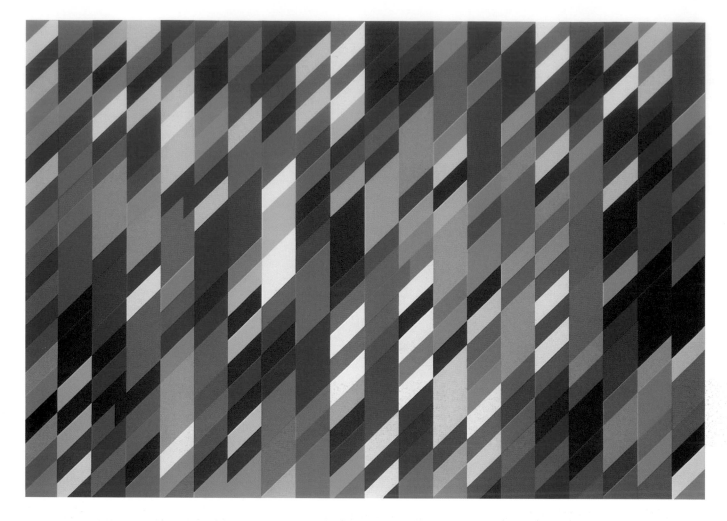

fig.145 *Nataraja* 1993, oil and acrylic emulsion on canvas 165.1 x 227.7 cm.

in relation to each other. At a certain stage of development, these can be marked on an underdrawing of the basic framework onto which any colour can be noted. Studies followed by a full-scale cartoon are made, all of which are 'continually open to modification'. As Smith explains, 'this system is her working palette, this is really like her brushes and paints'.

The linen canvas for this painting was prepared in a slightly different way:

The linen is stretched and primed on a stretcher larger that the final image. The final stretcher is [only] ordered when the painting is finished. This is because the oil paint is applied with the canvas flat on a table, so the whole process occurs off the stretcher. The canvas is thus unstretched for quite a long time and it was found that too much shrinkage occurred for the canvas to be safely replaced on a stretcher ordered to the cartoon size.

When the canvas is ready, the composition is transferred onto it and the acrylic painting can begin. All the colours in her palette, both in oil and acrylic (and gouache for the studies), are initially mixed by Riley, but subsequent batches can be exactly matched by an assistant. Smith explains that 'the acrylics are mixed as a good match to the original gouache of the cartoon, but the oil paint has its own richer colour characteristics and Bridget works with the oil colour on its own terms using oil colour tests on canvas. So the final colour is often different from the acrylic. It is usually deeper and more vibrant in colour.' The acrylic undercoat of *Nataraja* was ruled on the edges with a ruling pen using thinned acrylic emulsion paint, mixed to the 'consistency of single cream', which was the consistency used for all acrylic coats (and also gouache for the studies). The colour was then filled in with a brush, though more recently the acrylic has been entirely hand-painted. 'When the acrylic has reached the required density (some colours require more coats than others) the final layer of oil colour is applied entirely by hand, using the acrylic edges as a guide. The malleability and flowing quality of oil paint means that with skill and practice a very fine edge can be achieved.' The precision of the edges becomes apparent when viewed at magnification (fig.146) and on close examination brushstrokes are just visible. Also seen in this detail is an example of a very rare occurrence in Riley's paintings, where one of the layers of paint does not entirely cover the previous layer. The small area of a slightly lighter green that is visible in the dark green area at the bottom-right corner of this detail is actually the acrylic emulsion underlayer, which was not covered with the final layer of oil paint.

Throughout her career, Bridget Riley has used most of the various types of synthetic paint as well as oil, although her options were often been restricted by what was available. However, Andrew Smith thinks it is possible to generalise about each choice of paint. 'All the mediums … were chosen as the best technical means available to achieve a certain visual result. In the earliest works the need was for a flat, matt, uninflected surface and this has remained important, although the need for intensity of colour has become increasingly vital'.

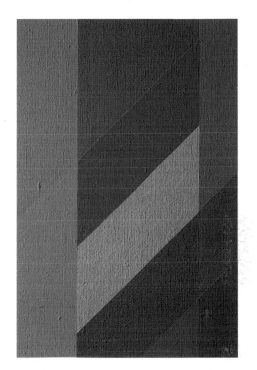

fig.146 Detail from *Nataraja* taken in raking light from the left.

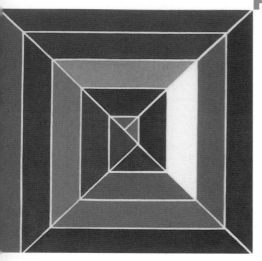

Frank Stella born 1936

Frank Stella recalls that, as a student in New York in the early 1950s, he often explored and speculated about the techniques of the Abstract Expressionists: 'how did Kline put down that colour? ... Why did Helen Frankenthaler use unsized canvas?'[1] Their large canvases and 'wholeness of gesture' inspired Stella to imitate them for a while before finding his own direction that became based on the concept 'that a good pictorial idea is worth more than a lot of manual dexterity'.[2] His work started to evolve as series of paintings that initially combined a simple design with bands of a single colour in which he 'tried for evenness, a kind of all-oneness, where intensity, saturation and density remained regular over the entire surface'.[3] His use of a regular pattern was his way of resolving 'the painterly problems of what to put here and there and how to do it to make it go with what was already there'.[4] Once the symmetry in the design had been established, 'the remaining problem was simply to find a method of paint application which followed and complemented the design solution. This was done by using the house painter's techniques and materials'.[5]

Stella's early series were painted in housepaints that 'were relatively glossy. They were normal household enamels ... I used mainly the ones that were being discounted – the colour would go out of style. I just took what the regular paint stores had to offer ... I took whatever was discounted for the day's special.' His use of commercial products expanded in the early 1960s to include paints designed primarily for other applications. The paintings from the 'Aluminum' series from 1961, were executed in a 'commercial aluminum paint' that was primarily intended for exterior use, but was also 'probably one of the things that was used for painting radiators'. The copper metallic paint, used for the subsequent series was a barnacle-inhibiting paint he had employed the previous summer on the hull of his father's boat.

Six Mile Bottom (fig.148) is one of the twelve paintings on shaped canvases that make up the Aluminum series. Stella had shown the artist Walter Darby Bannard preparatory sketches for the series in conven-

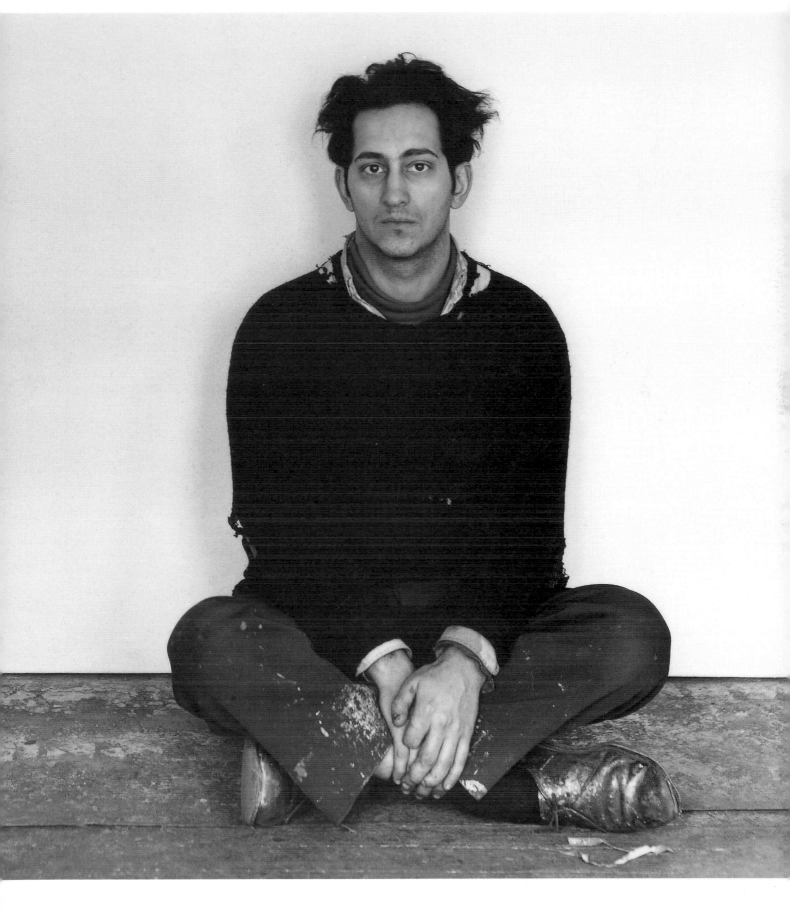

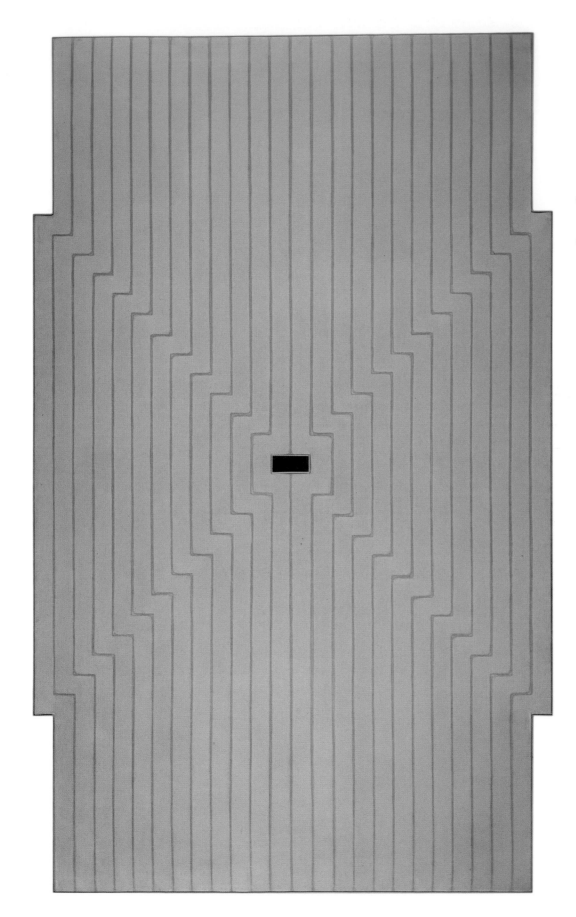

fig.148 *Six Mile Bottom*
1960, alkyd industrial paint
on canvas 300 x 182.2 cm.

tional rectangular format (see fig.149) and indicated his concern that the corner areas were superfluous to the composition. Bannard replied, 'Well, if you don't want them, then just take them away'.[6] Stella built the stretchers 'leaving out the part I didn't want. And once I started with the aluminum paintings, they kept suggesting more and more possibilities for shaped pictures.'[7] The stretcher was butt-ended together for reasons of convenience and speed. 'It looked OK, it was a quick way of doing it and I didn't want to make mitred corners. I didn't want to become a carpenter'. The resulting box-like structure was approximately three inches deep and set the surface of the painting off the wall. Stella used similar structures for his subsequent shaped works on canvas.

Stretching the canvas over the complicated shape of the structure was one of the more difficult parts of making the painting. In particular, there was 'a problem with the interior angles. You have to cut [the excess canvas] away. Eventually it could be rewoven, pieces put in it, but as it stands now, it's just cut out.' Stella had tried using board as a support, 'but it kills the paintings. I made a lot of small ones on wood. They looked terrible. We did one big one, a six-foot square one, and it looked terrible too. It just looks like it's been plastered down. It takes all the life out of the painting'. He also found that a painting on a solid support 'becomes hard to handle … you can't roll it up if it's on board', which became an important consideration with his larger works. He therefore chose to continue working on cotton canvas, 'the lightest and most economical' support.

Stella began *Six Mile Bottom* by drawing the stripes in pencil onto the stretched canvas, two and three-quarter inches apart, using a straight piece of lath as a hard edge. The Aluminum series was the first time that he had painted directly onto unprimed cotton canvas. Previously, Stella had primed his canvases but had observed that some types of paint were absorbed more into the primer, producing uneven surface gloss. Although he was not particularly concerned about this sinking effect, one of the reasons for not priming the canvases for the Aluminum series was an attempt to correct this. The yellow colour of the visible areas of canvas resembles an unpigmented priming, but the canvas was unsized: 'the colour is the bleed of the oil out of the paint'. The aluminium paint has a particularly high oil content compared to other types of alkyd paint, and was therefore especially likely to bleed. Stella accepted it as 'the problem with using unsized canvas'. The raking-light detail focusing on the centre of the painting (fig.150), reveals the texture of the unprepared cotton canvas where the yellow bleed of the oil has occurred. Another effect of the bleed from the paint can be observed across the surface when it is viewed into a raking light, as seen in fig.151. Some of the medium from the outer sections of each band of colour has bled into the canvas, resulting in a covering of paint that is high in aluminium content. The surface subsequently has a more reflective and lighter appearance.

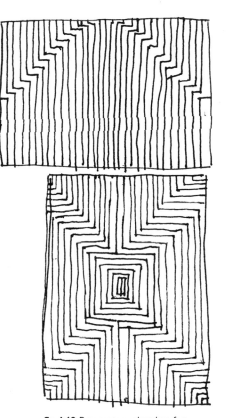

Mrs. Frank Stella
Quay Rd.
Ipswich, Mass.

fig.149 Preparatory sketches for
Six Mile Bottom, 1959, blue ink on paper
20.3 × 15.3 cm. Kunstmuseum, Basel

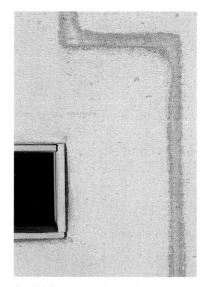

fig.150 Detail from *Six Mile Bottom*
taken in raking light from the left.

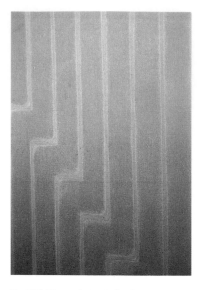

fig.151 The variation in binder content within each aluminium band is seen in this detail from *Six Mile Bottom*, taken *into* a raking light.

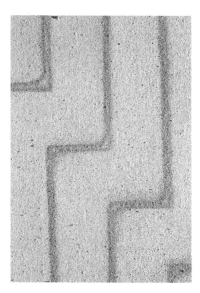

fig.152 A third detail from *Six Mile Bottom* taken in raking light from the right, showing the texture of the paint surface and exposed cotton canvas between the bands of aluminium paint.

Stella purchased the aluminium paint from a local hardware store. 'The aluminum surface had a quality of repelling the eye in the sense that you couldn't penetrate it very well … I felt that it had the character of being slightly more abstract.'[8] *Six Mile Bottom* is one of nine works in the series that were painted with an aluminium paint of a slightly lighter shade than that used for the other three. Stella preferred the lighter shade: 'the darker ones just looked different. I guess it didn't look quite as metallic'.

Stella applied the paint in 'just three or four coats onto the unsized canvas' using a house painter's brush two and a half inches wide. He used only the pencil lines as a guide in applying the paint bands, which have somewhat uneven edges as a result. It is often assumed that he used masking tape; he notes that '[mentally] everybody straightens them out, everybody wants to improve them', and that although the works are, 'silver and white. I'm sure most people think there's a white ground, even though it doesn't look that way. People make it into what they want'.

He used multiple-coat applications not only because 'one layer won't cover it' but also to build up a sufficiently high density in the metallic effect. The brushstrokes are still evident on the painting's surface and follow the direction of the bands, continuing at each turn in the pattern, setting up a gentle rhythm over the metallic surface (fig.152). Stella had realised in his early striped paintings that by using a high colour density it 'forces illusionistic space out of the painting',[9] even with a uniform and monochrome pattern that might be expected to appear extremely flat. The shimmering, metallic surface has 'its own kind of surface illusionism, its own self-contained space … And it holds itself in a nice way on the surface.'[10]

Later the same year, Stella began to paint with interior housepaints made by Benjamin Moore, an American paint company whose paints were considered to be of very high quality. The first series painted using these was named the 'Benjamin Moore' series. However, he continued to use these for the 'Mitred Mazes', a series consisting of twenty large canvases painted in 1962 and 1963, and the series to which *Hyena Stomp* (fig.153) belongs. Stella's choice of this paint was primarily an aesthetic one; he wanted 'to keep the paint as good as it was in the can … It had the nice dead kind of colour that I wanted'.[11] These were interior paints, designed as a matt finish for walls, as opposed to the metallic commercial paints he had used previously that were inherently more glossy and made for exterior use. Although alkyd resins normally confer gloss to a housepaint, matt alkyd paints can be produced by reducing the amount of resin binder relative to the pigment and extender content. The paint had a markedly different quality from artists' colours that suited the formalised, programmatic field of colour he wanted to project. Although he was aware of the artists' acrylic emulsion paints that were being introduced onto the market, he considered them too 'sophisticated or something'

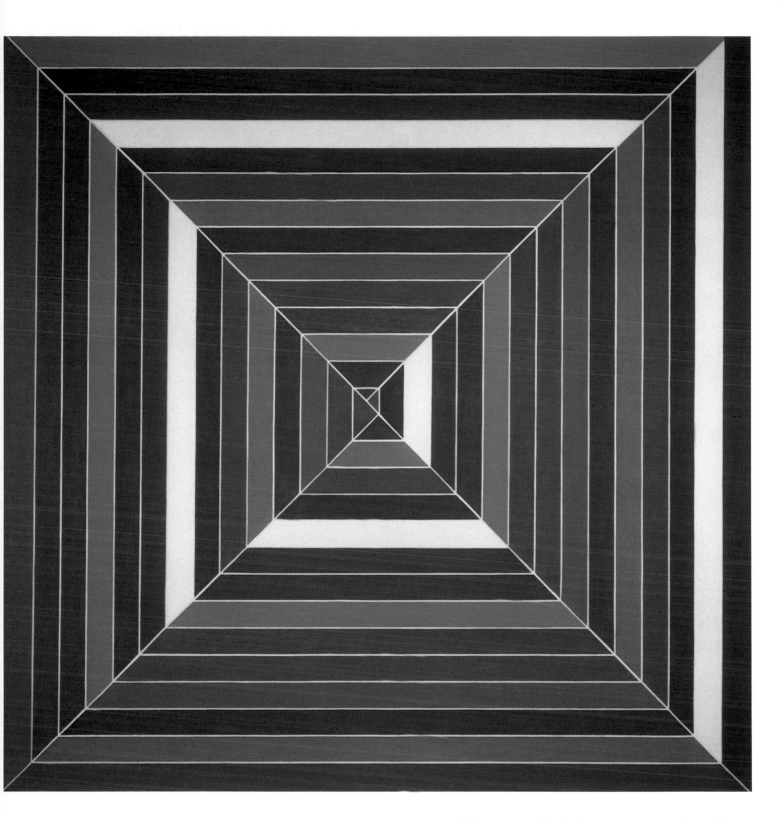

fig.153 *Hyena Stomp* 1962, alkyd housepaint on canvas 195.6 x 195.6 cm.

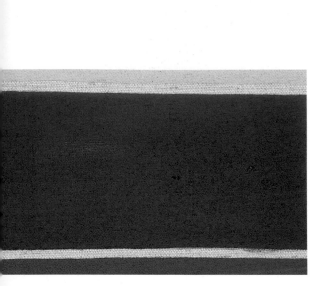

fig.154 Detail from *Hyena Stomp* showing traces of pencil lines between the bands.

and instead, chose to paint with what was more immediately available to him and also less expensive.

Hyena Stomp is a sequence of repeated combinations of coloured bands that spiral into the centre of the canvas. An array of optical tension is formed between each band and the various colours that surround it; the overall effect is a remarkable illusion of space and depth. The series was planned out in sketches, sometimes on tracing paper to enable Stella to repeat the same design with different groupings of colour. Drawings were made of the design, the colours indicated by notations. The pattern was drawn out in pencil onto the canvas, and little effort was made to remove the pencil lines completely after the colour had been applied. Fig.154 shows faint horizontal pencil lines on the bare areas of canvas between the painted bands. Built up in two to three layers of paint on the unsized cotton canvas, the paintings were, 'very symmetrical … and very all over'.[12]

Stella used six colours from the Benjamin Moore range: red, yellow, blue, green, orange and purple, the three primaries and their complements. These were used directly from the tin, 'and then I made half steps from the colours. I literally mixed the orange and the red to get this red-orange in between. So there was no attempt to adjust the colour, it was just a mechanical use of their colours.'

The bands of colour were applied with a house painter's brush, but the edges appear far more precise than in *Six Mile Bottom*. The absence of any bleed into the canvas was largely due to the relatively low binder content in these interior, matt housepaints. A close inspection of the diagonal borders of the coloured bands, especially when viewed in raking light (fig.155), reveals the sharp and slightly raised edges characteristic of masking tape. However, no such ridges are visible along the horizontal and vertical edges, indicating that these are painted freehand. In this detail and one taken in normal light (fig.156), the complete absence of brush-marks is observed in the bands, revealing that Stella was exploiting one of the main properties of interior paint, which is formulated to dry to a very flat finish.

As he progressed through further series of paintings, Stella began to explore the properties of other kinds of paint, which involved practical as well as aesthetic considerations. For example, in the series titled 'Notched V' and 'Running V', painted in 1964–5, he mixed metallic powder into a clear acrylic emulsion binder. He chose acrylic largely because he 'wanted to roll the paintings … You couldn't roll the oil-based paints with the metallic powder, I mean they would crack right away'. On this occasion, the practical consideration of being able to roll up the canvas outweighed his preference for the slight bleed that was given by the metallic alkyd paints. 'I didn't like [the emulsion] quite as much because it didn't have the bleed. The bleed really made it nicer'. Despite being the preferred choice of many artists, Stella found Liquitex acrylic emulsion paint to be 'just horrible. I used it for just about a day and then I threw it away … I think that was one of the most awful paints ever made.' Then, for a period in the early 1970s, Stella used Magna acrylic paint, for example on the series of large 'Concentric Square' paintings. 'Magna never had any problems. It was really a great paint. It was an oil [miscible] paint [and] it was an acrylic. I don't know if you could ask for anything more'. In particular, he found the paint 'easier to handle and for some reason more suitable to being in a bigger scale.'

During the early 1970s, Stella's painting style evolved in new ways. This occurred at a time of widespread talk about 'the death of painting'[13] when Stella witnessed a hesitancy among many of the 1960s abstract painters about the direction in which they should take their work. 'I was worried during the 'seventies that people would actually forget how to paint.'[14] Stella persisted in his method of working, researching through an idea in each series of paintings, taking it as far as he could, sometimes leading to further variations in the next series, or just allowing the idea to play itself out as he moved on to something else. 'By the early 'seventies I had more or less "had it" with the art world … As long as I felt confident about the new work, why not just do as I please.'[15]

Stella began to experiment with collage, initially onto stretched canvas. However, he soon discovered the impracticalities of this, especially the problem of the canvas warping under the weight of the collaged materials. He then found that by gluing canvas onto a panel of KachinaBoard (a heavy cardboard), which could be braced by rigid battens, he was able to glue a variety of materials of varying shapes and thickness onto the support. He proceeded to use foamcore as a support material, and then by the mid-1970s, aluminium alloy honeycomb, using a company of fabricators to cut and assemble his structures. 'It was a pretty natural way to translate foamcore, which was easy to work with, into another material.' The aluminium honeycomb panels, initially developed for use in the aircraft industry, combined strength and lightness, and could be shaped easily by cutting with a saw. The material made it possible for Stella to assemble works on a large scale.

This was not the first time that Stella had employed others in the production of his work. His use of assistants had begun in the mid-1960s, as the serial production of the 'Irregular Polygons' paintings increased in number. Their involvement in all aspects of the creation process allowed Stella to 'finish the paintings that I had it in my mind to do. But you know, it sounds a little dramatic, being an "art worker". I just wanted to do it and get it over with so I could go home and watch TV'.[16] His metal-relief structures were dependent on fabricators for their production, built in a factory as opposed to a studio environment, 'a place like a huge junk yard. There's so much available, it's hard to keep your hands off the things that

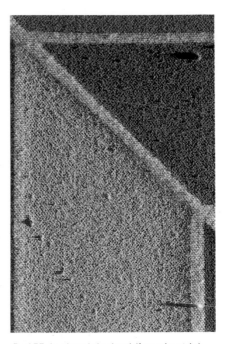

fig.155 A raking-light detail (from the right) of *Hyena Stomp* reveals the thinness of the paint film.

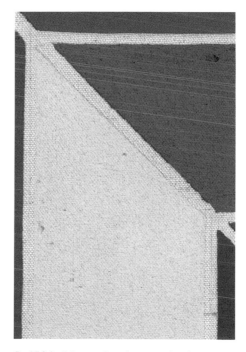

fig.156 Stella's use of masking tape for the diagonal borders can be seen in this detail.

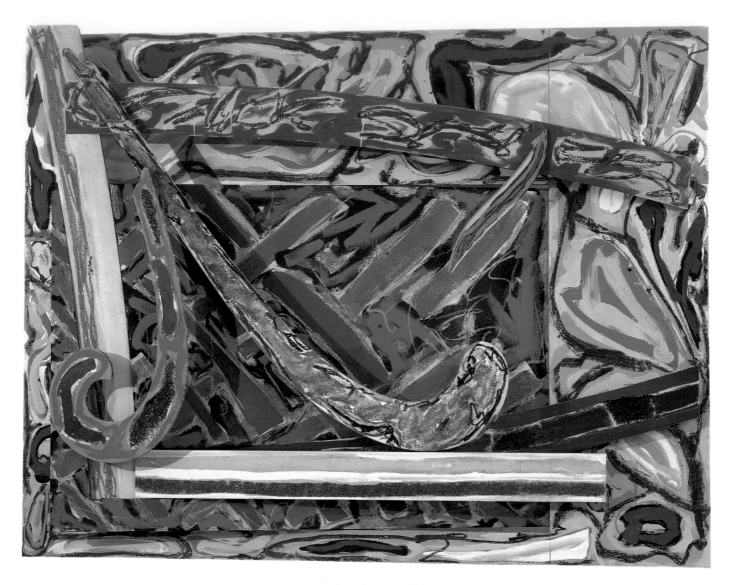

fig.157 *Guadalupe Island, Caracara* 1979, oil stick, industrial enamel paint and collage on aluminium honeycomb 238.1 x 307.3 x 45.7 cm.

go flying by you all the time. There's a tremendous physical, material turnover of things'.[17] But while labour was certainly required for the fabrication of the supports, it was Stella's hand that covered the surfaces in paint: 'my gesture is recorded in the painting'.[18]

Guadalupe Island, Caracara (fig.157) was painted in 1979 and belongs to a series of paintings entitled 'Exotic Birds'. The construction was first conceived by moving around a set of asymmetric French curves – the draftsman's templates that Stella collected – on a large piece of graph paper. Once he was satisfied with the motif, the shapes were marked out on the paper, which then became a working drawing for a number of small models. For *Guadalupe Island, Caracara* three early stages of the preparation are shown in figs.158–60. Fig.158 shows the design drawn in pencil on graph paper and fig.159 shows an initial maquette, assembled out of 'tycore' (a lightweight paper board), in which the shapes of the individual cut-out pieces are based on the initial graph paper design. The next stage was to construct a foamcore maquette, shown in fig.160. It

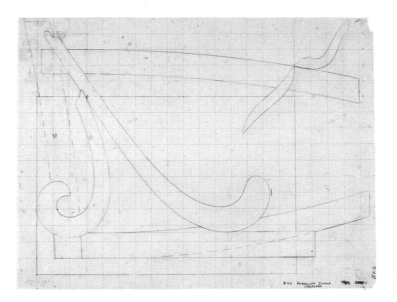

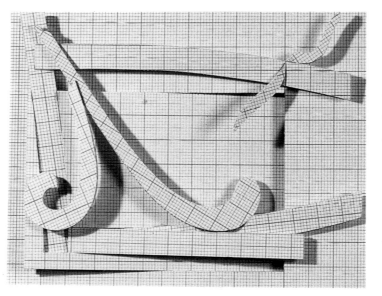

figs. 158–60 Preparatory
works for *Guadalupe Island,
Caracara* 1979. The first is
pencil on paper, the second
tycore and graph paper, the
third pencil on foamcore.
All 43.2 x 55.8 cm.
Courtesy of the artist

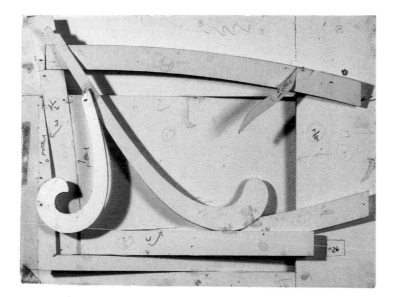

was at this point that Stella removed the small relief piece that had been located in the top right corner of the earlier models. Stella then arranged for a commercial fabricator to construct the model out of aluminium honeycomb following his prototype. 'I make the models. The models go to a factory where they are built and in that part I don't have much say. They're following a model that I'm giving them and then I'll go and check

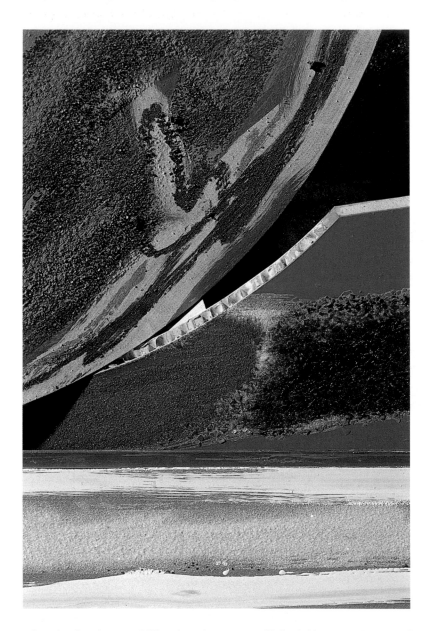

fig.161 Detail from *Guadalupe Island, Caracara* taken in raking light from the left, showing the different edges of the aluminium panels and a variety of textures in the paint surface.

what they've done and I'll make adjustments if I don't like something, or if they've made mistakes.'[19] Stella wrote a number of instructions to the fabricators on the foamcore model (fig.160), such as the thickness of each panel (given in inches) and some additional cuts (the vertical dotted lines that run down the right-hand side of the rear panel). He also indicated how some of the aluminium honeycomb panel edges should be filled. Three different types of edging were used as 'it gets a little boring when they're all the same'. Those marked 'open' were to be left with the honeycomb centre showing, those marked 'potted' were to be filled with an epoxy resin ('a kind of auto[mobile] body putty') and those marked 'U' were to be filled with a strip of U-section aluminium channelling. Fig.161 shows the three types of edging in the final work. The open and potted options are seen in the upper edge of the curved piece, whereas the aluminium channelling was used in the top edge of the horizontal piece. Stella could also request various surfaces on the metal sheets. 'I like the metal surfaces because you can etch them and so [for example] I can bite into the metal and have a rough surface.'[20]

The actual painting was a spontaneous process. 'I never thought about painting until I got into the studio and [the structure] was taken apart. Even then it just got thrown into the stew with all the other paintings.' The construction was disassembled and then each piece was painted separately. 'Ninety percent of it was done flat' on the floor as separate pieces. 'Then it would get put together and I might paint on it [further], but [only a] relatively small amount compared to the whole thing.' Different types of paint and other materials were incorporated into the piece, and various kinds of alkyd, industrial acrylic and epoxy resins have been identified through analysis. However, Stella recalls that 'mostly I was using oil sticks and industrial enamel paints ... [such as] two part epoxies made for metals ... We had a pretty strong palette of epoxy paints ... [but] if I wanted a stronger [colour] I'd paint an oil paint or something over it' once the epoxy had dried. Stella recalls that pearlescent colours were also used, in particular a 'funky paint that's underneath most of the oil stick ... It has a different texture [so] you could scumble the paint stick on it'. The fluid consistency of the industrial paint and the waxy lines of the oil stick drawn over it, are combined with other materials, the texture of which is revealed in raking light (fig.162). Whatever else was lying around the studio could also be incorporated into the wet surface. 'We had cans of those sequin things and [pigment] powders ... We did throw a lot of ground glass around into the clear [binder].' In the lower metal panel shown in fig.161, ground glass is distributed in a band along the section. In addition, areas of bare etched-metal surface were deliberately left exposed in places to show through the scumbled brushwork.

In 1982, Stella and his assistant Earl Childress began work on another series of complex metal reliefs employing a new motif, 'Cones and Pillars'. Stella recalls: 'They represented a slightly aggressive step backwards ... there was more surface to paint on. Not only because of the surface area of the big, hollow aluminium forms, but they [also] had a canvas background.' Painted in 1984, *Salto nel mio Sacco* (fig.163) belongs to this series. The canvas background is the area of the work displaying broad cream, red and blue brushstrokes over a white priming. As with *Guadalupe Island, Caracara*, the construction of the piece was first established with drawings

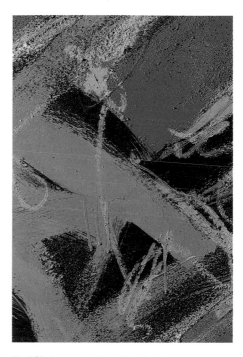

fig.162 A second raking-light detail (from the left) of *Guadalupe Island*, showing the different applications and texture of painting materials used.

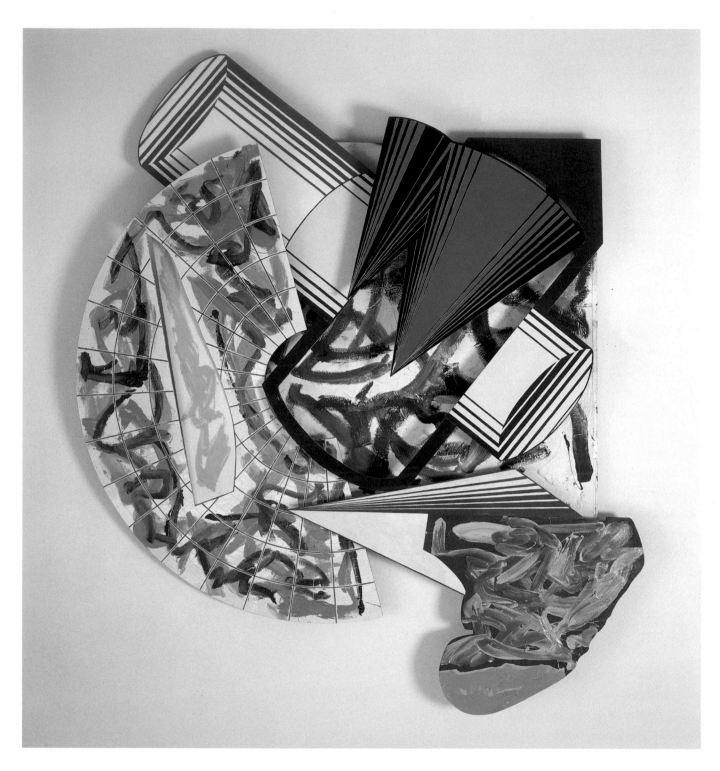

fig.163 *Salto nel mio Sacco* 1984, oil and industrial enamel paint on etched magnesium, aluminium honeycomb and canvas 373.5 x 325 x 39 cm.

and models. The various sections were then taken apart for the painting stage and reassembled to produce the finished work. An indication of the complexity of the structure is given in fig.169, a view taken from the left side and looking up at the assembled work. Stella explains that the canvas 'is not stretched [but] fitted' over an aluminium panel. 'It's quite cute, it has an edge and it's sewn and it fits over the aluminum.' The relief pieces were made from aluminium honeycomb panels, onto most of which were attached sheets of etched magnesium to give additional relief to their surfaces.

Prior to painting, the canvas was 'coated with fibreglass', followed by a layer of white artists' oil paint, used straight from the tube, which covers most of the canvas surface apart from the occasional area where the pale brown fibreglass remains visible. By contrast each of the aluminium/magnesium relief sections was laid flat and primed first with a layer of the epoxy resin and then a thin layer of white industrial enamel paint (again based on epoxy resin). The fluid consistency of the white priming paint and the horizontal orientation of the panels during this stage are evident by the drips visible around the edges of some of the sections, as seen in fig.164. Once the white primers had dried, the other colours were applied. On most of the relief pieces the uniform areas of colour consist of various types of industrial enamel paints, although the gestural brushwork visible in many areas was executed in oil. With some colours, most notably the bright yellow, the paint did not flow quite as well compared to the smooth fluency of the gloss green applied alongside it. The raking-light detail of this section (fig.165) shows the drag of the brush marks in the yellow paint. Masking tape was also employed in those sections where oil paint was used alongside the high gloss enamel, as seen in the raised edges of the yellow paint. The artists' oil paint has been squeezed directly from the tube onto the surface in sections, and in some areas, 'driven right into the wet epoxy'. The combination of the glossy enamel, which often contained fluorescent pigments, and artists' oil paint sets up contrasts in the paint surface that for Stella 'are just meant to be this way, some of the choices are already made'.

Much of Stella's work has been characterised by the use of synthetic paint, including several types of housepaint and industrial coatings. His willingness to experiment with these products gave him a wide choice of paint, even before the introduction of acrylic, and was fundamental to his approach. Which paint to use was clearly an important consideration in his work, despite his claim that he 'usually uses whatever there is. I mean I'm not in the paint business'. The liberating aspect of having large volumes of cheap paint with which to work, prompted another way of thinking about painting that 'was economical … It was also pedestrian, which personally appealed to me. I opted to push through, to try for something like a house painter's technique.'[22]

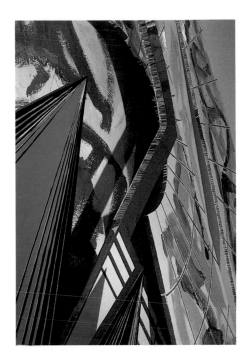

fig.164 Detail from *Salto nel mio Sacco* taken from the left side of the painting. It shows the complexity of the structure and some of the paint textures and consistencies.

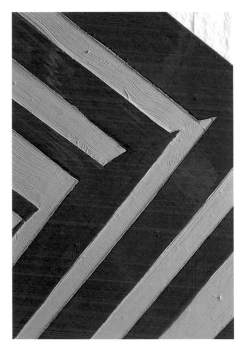

fig.165 A raking-light detail (from the right) of *Salto nel mio Sacco*, showing the yellow and green paint surfaces.

Andy Warhol 1928–1987

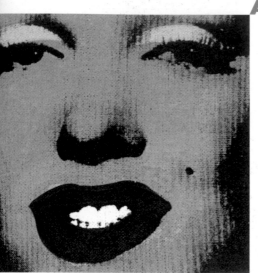

Andy Warhol initially established himself as a successful commercial artist. In the early 1960s he began making paintings of comic strips and magazine advertisements. By 1962, he was producing meticulous reproductions, in which he attempted to avoid artistic gesture, especially brushstrokes.

I still wasn't sure if you could completely remove all the hand gesture from art and become noncommittal, anonymous. I knew that I definitely wanted to take away the commentary of the gestures – that's why I had this routine of painting with rock and roll blasting the same song … The music blasting cleared my head out and left me working on instinct alone.[1]

Accordingly, he switched from oil paints to acrylic emulsion, which had been available in America for a few years and which tends to produce a flatter and more uniform paint film compared to oil colours.

The types of images depicted in these paintings closely resembled those of Roy Lichtenstein, and Warhol employed similar techniques, for example in the use of an opaque projector to transfer the image onto primed canvas. Warhol was unaware of the similarity in their work until early in 1962 when Ivan Karp, a gallery assistant at Leo Castelli's Gallery, pointed this out. 'Ivan had just shown me Lichtenstein's Ben Day dots and I thought, "Oh, why couldn't I have thought of that?" Right then I decided that since Roy was doing comics so well, that I would just stop comics altogether and go in other directions where I could come out first – like quantity and repetition.'[2]

Warhol experimented with various methods for the serial reproduction of his images, such as stencils and rubber stamps, at a time when he found it 'too much trouble to paint'.[3] He recognised such mechanical methods as representative of the time, and saw them as a way of taking 'art' to a far wider audience. The breakthrough came with the silk-screen. 'The rubber stamp method I'd been using to repeat images suddenly seemed so home-made; I wanted something stronger that gave more of an assembly-line effect.'[4] The printed effect created by a silk-screen was

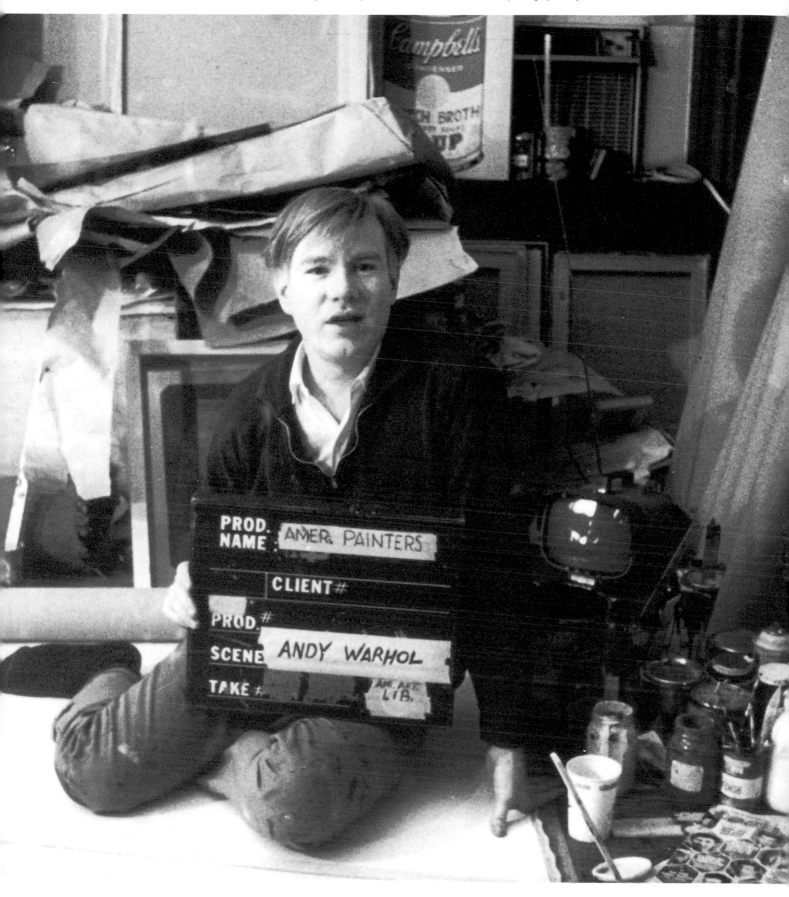

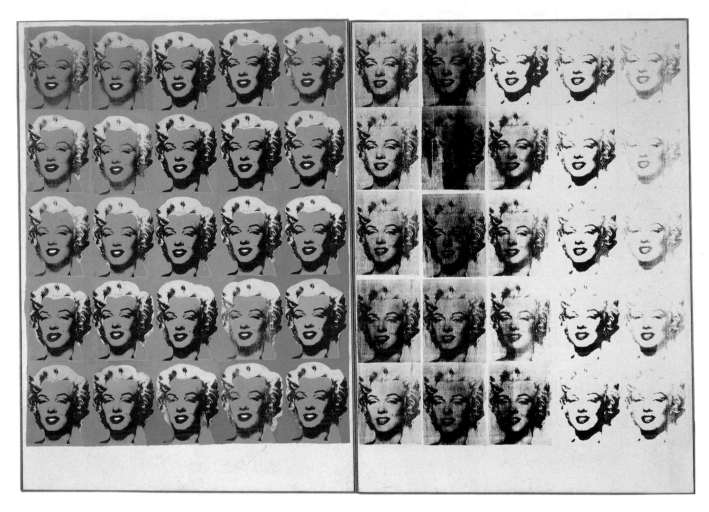

fig.167 *Marilyn Diptych* 1962, alkyd silk-screen ink
and acrylic emulsion on canvas 207 x 292.5 cm.

not only entirely appropriate in this respect, but it was also effective in further removing the sign of his hand. 'One of my assistants, or anyone else for that matter, can reproduce the design as well as I could.'[5]

The early silk-screens were hand-cut from an outline drawing, but the technique was quickly developed to incorporate black and white photographs using a photo-mechanical process.

With silk-screening you pick a photograph, blow it up, transfer it in glue onto silk, and then roll ink across it so the ink goes through the silk, but not through the glue. That way you get the same image, slightly different each time. It was all so simple – quick and chancy. I was thrilled with it.[6]

The 'glue' to which Warhol refers is a light-sensitive material that hardens when exposed to light so that it cannot be re-dissolved. The areas of glue that were left unexposed, however, can be re-dissolved and washed

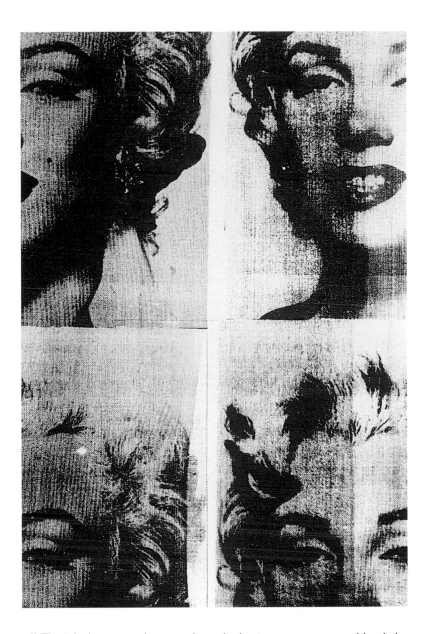

fig.168 Detail from the right canvas of *Marilyn Diptych*.

off. The ink that was subsequently applied using a squeegee could only be pushed through the silk fabric in areas where the glue had been washed off, and was deposited as a pattern of dots.

The *Marilyn Diptych* (fig.167) was one of Warhol's earliest paintings made using this process (the first work, *Baseball*, was produced in the same year). Warhol worked on the diptych alone, although he employed assistants throughout most of his career. His assistant at this time, Nathan Gluck, was employed only to work with him on the commercial assignments that continued to finance his work.[7] The photograph of Marilyn used for the *Marilyn Diptych* and other Marilyn pictures was taken from a publicity still for the film *Niagara*, made in 1952. The process of transferring the final image from the photograph to the silk-screen was carried out by a commercial silk-screen company who would make up the screen for him. The photograph was first enlarged and then a photostat was

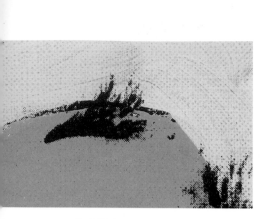

fig.169 A magnified area from the left canvas of *Marilyn Diptych*, where the lower silk-screened image is visible.

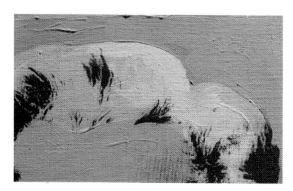

fig.170 A raking-light detail (from above) of *Marilyn Diptych*, showing the brushwork in the acrylic emulsion paint.

made on an acetate sheet. Subsequently, Warhol made some final adjustments to the image on the acetate before it was made into a screen, such as annotating where the photograph should be cropped. He also specified that the tonal contrast in the image should be maximised by removing areas of half-tone, which had the effect of further flattening the image.

For each part of the diptych, a piece of commercially primed linen canvas was laid out on the studio floor, having been cut to allow for the extra fabric needed for fixing it to the stretcher on completion.[8] For the right-hand (black and white) canvas, a grid was first drawn in pencil to indicate the intended positions of each screened image. This grid is still visible in many areas between the heads on the right-hand canvas (fig.168). Warhol then applied the screen twenty-five times using an oil-based, matt black, silk-screen ink made by the American paint company Naz-Dar. The ink was formulated to give a matt finish by reducing the amount of alkyd resin binder normally present in gloss silk-screen inks. The surface gloss could have been reduced further by incorporating extra solvent thinner, which would have the added benefit of ensuring that the ink flowed properly through the silk-screen.

The first image to have been screened onto the right-hand primed canvas was probably the one in the lower left corner. It is certainly the clearest printing. Warhol then appears to have worked up the left column, before continuing at the bottom of the next column. The resulting twenty-five heads show a huge amount of variation in terms of clarity and darkness. All the variations are due either to the fact that the screen was not cleaned thoroughly before each use, or to an inconsistency in the amount of ink used. Given that the heads become increasingly faint towards the right-hand side, it is probable that no additional ink was added to the screen. In the second column from the left, however, the images are very dark indeed, indicating an excess of ink. This can cause the ink to run under the screen so it smudges, or clog the pores in the fabric, resulting in a faint transference of the imprint of the fabric onto the image. The latter has occurred along the second column on this canvas, where the image is almost obliterated. In some heads, the squeegee was pressed at least twice over the screen. The lower-left head in fig.168 shows an upper application with a curved right edge, caused by the edge of the squeegee. No such curve was made in the initial screen print, which, despite being much fainter, remains visible. However, Warhol was unconcerned by the irregularities that occurred when working by hand and when Gluck later suggested a method of perfecting the registration for a later portrait of Elizabeth Taylor, 'Andy couldn't be bothered with this ... [he] would say, "I like it that way", and that's how it went'.[9]

Although the left-hand canvas appears to consist of screened images applied over areas of coloured paint, in fact it was started in exactly the same way as the right-hand one. Here, the initial twenty-five silk-screened images (applied directly onto the primed canvas) were the equivalent of an underdrawing, guiding Warhol to where the areas of colour should be painted. Once the silk-screen ink had dried the colours were applied by brush. The paint is all Liquitex acrylic emulsion, whose rapid drying qualities would have been an important property in the process, enabling him to apply the final silk-screen layer soon after. However, in the few areas where no paint was applied, this lower screen print remains visible. Fig.169 shows a section of the lower silk-screen image, visible between the purple and yellow colours. The section mimics the shape of the hair 'shadow' from the upper screen, although it can be seen that the lower screen was positioned slightly higher than the upper one and that additional dots were applied through the lower one.

Unlike some of his earlier works, where Warhol attempted to hide his brushwork, in this painting they are extremely apparent, particularly when viewed in a raking light (fig.170). They become even more visible when the painting is photographed using a film sensitive to infrared radiation (fig.171), which can penetrate a painting's surface more effectively than visible light. In this work it can reach the black ink of the initial screen print if the acrylic emulsion paint above it is sufficiently thin, so the IR image appears darker in areas where the paint is thinner. Fig.171 shows that the black ink is present beneath most areas of paint, which suggests that it was partially dissolved by the wet acrylic emulsion paint.

Examination of the painting's surface under raking light helps deduce the order of paint application. The first colour to be applied was the light green of Marilyn's collar and eye-shadow, followed by the violet paint used for the face. In the top-right corner of the detail (fig.170), the violet clearly lies over the green. The yellow for the hair was painted next, which can be seen to overlap the violet of the face. The red lips and white mouth were then added, followed by the orange background.

Warhol often used pure colour directly from the tube, but sometimes modified it with varying amounts of titanium white paint. Fig.170 shows two different shades of yellow that were used for the hair; a larger quantity of white paint would have been added to produce a lighter shade. Mark Lancaster, an assistant working at the Factory during the summer of 1964, recalls watching Warhol preparing his materials for painting.

Andy was one day found kneeling on the floor with tubes of acrylic paint, bits of canvas, brushes and a can of water … He spent several hours mixing paints – yellow, brown, ochre, white – making a vaguely off-white creamy colour, hardly a colour at all, one thought. But he would not stop until it was 'right'. This was the background as it were for the silk-screened image to be added.[10]

The final layer is made up of the same silk-screened image repeated in the same matt black silk-screen ink over the coloured images (fig.170). These still vary in darkness and clarity, but not in such an extreme way as those on

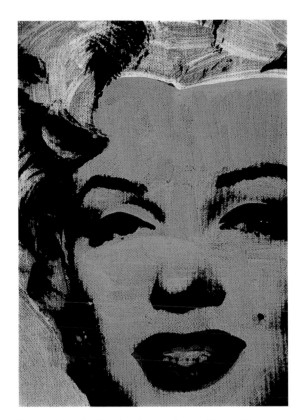

fig.171 A detail of *Marilyn Diptych* taken on infrared film.

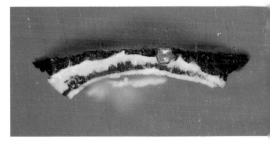

fig.172 Cross-section of paint from the lower left painted head in *Marilyn Diptych*, photographed at 200 x magnification. There are two distinct applications of black silk-screen ink.

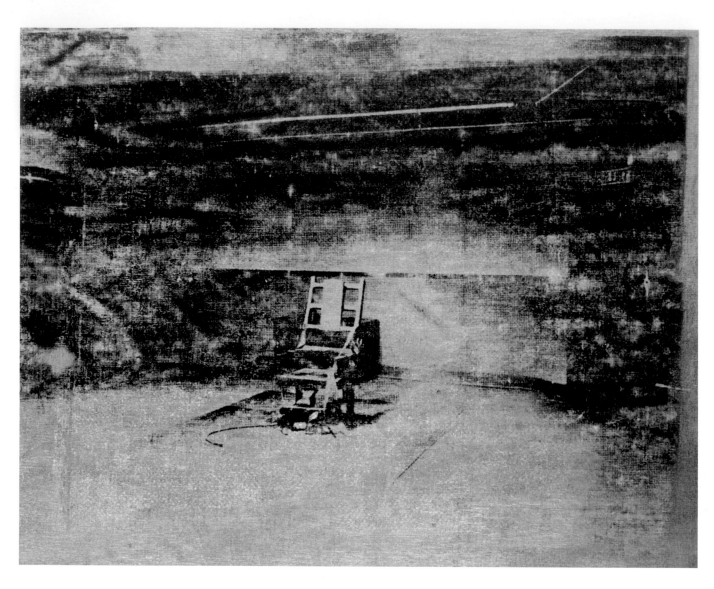

fig.173 *Electric Chair* 1964, acrylic solution and acrylic silk-screen ink on canvas 56.2 x 71.1 cm.

the right-hand canvas. The overall layer structure can be seen in fig.172, which shows a cross-section taken from the left edge of the lower left head, where the yellow hair is clearly covered by the upper black silk-screen. The two shades of yellow paint are clearly visible, with the lighter shade applied over the deeper shade. Working down through the layers, a second black layer is visible, which corresponds to the initial black silk-screened image, and beneath this lies the white of the commercial priming layer.

This 'double-screen' technique was used in the coloured *Marilyn* and *Liz* paintings dating from mid-1962 to late 1963. After that date, Warhol discovered methods for transferring an image onto canvas that did not require a first screen to mark out areas of colour. He would simply make a pencil drawing of the image to be transferred onto the primed canvas. This could be carried out either by tracing the image, using an opaque projector, or by making stencils for each colour, cut from the appropriate area in the acetate. This was a much cleaner system that avoided any pick-up of the initial silk-screen ink by the acrylic emulsion paint.

Warhol had stopped using the double-screen technique by the time he employed Gerard Malanga in the summer of 1963. Malanga, a graduate student with previous experience of working with silk-screens, was Warhol's first assistant to work specifically on the screened images and frequently transferred the image to the canvas. Malanga reported that when working with Warhol on the early portraits, 'I would put the tracing paper on top of the acetate and trace the shapes, the hair, the eyes, the eyebrows and the lips'. The outlines were then transferred onto the canvas 'by pressing along the acetate ... and then I would take the masking tape and create sections, or areas, or shapes ... based on those lines'. He was also frequently Warhol's photo researcher, finding images in magazines and newspapers, and suggesting ideas. Warhol 'was never embarrassed about asking someone, literally, "What should I paint?" because Pop comes from the outside and how is asking someone for ideas any different from looking for them in a magazine?'[11]

For works with a single colour beneath the screen, it was not necessary to transfer the image before applying the paint. In *Electric Chair* (fig.173), painted in 1964, the image has been simply screened onto an acrylic-based silver-coloured background. Warhol had been excited by the 'Aluminum' paintings of Frank Stella which he had seen exhibited in 1960, for which Stella had employed an aluminium industrial paint. Warhol is known to have applied the aluminium paint by brush as well as by spraying it; here, the visible brushstrokes (see fig.174) confirm that it was a brushed coat, 'either a silver Liquitex, or a regular silver paint from a hardware store'.

For the series of Electric Chair paintings, Warhol employed the same anonymous photograph of the chair, which he considered would eventually become nullified of meaning through repetition. The image varied

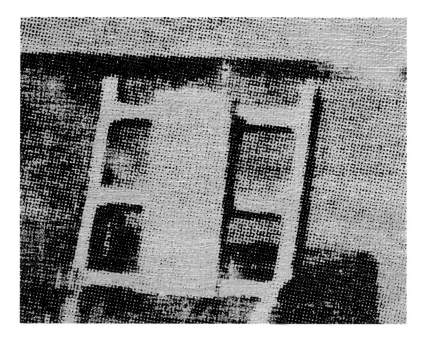

fig.174 Detail from *Electric Chair* taken in raking light from above, showing brushmarks in the aluminium paint.

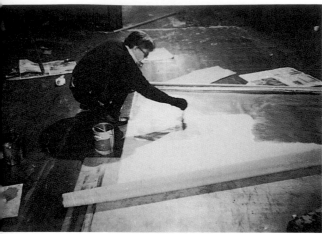

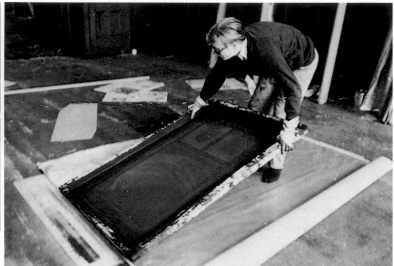

fig.175 Warhol in his studio in 1963 applying aluminium paint onto a large piece of unstretched canvas in preparation for the *Tunafish Disaster* series. Figs.175–80 photographed by Edward Wallowitch.

fig.176 The silk-screen is placed onto the painted canvas.

fig.177 Having poured some black silk-screening ink onto the screen, Warhol drags the squeegee across it.

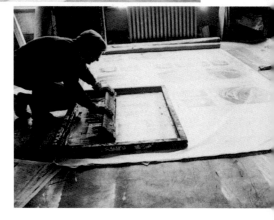

only in the cropping. Different sized photo-screens were made up for re-use in new works. For *Tunafish Disaster*, produced in the previous year, various stages of the silk-screening process were photographed. The materials and techniques were similar to those used for the 'Electric Chair' series. Fig.175 shows Warhol painting a large piece of unstretched canvas, as yet uncut from the roll, with aluminium paint on a wide, house-painter's brush. The paint was applied as a fairly thick, single coat, and after it had dried thoroughly, Warhol placed the silk-screen onto the painted canvas, as seen in fig.176. The screen was attached to a simple wooden batten frame, which would have kept it taut and acted as a tray into which the ink was poured. Fig.177 shows the silk-screen in place

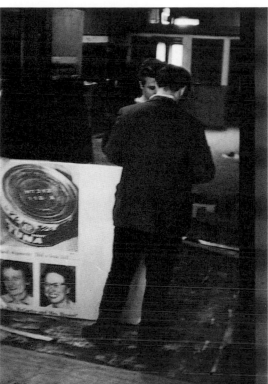

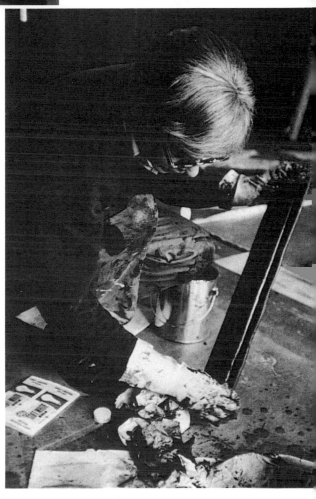

fig.180 Warhol cleans the squeegee
in preparation for the next printing.

fig.179 Warhol and Malanga
stretch the canvas.

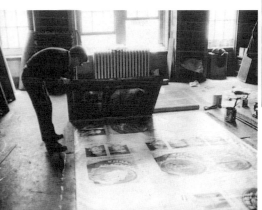

fig.178 The screen is carefully
removed and the result is inspected.

with the ink poured onto it. Warhol is dragging the squeegee across the
surface of the silk-screen, pushing the ink through the holes in the fabric
onto the painted canvas beneath. By the time this photograph was taken,
Warhol had already made a number of screen prints further down the
roll of canvas. In fig.178 the screen is being carefully removed from the
canvas while Warhol inspects the result. Each image will then have been
cut from the rest of the canvas, and attached to a stretcher. Fig.179 shows
Warhol and Malanga stretching the canvas and in fig.180 Warhol is cleaning the squeegee in preparation for the next printing.

Four years later, Warhol produced a series of self-portraits, based on a
photograph of the artist in a pensive pose. Malanga assisted him in mixing

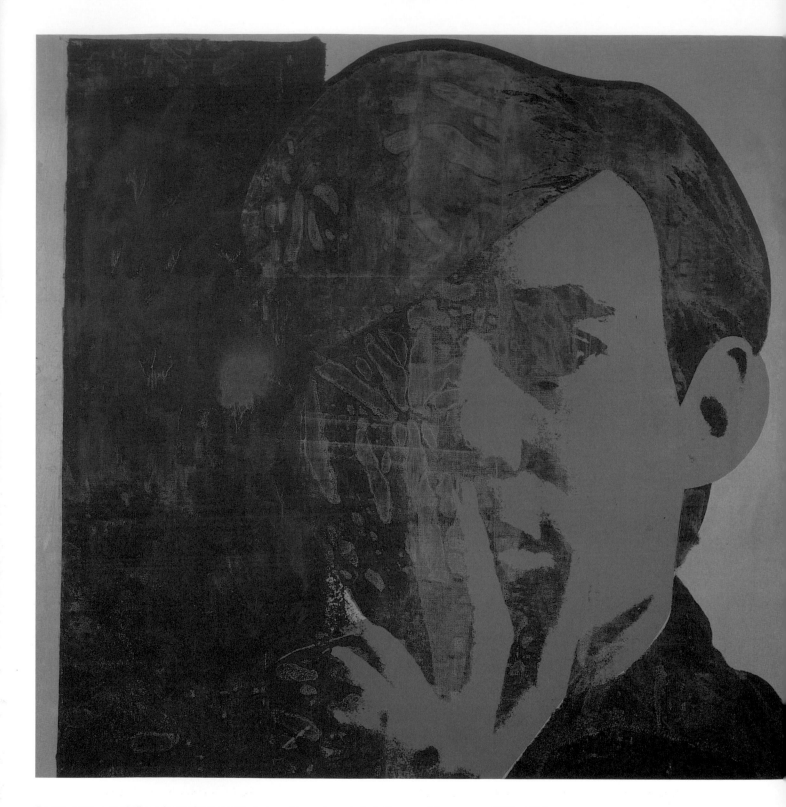

fig.181 *Self-Portrait* 1967, acrylic emulsion, acrylic-vinyl emulsion paint and alkyd silk-screen ink on canvas 183.2 × 183.2 cm.

the colours to the right consistency – 'with the water-based paints, we wanted to thin it out a little bit'. In *Self-Portrait* (fig.181), painted in 1967, the salmon-pink background colour is a thin layer of Liquitex acrylic emulsion, diluted with water and brushed over the primed face of the canvas. An outline of the head, eyes and hand was made in pencil over the colour, using either a tracing or an acetate stencil. These lines are still visible in a number of places.

Malanga recalls that the areas to be painted were then divided into sections with masking tape. 'Andy and I would paint in by hand with a brush the different colours that we wanted with the water-based Liquitex.' In this painting the light-blue colour used for Warhol's skin is an acrylic emulsion paint (Liquitex) although the red paint used for the highlights in his hair has been analysed as a acrylic-vinyl emulsion (probably New Masters). Analysis of the blue acrylic paint also revealed the presence of a small amount of thickening agent, such as an acrylic gel medium. This would have increased the consistency of the pure acrylic to that of the acrylic-vinyl paint, making the brushmarks clearly visible in both colours (fig.182). Once the paint had dried, the tape was gently peeled away from the shape, leaving the characteristic sharp, slightly raised edges seen in the red area in this detail. Each area was painted one section at a time to allow the paint to dry before the tape could be re-applied to the surface; 'in this way, when we painted in the next area it would abut seamlessly'.

This work differs from the others in the series in that the silk-screen layer consists of two colours, applied through the same screen. This was probably so that the deep-pink final layer (which is a slightly transparent colour) would show up more strongly against the cadmium-red under-layer. The first silk-screen colour was a light off-white, followed by the very glossy deep pink ('enamel') ink. The two screened applications seem to match up perfectly, which would have necessitated accurate reference marks.

Andy and I would lay the screen down on the canvas, trying to line up the registration with the marks we'd made where the screen would go. Then oil-based paint was poured into a corner of the screen's frames and I would push the paint across the mesh surface with a squeegee. Andy would grab the squeegee still in motion and continue the process of pressuring the paint through the screen from his end. We'd lift the screen and I would swing it away from the painting and start cleaning it with paper towels soaked in a solution called Varnolene. If this was not done immediately, the remaining paint would cake up and clog the pores.[12]

Varnolene is a turpentine substitute, which was also used 'to thin out the ink if we thought it was too thick'.

Warhol still used the silk-screen inks made by Naz-Dar, and the significant difference in gloss between the pink used here and the black used in

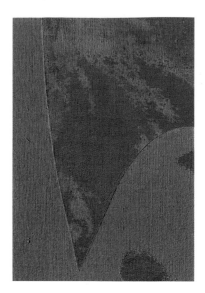

fig.182 Detail from *Self-Portrait* (1967) taken in raking light from the left, showing evidence of the masking techniques used for applying the emulsion paint.

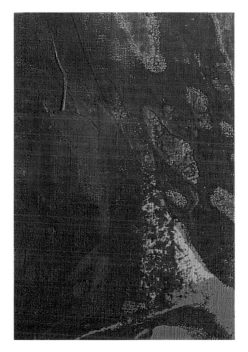

fig.183 A second raking-light detail (from the right) of *Self Portrait* reveals the variation in surface effects made by the pink silk-screen ink.

fig.184 Detail of *Self-Portrait* (1986) taken in partial raking light from the right, showing the precision of the black silk-screened dots.

Marilyn Diptych was due to the presence of considerably more alkyd binder in the ink. A large amount of ink appears to have been applied to the screen and the pitted bubbles that are visible in many areas suggest it was vigorously mixed before use. In many areas it has wrinkled or run down the surface in dribbles (fig.183); it was also responsible for several blotchy areas. This was, according to Malanga

a technical accident … that's created when you're silk-screening and there's too much ink on the screen and when you put it down you're putting down a big blotch of ink that's already coming from the screen before you've actually silk-screened through it … That wasn't really the way it was suppose to be.

However, nothing silk-screened was rejected: 'we embraced the mistakes'.

Warhol continued to employ silk-screening techniques in his paintings until his death in 1987. The technique used for *Self-Portrait* (fig.185), painted in 1986, is typical of his later works. The red acrylic emulsion paint was applied to a piece of unstretched canvas that was stapled to the wall of his studio (a ladder was used to reach the upper half of the painting). The canvas was then spread out on the floor and the portrait was silk-screened with black, gloss silk-screening ink that was bound in an alkyd resin. A detail of the side of his nose is seen in fig.184, which shows the flat, neat surface of the silk-screened image. By the mid-1980s his screened images had become noticeably neater and more precise. As Warhol said in the mid-1960s: 'If you want to know all about Andy Warhol, just look at the surface of my paintings and me, and there I am. There's nothing behind it.'[13]

fig.185 *Self-Portrait* 1986, acrylic emulsion paint and alkyd silk-screen ink on canvas 203.2 x 203.2 cm.

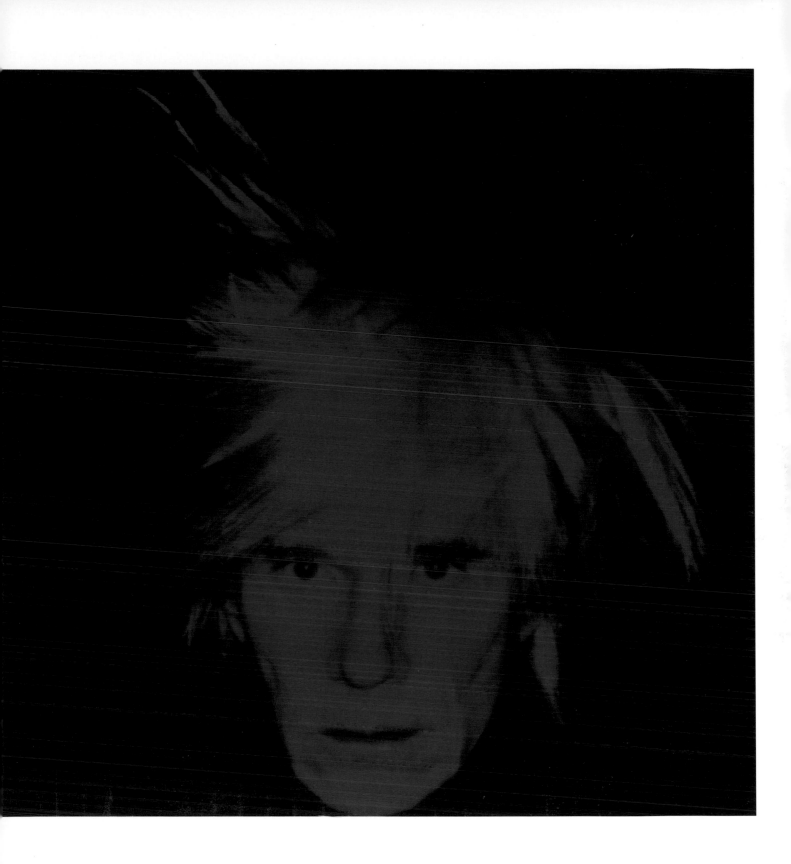

Notes

Introduction

1 Pollock quoted in a taped interview with William Wright for presentation on the Sag Harbor radio station, but never transmitted, 1950. Reprinted in Hans Namuth, *Pollock Painting*, New York 1978, n.p.

2 Kenneth Noland quoted in a videotaped interview with Carol Mancusi-Ungaro and Leni Potoff at the Museum of Fine Arts, Houston, 12 November 1993.

3 Diane Waldman, 'Color, Format and Abstract Art: An Interview with Kenneth Noland', *Kenneth Noland*, exh. cat., Salander O'Reilly Galleries, Inc., New York 1989, p.35.

4 Gertrude Stein, *The Autobiography of Alice B. Toklas*, New York 1961, p.154 (originally published New York 1933).

5 Alex Horn, 'Jackson Pollock: The Hollow and the Bump', *Carleton Miscellany*, no.7, Northfield, Minn., Summer 1966, pp.80–7.

Modern Paints

1 Correspondence with the Tate Gallery, 8 July 1995.

2 David Alfaro Siqueiros, 'Como se pinta un mural', *Cuernavaca, Edición del Taller Siqueiros*, transl. Jan Marontate, 1951. Reproduced in Jan Marontate, 'Synthetic Media and Modern Painting: A Case Study in the Sociology of Innovation', unpublished Ph.D thesis, Université de Montréal 1996.

3 David Alfaro Siqueiros, 'Muere el Fresco y Nace el Duco', *Me llamaban el Coronelazo (Memorias)*, Grijalbo, Mexico 1977, pp.314–15 (posthumous publication of memoirs dictated to Julio Scherer García while in Lecumberri prison in 1960–4, edited by Angélica Arenal de Siqueiros). Transl. Jan Marontate, reproduced in Marontate 1996.

4 B.H. Friedman, 'An Interview with Lee Krasner Pollock', *Jackson Pollock: Black and White*, exh. cat., Marlborough-Gerson Gallery, Inc., New York 1969, pp.7–10. Reprinted in Namuth 1978.

5 Pollock quoted in a taped interview with William Wright for presentation on the Sag Harbor radio station, but never broadcast, 1950. Reprinted in Namuth 1978.

6 Pablo Picasso, letter to Daniel Henry Kahnweiler, 20 June 1912, Catalogue Donation Louise et Michel Leiris, Collection Kahnweiler-Leiris, Centre Georges Pompidou, 22 November 1984–28 January 1985, p.169.

7 Françoise Gilot and Carlton Lake, *Life with Picasso*, Paris 1965, p.128.

8 Susan C. Lake, 'The Relationship between Style and Technical Procedure: Willem de Kooning's Paintings of the Late 1940s and 1960s', Ph.D thesis, University of Delaware, Ann Arbor, Mich., University Mircofilms 1999.

9 Gillian Ayres quoted in an interview with the authors, 22 June 1999.

10 Ibid.

11 Sidney Nolan quoted in a radio interview with Colin MacInnes, 'The Search for an Australian Myth', 4 July 1957.

12 Noël Barber, *Conversations with Painters*, London 1964, p.99.

13 Kenneth Noland quoted in a videotaped interview with Carol Mancusi-Ungaro and Leni Potoff at the Museum of Fine Arts, Houston, 12 November 1993.

14 Transcript of an interview with Leonard Bocour, tape nos.30–3, New York, 10 February 1979, p.6. Morris Louis Papers and Morris Louis Estate Papers, Archives of American Art, Smithsonian Institution.

15 Ibid., p.3.

16 See note 13.

17 Bert Marshall, unpublished interview with Henry Levinson, Hallandale, Florida, 30 November 1986.

18 Helen Frankenthaler quoted in Gene Baro, 'The Achievement of Helen Frankenthaler', *Art International*, September 1967, p.33.

19 Henry Geldzahler, 'An Interview with Helen Frankenthaler', *Artforum*, October 1965, p.38.

20 Typescript of an interview with Helen Frankenthaler by John Jones, 1965, p.1. Reprinted in John Elderfield, *Frankenthaler*, New York 1989, p.166.

21 *David Hockney: Paintings, Prints and Drawings 1960–1970*, exh. cat., Whitechapel Art Gallery, London 1970, pp.11–12.

Patrick Caulfield

1 Patrick Caulfield quoted in a taped interview with Bryan Robertson, *Chicken Kiev by Candlelight*, Lecon Arts, 1988–90.

2 Ibid.

3 Ros Mitchelmore, 'Patrick Caulfield: A Touch of Realism', *The Artist's and Illustrators Magazine*, no.1, Oct. 1986, p.13.

4 Ibid.

5 Robertson 1988–90.

6 Mitchelmore 1986, p.11.

7 Robertson 1988–90.

8 Ibid.

9 Marco Livingstone, *Patrick Caulfield, Paintings 1963–81*, exh. cat., Tate Gallery, Walker Art Gallery, London 1981, p.15.

10 Mitchelmore 1986, p.11.

11 Patrick Caulfield in a letter to Christopher Finch, June 1969, printed in Christopher Finch, *Patrick Caulfield*, Harmondsworth 1971, p.59.

12 Robertson 1988–90.

13 Livingstone 1981, p.28.

14 Mitchelmore 1986.

15 Robertson 1988–90.

16 Ibid.

Richard Hamilton

1 Christopher Finch, *Image as Language: Aspects of British Art 1950–1968*, Harmondsworth 1969, p.35.

2 Richard Hamilton, Interview with Jo Crook and Tim Green, Tate Gallery, 16 October 1996.

3 Richard Hamilton, *Collected Words, 1953–1982*, London 1982, p.65.

4 Richard Hamilton, Interview with Jo Crook and Rosanna Eadie, Tate Gallery, 12 June 1992.

5 Richard Hamilton in conversation with Sarat Maharaj, taped interview, Lecon Arts 1990–1.

6 Ibid.

7 Hamilton 1982, p.32.

8 Ibid., p.135.

9 Ibid., p.36.

10 See note 2.

11 Ibid.

12 Correspondence with Tate Gallery, 1 January 1965.

13 Ibid.

14 See note 4.

15 Hamilton 1982, p.32.

16 Unpublished transcript of Richard Hamilton talking about his works in the 1973 Guggenheim retrospective exhibition, Tate Gallery Conservation files, p.8.

17 Ibid.

18 Ibid.

19 Conversation with Christopher Finch and James Scott, Maya Film Productions, 1968. Unpublished pre-edited transcript of tape made for James Scott's film.

David Hockney

Unreferenced quotes are taken from Nikos Stangos (ed.), *David Hockney by David Hockney*, London 1979; reprinted in paperback in 1986.

1 Marco Livingstone, *David Hockney*, new enlarged ed., London 1996, p.207.

2 Correspondence with Tate Gallery, 15 August 1963.

3 Correspondence with Conservation Department, Tate Gallery, January 1982.

4 Ibid.

5 Ibid.

6 Ibid.

7 Ibid.

8 *David Hockney: Paintings, Prints and Drawings, 1960–1970*, exh. cat., Whitechapel Art Gallery, London 1970, pp.11–12.

9 Ibid.

John Hoyland

1 Thomas Maloon, 'Hoyland Retrospectively' in *John Hoyland: Paintings 1967–79*, exh. cat., Arts Council tour 1979–80, pp.33–4.

2 John Hoyland quoted in William C. Seitz, *Hans Hofmann*, with selected writings by the artist, exh. cat., Museum of Modern Art, New York 1963, p.27.

3 Adrian Searle, 'John Hoyland', *Artlog*, no.3, 1979.

4 Ibid.

5 Ibid.

Roy Lichtenstein

1 Milton Esterow, 'How Could You Be Much Luckier Than I Am?', *Roy Lichtenstein: Interiors*, exh. cat., Galerie Ulysses, Vienna 1992, p.13.

2 John Coplans (ed.), *Roy Lichtenstein*, London 1972, pp.68, 168.

3 Lawrence Alloway, *Lichtenstein*, New York 1983, p.73.

4 'I make a drawing from the original cartoon, or rearranged from a group of cartoons. Or they might be made up: they range from being completely made up by me to being very close to the original.' *But once you've done the drawing, do you ever refer back to the original cartoon?* 'Rarely. Rarely.' Quoted in David Sylvester, *Some Kind of Reality: Roy Lichtenstein interviewed by David Sylvester in 1966 and 1997*, London 1997, p.11.

5 'This is a rather recent development; I used to do them just fresh and from the cartoon itself. Everybody thought that I was projecting them up, so I did.' Quoted in Sylvester 1997.

6 Interviews by G.R. Swanson, 'What is Pop Art?', *Artnews*, vol.62, no.7, Nov. 1963, p.63.

7 Coplans 1972, p.87.

8 Sylvester 1997, p.36.

9 Sylvester 1997, p.37.

10 Michael Brenson, 'The changing world of Roy Lichtenstein', *New York Times*, 10 August 1982, sec.C, p.9. Reprinted in Alloway 1983.

Morris Louis

1 Marcella Louis Brenner, letter to the authors, September 1998.

2 Diane Upright, *Morris Louis: The Complete Paintings*, New York 1985, p.35. The book contains a chapter entitled 'The Technique of Morris Louis', in which the author draws conclusions on Louis's painting methods based on his entire *oeuvre*.

3 *Morris Louis*, exh. cat., Hayward Gallery, London 1974, p.9.

4 Kenneth Noland quoted in a videotaped interview with Carol Mancusi-Ungaro and Leni Potoff, Museum of Fine Arts, Houston, 12 November 1993.

5 Noland quoted in Kenworth Moffet,

Kenneth Noland, New York 1977, p.22.

6 Ibid.

7 Hayward Gallery 1974, p.35.

8 Interview with Leonard Bocour by Paul Cummings, 8 June 1978, Archives for American Art, Smithsonian Institution, Washington, Tape 1, Side A, p.35.

9 The first series of 'Veils' from 1954 were slightly smaller.

10 Upright 1985, p.54.

11 Ibid., p.58.

12 Diane Waldman, *Kenneth Noland*, exh. cat., Salander O'Reilly Galleries Inc., 1989, p.35.

13 Louis obtained the Acryloid F-10 direct from Rohm and Haas.

14 Kenneth Noland quoted in a videotaped interview with Carol Mancusi-Ungaro and Leni Potoff, Museum of Fine Arts, Houston, 12 November 1993.

15 Ibid.

16 Upright 1985, p.58.

17 Marcella Louis Brenner, letter to the authors, September 1998.

18 Marcella Louis Brenner, personal communication, April 1999.

19 Clement Greenberg, 'Postscriptum', 1966 in *Morris Louis 1912–1962*, exh. cat., Museum of Fine Arts, Boston, 1967, p.84.

20 Kenworth Moffett, *Morris Louis*, exh. cat., Museum of Fine Arts, Boston, 1979, p.6.

21 Interview with Leonard Bocour, New York, 19 February 1979, p.34. Morris Louis Papers and Morris Louis Estate Papers, Archives of American Art, Smithsonian Institution.

22 Kenneth Noland quoted in a videotaped interview with Carol Mancusi-Ungaro and Leni Potoff, Museum of Fine Arts, Houston, 12 November 1993.

23 Morris Louis, letter to Leonard Bocour, 21 October 1958, Morris Louis Papers and Morris Louis Estate Papers, Archives of American Art, Smithsonian Institution.

24 Morris Louis, letter to Leonard Bocour, 21 May 1958, ibid.

25 Interview with Leonard Bocour, New York, 19 February 1979, p.6, ibid.

26 Leonard Bocour, letter to Morris Louis, 8 June 1962, ibid.

27 Morris Louis, letter to Leonard Bocour, 22 May 1982, ibid.

28 Interview with Marcella Louis Brenner by Alan Solomon, 11 January, 1966, ibid.

29 Ibid.

Bridget Riley

1 Felix Fénéon, 'Les Impressionistes', *La Vogue*, Paris 13–20 June 1886, pp.261–75. Part of text reprinted in John Russell, *Seurat*, London 1965, p.182.

Frank Stella

1 Frank Stella, *Working Space*, The Charles Eliot Norton Lectures, Cambridge, Mass. 1986, p.162.

2 William S. Rubin, *Frank Stella*, exh. cat., Museum of Modern Art, New York 1970, p.32.

3 Ibid., p.29.

4 Stella 1986, p.162.

5 Frank Stella, text of a lecture given at the Pratt Institute, Winter 1959–60, Appendix in Robert Rosenblum, *Frank Stella*, Harmondsworth 1971, p.52.

6 Sidney Guberman, *Frank Stella: An Illustrated Biography*, New York 1995, p.56.

7 Rubin 1970, pp.48–50.

8 Ibid., p.60.

9 Stella in Rosenblum 1971, p.52.

10 Rubin 1970, p.60.

11 Lucy Lippard (ed.), 'Questions to Stella and Judd', *Artnews*, Sept. 1966, pp.55–61. Reprinted in Rubin 1970, p.75.

12 Rubin 1970, p.73.

13 William S. Rubin, *Frank Stella: 1970–1987*, exh. cat., Museum of Modern Art, New York 1987, p.28.

14 *Audio Arts Magazine*, vol.7, no.4, Frank Stella talking during the installation of his exhibition at the Institute of Contemporary Arts, London 1985.

15 Rubin 1987, p.14.

16 Caroline A. Jones, *Machine in the Studio: Constructing the Postwar American Artist*, The University of Chicago Press, Chicago and London 1996, p.121.

17 Jones 1996, p.182.

18 Stella quoted by Douglas C. McGill, 'Art People: A New Stella in Office Lobby', *New York Times*, 25 April 1986.

19 *Audio Arts Magazine* 1985.

20 Ibid.

21 Guberman 1995, p.205.

22 Jones 1996, p.123.

Andy Warhol

1 Andy Warhol and Pat Hackett, *Popism: The Warhol 60s*, London 1980, p.7.

2 Ibid., p.18.

3 Patrick Smith, *Andy Warhol's Art and Films*, Michigan 1981, 1986, p.315.

4 *Andy Warhol, Cars*, exh. cat, Solomon R. Guggenheim Museum, New York 1988, p.24.

5 Quoted in Andy Warhol, Kasper Konig, Pontus Hulten and Olle Granath (eds.), *Andy Warhol*, exh. cat., Moderna Museet, Stockholm 1968, n.p.

6 *Andy Warhol, Cars* 1988, p.24.

7 Warhol worked on it either in a room at his house or at his first studio space, the Firehouse. Both spaces would have been small, which which indicate that he couldn't step back and view the work effectively, so was likely to have been working on a section at a time.

8 Occasionally he would work on uncut rolls, as with the paintings of Elvis Presley made in the same year, which were then sent to his dealer rolled with stretcher bars, with instructions as to how they should be cropped.

9 David Bourdon, *Warhol*, New York 1989, p.126.

10 The colour was mixed for the background of the silk-screen painting, *The American Man –Watson Powell* 1964.

11 Warhol and Hackett 1980, p.16.

12 Gerard Malanga, 'Working with Warhol', *Andy Warhol: Thirty Are Better than One*, exh. cat., New York 1997, p.4.

13 Warhol and Konig 1968, n.p.

Glossary

Acrylic resin
A synthetic resin produced from acrylates and/or methacrylates. See the Modern Paints chapter, pp.12 ff.

Acrylic gel medium
An acrylic emulsion medium containing thickening agents – typically cellulosic or polyacrylate materials – which can be added to an emulsion paint if a thicker consistency is required.

Acrylic gesso
A primer, usually white, which contains an acrylic emulsion binder. It contains less binder than acrylic emulsion paint and is therefore more absorbent. It can be used as a primer for all types of paint and adheres well to most supports. The term 'gesso' is Italian for gypsum (calcium sulphate), and is also traditionally used to describe a white aqueous primer containing gypsum.

Acrylic primer
Material containing an acrylic emulsion binder that is applied to a support prior to painting.

Acrylic-vinyl
Synthetic polymer produced by combining acrylic and vinyl acetate components.

Acryloid F-10
An acrylic resin (poly n-butyl methacrylate) produced by Rohm and Haas. It is the binder used in Magna and MSA acrylic solution paints.

Air brush
A small pen-like spray gun which uses compressed air to atomise paint or varnish and apply it in a fine spray.

Alkyd resin
A specific type of synthetic polyester resin that can be modified with a drying oil to form an excellent paint binder. It remains the most important binder in all oil-based household and industrial paints since the mid-1950s. See the Modern Paints chapter, pp.12 ff.

Aluminium honeycomb panel
A panel made from two sheets of aluminium metal that sandwich a transverse honeycomb made from aluminium foil. The material is extremely strong, rigid and light.

Artists' colourman
A maker or supplier of artists' materials.

Batten
Strip of wood, used, for example, to stiffen a board support, or to surround a painting as a batten frame.

Ben Day dots
Small dots produced in the photo-engraving process developed by the New York printer, Benjamin Day (1828–1916). The tonal range of an image is achieved by breaking it up into a series of dots.

Binder
The component of paint into which pigments are mixed and which holds them in place after the paint has dried.

Binding medium see Binder

Bitumen
Black or brown tarry compound derived from crude oil, or from purer sources such as natural tar deposits.

Bleeding
The migration of a pigmented layer after its application. It may refer to migration into an adjacent paint layer (in which it would be slightly soluble), into a canvas support via capillary action or under a strip of masking tape.

Blackboard paint
Extremely matt paint, usually black or green, used to coat blackboards. The term does not specify the binder.

Blockboard
Board commonly made of softwood strips glued edge-to-edge forming a core, which is faced on each side with a single thin veneer of usually birch or poplar in 'three-ply' and two veneer layers in 'five-ply'.

Bloom
Term describing the appearance of a white haze in a paint or varnish film, either at the film's surface (e.g. if a material crystallises out of the film) or within it (e.g. if its various components separate out to leave air pockets). Sometimes referred to as hazing or blanching.

Cadmium red
Commonly used opaque, scarlet pigment made from cadmium sulpho-selenide and available throughout the twentieth century.

Cadmium yellow
Commonly used opaque, yellow pigment made from cadmium sulphide and available throughout the twentieth century.

Canvas
Strong, woven cloth traditionally used for

artists' supports. Commonly made of either linen or cotton thread, but also manufactured from man-made materials such as polyester.

Canvas weave
A term describing the different textures of a canvas surface according to the way in which the canvas threads are woven together.

Cartoon
A preparatory drawing for a painting made on paper. Cartoons are often made in precise detail and in colour so that craftsmen or studio assistants carry out the execution of the final work of art.

Cellulose
Naturally occurring organic material found in all plant fibres and therefore present in paper, wood, canvas etc. The term is sometimes loosely used when referring to nitro-cellulose paints.

Cellulose nitrate
Semi-synthetic plastic produced by treating cellulose with nitric acid. It was used for early cinematic 'celluloid' films.

Chalk
White or off-white inorganic material composed of calcium carbonate. Naturally occurring, although also produced industrially throughout the twentieth century.

Chipboard
Rigid panel made by the compression of chips of wood with synthetic resin glue. It is often used as a laminating material in the manufacture of furniture.

Chlorinated rubber
Synthetic resin made by incorporating chlorine into natural or synthetic rubber. Because of its exceptional resistance to corrosion it is used in high-performance industrial paint such as that for road-marking.

Commercially prepared canvas
Canvas purchased with a white pigmented priming already applied.

Cotton duck
Canvas made with cotton fibres. The grades of good-quality cotton duck canvas

commonly used by artists range in weight from 10 to 12 ounces per square yard (or 340 to 410 grams per square metre).

Cropping
Reducing the dimensions of a painting after (or during) its execution.

Cross-section
An analytical technique involving the removal of a microscopic sample of paint and viewing it under magnification from the side, revealing its layers.

Diluent
A liquid that can be added to a paint to reduce its consistency, increase its transparency and increase the area over which it can be applied (used extensively, for example, for staining). Turpentine has been the traditional diluent for oil paint, although white spirit is now more commonly used. Emulsion paint is diluted with water.

Dispersal
The spreading of insoluble solid particles (e.g. pigment) into a liquid (e.g. a paint binder), usually by grinding.

Dispersion
Suspension of solid particles in a liquid. All paints are dispersions of pigment in binder. Some unpigmented binders are themselves dispersions in water, but are more commonly termed emulsions (e.g. acrylic or PVA)

Drying oil
Vegetable oil, often made by crushing nuts or seeds, that dries to a tough film on exposure to air. For paints, linseed oil is most commonly used, but poppy, sunflower, safflower, soya-bean and walnut oils have also been used.

Emulsion
The suspension of one liquid in another liquid with which it is immiscible, such as oil and water. An emulsion can be stabilised with an emulsifier, a component that mixes with both liquids. Milk is a natural emulsion, with the protein casein acting as the emulsifier. The term is also used to describe water-borne polymer paints (see Dispersion) in which the emulsifier is usually a strong detergent.

Enamel paint
Term loosely used to describe industrial paints and housepaints of very high gloss which bear a superficial resemblance to vitreous enamels. When unpigmented or transparent they are often termed 'lacquer'.

Epoxy resin
Synthetic resin used mainly in two-pack adhesives (e.g. Araldite), but also in industrial paints with high resistance to corrosion.

Etching
Method of printmaking whereby the lines or tones of the design are transcribed into a prepared ground on a metal plate. The exposed lines or areas are etched (i.e. corroded) by the action of acid before it is printed.

Ethyl silicate
Early synthetic resin used mainly for weather-resistant exterior coatings.

Extender
White powdered solid, distinct from a white pigment in that it becomes transparent when properly dispersed in a paint binder. It is often used to reduce cost, but it can also modify a paint's handling qualities.

Fibreglass resin
A strong composite material made from glass fibres embedded in a resin, often polyester or epoxy, which has been 'cured' by a hardener. It can be easily moulded and is used to make boat hulls and vehicle bodies. Also known as 'glass-reinforced plastic' (GRP).

Filler *see* Extender

Flourescence
Visible light emitted from an object when exposed to (invisible) ultraviolet radiation.

Foamcore
Lightweight board with a foam centre, usually faced on both sides with white, plastic-coated paper.

Fringing
Term used to describe the uniform bleeding of a binder away from a pigmented area of paint.

Glaze
Layer of translucent paint often applied as a

thin layer over another colour to modify its colour or alter its tone.

Glue size *see* **Size**

Gouache
Similar to watercolour, but made opaque through the addition of a white pigment or extender.

Ground
Layer of pigmented priming. Usually a lean, opaque paint applied as a single, unmodified colour to the support.

Hardboard
Generic term for a panel manufactured by consolidating felted wood fibres under heat and pressure. The fibres are bound together by a combination of resin and the lignin content in the wood. Panels usually have one smooth and one textured surface.

Hard-edge painting
Form of painting in which boundaries of areas of colour are extremely rigid and precise (i.e., there is no bleeding).

Housepaint
Paint made for use in either exterior or interior household decoration.

Impasto
Thickly applied paint that stands out from the surface in relief.

Incised lines
Technique of scoring the support or primer prior to paint application so that the relevant preparatory drawing remains visible through the paint layer.

Infrared
Region of radiation, just beyond the red end of the visible spectrum, which can be detected by special photographic films.

Lacquer *see* **Enamel**

Linen
Thread or woven cloth made from fibres of the flax plant.

Linseed oil
Oil extracted from flax seeds. It has the shortest drying time of all vegetable oils and is consequently widely used in oil paint.

Mahlstick
A light stick with a ball of material, often covered with soft leather, at one end. It is used to support the painter's hand.

Maquette
A model made as a preliminary design, usually for sculpture but also for paintings incorporating areas of relief.

Masonite
Hardboard produced by a process discovered and patented in 1924 by W.H. Mason, in which wood chips are reduced to cellulose fibres under high pressure.

Medium *see* **Binder**

Mineral spirit
Organic solvent derived from petroleum. White spirit and Stoddard's solvent are grades of mineral spirit.

Nitro-cellulose
A paint binder containing cellulose nitrate. See Modern Paints chapter, pp.12 ff

Ochre
A term encompassing a range of iron oxide pigments of moderate intensity. They are often shades of yellow but can also be red, orange or brown. They occur naturally, but synthetic iron oxides are now more commonly used.

Oil *see* **Drying oil**

Oil-based paint
Either oil paint or alkyd paint. Sometimes loosely used to describe a paint that is thinned in organic solvents.

Oil stick
Painting material containing pigment, a drying oil (often linseed oil) and wax, which is moulded into stick form.

Opaque projector
Device used for the projection of an image on to a blank surface by placing it under glass and illuminating it strongly to a magnified image. Referred to as an Epi[dia]scope in the UK.

Organic solvent
Volatile liquid capable of dissolving an organic resin. Organic solvents used in paints include mineral spirits and turpentine.

Overpaint
Paint applied over other (dried) paint layers. If used to describe paint applied over specific areas of loss or damage it is often termed retouching or inpainting.

Paint
Liquid material in which coloured pigments are dispersed in a binder and which forms a solid film on drying.

Palette
Board used for mixing colours. The term is also used to describe the range of colours used by an artist.

Palette knife
Flexible steel spatula made with a straight or cranked blade in different sizes which is used principally for the mixing of paint and painting-media on the palette.

Painting knife
Designed for the application of paint to the canvas, the painting knife has a thin and flexible steel blade at the end of a curved steel shank. A variety of sizes and shapes, such as 'diamond' and 'pear', produce different painting effects.

Panel
Rigid support for painting on, traditionally made of joined planks of wood, but more recently boards and composites.

Patina
Term describing the alteration of the surface of a painting or sculpture through natural ageing.

Pearlescent paint
Paint made from transparent mica flakes that are coated with thin films of pigment to reflect and transmit light. The painted effect is one of pearly luminescence. Also known as iridescent paint.

Pestle and mortar
Bowl (mortar) and grinding stick (pestle) often made from agate and used to grind materials by hand. Prior to the development of ready-mixed tubes of paint, artists' paints

were usually prepared by grinding the dry pigments into a binder.

Photo-mechanical silk-screen
The combination of a photographic and mechanical process, whereby the reaction of light on chemical substances forms the printing surface from which impressions can be produced.

Pigment
Small coloured particles that are dispersed (mixed) into the binder to form paint.

Plywood panel
Panel made from thin sheets of wood veneer, glued together under pressure. The grain in each layer of veneer is set at right angles to the grain of the adjacent layer, producing a strong board, resistant to shrinkage.

Polyester resin
A synthetic resin containing ester linkages (made up of an organic acid and an alcohol). Alkyd resins are a form of polyester.

Polymer
An organic material of high molecular weight, consisting (typically) of thousands of small molecules known as monomers linked together, often in a chain. Polymers occur naturally (e.g. cellulose), but most are synthetic. Synthetic polymers are commonly referred to as plastics

Polyurethane
A synthetic resin used in paints where high durability is required, such as those used on boats.

Polyvinyl acetate or PVA
A synthetic polymer formed from vinyl acetate. As an emulsion, it is commonly used as wood glue, but is also used as a low-cost alternative to acrylic binders in paints. See Modern Paints chapter, pp. 12 ff.

Preparation (of support)
Term used to describe any preparation of a support before paint is applied, including the sanding of boards, washing of canvas, and all forms of priming.

Preparatory drawing
Preliminary drawing, often over the priming layers, in which the composition is established. Sometimes notes are made on materials and technique.

Primer
Substance applied to a support before the application of paint in order to improve the adhesion of paint to the surface. It can be either unpigmented (often referred to as 'size') or pigmented (often referred to as 'ground').

Priming see Primer

Pyroloxin see Nitro-cellulose

Rabbit skin glue
Aqueous glue made by extracting the collagen from rabbit skin. Traditionally used as a 'size' coating.

Raking light
See Methods of Examination, pp. 32–5.

Relief
The three-dimensional aspect of a work of art.

Resin
An organic solid, usually transparent. 'Natural' resins derive from either plants or insects, whereas 'synthetic' resins (e.g. alkyd and acrylic) are manufactured industrially. They can usually be dissolved in organic solvents to produce a clear solution, although many synthetic resins are produced as dispersions.

Retouching see Overpainting

Retouching varnish
A clear coating applied to a paint surface before retouching or overpainting to ensure proper adhesion between layers.

Rosin
The natural resin remaining from the distillation of material exuded from species of pine trees. The distillate is oil of turpentine.

Ruling pen
Instrument for drawing lines of uniform thickness in draughting. The point of the pen is made of two parallel blades that can be adjusted by a screw to set the width of the line. A small reservoir of ink or paint is placed between the two blades.

Saturation
The intensity of a colour in a work of art. For example, a depiction of a clear sky may be more saturated with blue than a hazy sky.

Scumble
A thin layer of opaque paint, frequently lighter in tone, that partially hides the layer beneath.

Silicone resin
Synthetic resin containing alternate silicon and oxygen atoms instead of a carbon chain. Often used in a rubbery form for mould-making, but also incorporated into weather-resisitant industrial paints.

Silk-screen
Method of printmaking in which the ink is forced with a 'squeegee' through areas of a fine mesh screen (usually made of silk, or polyester) that have not been blocked out by glue.

Sinking
When the paint medium is absorbed by a lean underlayer to produce a matt or dead surface.

Size
Traditionally a solution of animal glue (e.g. rabbit-skin glue) used as the first layer of primer on a canvas or panel, onto which a pigmented primer would be applied. Nowadays the term describes any unpigmented primer used to seal a support.

Solution
A liquid made by dissolving a solid in a solvent.

Solvent
A liquid that dissolves another material.

Spray gun
Large hand-held or fixed device usually powered by an air compressor to apply paint or varnish as a spray.

Spring compass
Compass incorporating a spring to ensure its two arms are kept at a constant distance. The tip of one arm can be modified to hold paint, rather like a ruling pen.

Squaring up
Method of transferring a drawing to another surface on a different scale, usually an enlargement. A grid of lines is drawn on both surfaces and each block is copied free-hand onto the new surface: the grid allows each small area to be transcribed as a simple shape.

Squeegee
The tool used in silk-screening to push the ink through the screen. The squeegee is a thick square-cut blade of flexible rubber or plastic, set into a wooden or metal handle.

Stain
Paint or varnish that has been entirely absorbed by a surface. It is usually applied in a very diluted form.

Stencil
Cut-out design in thin metal, plastic or cardboard through which paint can be applied to the surface on which the stencil is laid.

Stencil brush
Short brush, usually round in section, with stiff bristle hairs and flat ends, used for pressing paint through the cut-out holes in a stencil.

Stretcher
An expandable frame, traditionally made of wood, to which canvas is attached for painting. If it is a rigid construction (i.e. non-expandable) it is usually termed a strainer.

Studio
The room in which an artist works; alternatively the group of assistants or apprentices working with an artist, and using the same style and techniques.

Support
Any surface for painting on, for example canvas or hardboard.

Swatch
Sample of a paint's colour when dry, usually a small area painted out on card. Also, a number of such samples tied together.

Synthetic resin see Resin

Tacking edge
The area of canvas around the outer edge of a stretcher. Traditionally the canvas was secured to the stretcher with tacks along these edges, but nowadays the canvas is more commonly attached with staples, sometimes on the back of the stretcher.

Template
Piece of (usually) thin board or metal with one edge shaped to correspond to the outline of the desired pattern, or perforated with shapes and used like a stencil. The artist can make multiple reproductions of a pattern by following the contour of the edge or the perforations. Can be used for both preparatory drawing and the application of paint.

Thinner see Diluent

Thixotropic
Substance that flows when a force is applied to it, but holds its shape when left, such as a 'non-drip' housepaint.

Titanium white
Highly opaque white pigment made from titanium dioxide and used since the early twentieth century.

Turpentine
A volatile liquid made from the distillation of a material exuded from certain species of pine trees. Traditionally used as a diluent in paints.

Ultramarine
A blue pigment traditionally made from lapis lazuli. Since the 1820s a synthetic replacement has been available.

Ultraviolet illumination
Region of radiation just beyond the blue end of the visible spectrum.

Umber
Brown inorganic pigment made by refining naturally coloured earths containing a mixture of manganese and iron oxides, originally mined from Umbria in Italy.

Underlayers see Underpainting

Underpainting
Preliminary design for the image, executed in paint on the prepared surface, and usually not visible in the final work.

Varnish
Transparent coating usually applied as a protective layer, or to enhance the appearance of the paint surface underneath. Many unpigmented synthetic and natural resins can be used.

Veneer
A thin structured wood layer used to face thicker wood, making a decorative grain finish (e.g. birch ply used for the surface of plywood).

Wash
Thin application of dilute paint.

Watercolour
Paint containing a gum binder that is usually transparent and applied as a thin wash of colour.

Wet-and-dry paper
An abrasive paper, similar to sandpaper but usually much finer, which can be used either wet or dry.

Wet-in-wet
Application of one colour next to or onto another, before the first has dried, resulting in the earlier application being disturbed so both colours become blended.

White spirit
Organic solvent based on a distillate of petroleum and refined for use as a paint diluent. Also known as naphtha.

Working stretcher
Stretcher (or strainer) used while a painting is being made, but not retained when the work is finished, the canvas usually being re-stretched onto a permanent stretcher for display.

Wrinkling
A defect in a dried paint or varnish film, more common with thicker applications. It can occur when the lower part of the film contracts on drying after the surface has formed a skin.

List of Interviews

All interviews and correspondence with the artists were conducted
by Jo Crook and Tom Learner, unless otherwise stated:

Peter Blake: 29 October 1997 in his London studio.

Patrick Caulfield: 27 April 1994 and 24 November 1998, both in his London studio.

Richard Hamilton: 1 November 1988 in his studio, interviewed by Lucy Pearce;
3 January 1999, e-mail correspondence.

John Hoyland: 12 December 1996 in his London studio, and 5 November 1998,
at the Tate Store.

Gerard Malanga (assistant to Andy Warhol): 29 September 1998,
telephone interview.

Roy Lichtenstein: 26 May 1992 and 6 May 1997, both in his New York studio.

Bridget Riley: 24 November 1998 in her London studio.

Andrew Smith (assistant to Bridget Riley): 17 January 1995 in Riley's London studio.

Frank Stella: 6 May 1997 in his New York studio.

Index